Don't Cry at My Funeral

David Anderson

TABLE OF CONTENTS

PREFACE

This isn't an autobiography. I wasn't ambitious enough to have a life worthy of one. When ambition called, I usually said no. I declined when United Press International invited me to go to Washington as UPI's Supreme Court reporter. I declined when the dean of the University of Texas Law School asked me to be associate dean. I frittered away an opportunity to see if I could succeed in television journalism. So I have no great accomplishments to write about, only a life rich with fun — adventures, characters, pleasures, and discoveries.

My era — mostly in the second half of the twentieth century — left room for fun. You could play high school football and still be valedictorian and student council president. You could flirt with a life in rodeo and still get into Harvard. You could devote most of your college time to partying and not flunk out. You could get married and have a child and still be president of your fraternity. You could spend seven exhilarating years in journalism and still go to a good law school. You could choose an academic career over law practice and still represent memorable clients. You could teach law to four or five thousand students, edit casebooks, and write scholarly articles — while also running rapids, prowling junkyards, restoring old cars, chasing rodeos, and sampling honky-tonks. You could serve your university's interests while enjoying the enticements of London, Moscow, Sydney, Melbourne, Perth, and Stockholm.

A friend who read this manuscript said I should devote more space to my career as a law professor. If I had done so, I doubt you would want to read it; my career was rewarding, but not that different from other law professors' careers. I don't want to reprise my career; what I want to do is push back a little against our era's constant demand to focus, concentrate, specialize — in school, in career, even in avocation. This is a paean to dabbling, a celebration of the unfocused life.

CHAPTER 1

The Summer of '58

It was a summer when time stood still, dreams came true, transgressions weren't punished, and the whole world was beautiful. Everyday-life faded away, displaced by a new life of pleasure, adventures, and happy surprises.

My job in the summer of 1958 was guiding dudes on horseback rides in the mountains. I was 19, ranch-raised, and grateful for a break from the nerve-jangling pressures of my first year at Harvard, for which I had been woefully unprepared. The stable was part of a grand old resort in Colorado. The affluent, fun-loving, free-spending vacationers were a new breed to me; I was raised among sober, hard-working, penny-pinching country people.

I was in Colorado because my parents had decided that the entire family would benefit from a brief change of scene. They had just sold their place in Nebraska and arranged for the buyer to take care of the cattle for a share of the calf crop. For the first time in 20 years, they were liberated from the twice-a-day chores of looking after livestock. They opted for nothing as extravagant as a family vacation, though; we were all expected to find jobs.

Mother worked as a checker in a grocery store. Dad was a clerk in a western wear store. Nancy, age 17, worked as a maid at some creekside tourist cabins. Elaine, 15, worked as a motel maid in the mornings, at a candy shop in the afternoons, and as a waitress in the evenings. Ellen, 13, had some baby-sitting jobs, and Walt, 7, roamed the town on his own when Ellen wasn't watching him. All but me lived in a rented house in town. It was an eye-opening experience of all of us.

I got my job at the stable by walking in and asking. I told the boss about my ranch background. He pointed me toward a dozen or so horses tied in narrow one-horse stalls and said "Go back there and git acquainted with them horses.

Git in there and move round with 'em." That was my employment exam — an ingenious way of testing my claim that I knew horses.

He watched out of the corner of his eye and when I came back to the office he offered me a job. "I pay $100 month. You start at six and end at six, seven days a week. Board and room at the hotel." I must have hesitated a moment, because he said ""I'll make you head wrangler and pay you $150. After you finish here you git cleaned up and go in the lobby an' talk to people 'bout goin' ridin.'" I started the next day.

It was still barely above freezing at 6 a.m. when I made the 15-minute walk from my unheated concrete-block cell in the hotel dormitory to the stable, but the intense mountain sun quickly thawed me out. A couple of hours later, when I walked back to the hotel for breakfast, the mornings were glorious — dew on the grass, cool air and hot sun, and cloudless blue skies that seemed to stretch to infinity. All around were mountains, some tree-covered and some solid rock. The scenery and the smell of the pines made it seem like a perpetual vacation.

The Colorado Resort

The owner of the stable was Earl, an old bronc rider. He loved to pull up his shirt and show a foot-long scar that he said was the result of being stepped on by Five Minutes to Midnight, a famous bucking horse. Earl was now a serious alcoholic. He kept a bottle in his truck parked beside the stable, and several times a day, starting in the morning, he would slip out to the truck for a snort. His hands shook and by mid-morning he was tottering. Often he left at midafternoon, leaving his wife, Roberta, to close up at the end of the day.

Roberta really ran the business. She kept track of the scheduled rides, collected the money, and arranged the visits of the farrier and the veterinarian. She appeared to be about 15 years younger than Earl. She was like a rodeo queen 15 or 20 years after her reign: still pretty and graceful, but a little pudgy and saggy. As far as I could tell she didn't drink, and she seemed unperturbed by Earl's alcoholism.

Earl was the best drunk driver I ever knew, or maybe just the luckiest. His main herd of 70 or 80 horses was kept on a ranch 25 miles down the canyon toward the flatland. After a few weeks at the stable, horses got sour and had to be replaced with fresh ones from the ranch. So once or twice a week, Earl would load five or six horses in his truck, take them to the ranch, and bring back a like number of fresh horses. It was a two-lane mountain road, full of steep grades, sheer dropoffs, and switchbacks. Somehow Earl, in his alcoholic fog, was able to successfully navigate a trip that was a challenge for most of us stone sober.

———◆———

I was one of three wranglers. The other two were both named Jimmy — Little Jimmy and Big Jimmy. Big Jimmy wasn't much of a horseman, so Little Jimmy and I connived to make Big Jimmy do most of the manure-shoveling. Earl was a maniac about cleanliness. He wanted droppings removed from the corral and the stable the minute they hit the ground. If a horse relieved itself on the far side of the corral, shielded by 20 horses, Earl would somehow notice.

"Better git after that," he would say to whoever was closest. Sometimes he would just point a shaky finger, and we knew he meant "Git out there and git that cleaned up."

Little Jimmy was the best cowboy among us. He was 15, son of a shiftless ex-bronc rider and an Indian mother who, we eventually learned, was in a mental hospital. Little Jimmy was effectively an orphan, and Earl and Roberta, who had no children, took him in. He lived with them and Roberta tried to mother him, but Little Jimmy wanted no parenting. One weekend he got drunk and ended up in jail, until the police were able to locate his father. When he was released, the father disappeared and Little Jimmy was back with Earl and Roberta.

Little Jimmy occasionally told secrets of life with Earl and Roberta. He said Earl kept a fifth of whisky under the bed and took a long drink in the morning before he got up. He said Roberta once entertained the farrier in the bedroom when Earl was away hauling horses.

Roberta adored Little Jimmy, as did most women. He was small for a 15-year-old, quick and lithe. He had a round baby face, brown skin, flashing dark eyes, and a devastatingly white smile. I believe he could have seduced most of the women who came to the stable, but he evaded their flirtations. He was a natural horseman, sure-seated, carefree, totally confident of his abilities. He rode a three-year-old sorrel filly that had a smooth, nimble jog-trot. She and Jimmy moved as one, as if they were dancing to the music of the hoofbeats and the creaking saddle.

———◆———

We guided hotel guests on rides for an hour or two, half a day, or all day. We also had occasional midnight rides and cookout rides, and gave riding lessons. We worked from 6 a.m. to 6 p.m., seven days a week — which may explain why the summer seemed timeless. Our first task was to saddle a couple of horses that had been kept up overnight, ride down to the night trap, round up the full herd of 30 or 40 horses, and drive them up the long hill to the stable. Then we fed and brushed them, and saddled as many as we expected to need for the day. It didn't seem like work at all.

We tried to get people to ride in the mornings when the sun invariably shone, but they were on vacation and often weren't ready to ride until afternoon. Most afternoons, there was a rain shower, so we packed a rolled-up yellow slicker on the back of each saddle for the afternoon rides. Getting the slickers untied and on the dudes when the rain started was an adventure. Flapping slickers sometimes spooked the horses. Once I was halfway up a narrow, steep trail with six or eight dudes when the rain started. There wasn't room for the dudes to dismount, so I went back along the line, helping each rider to get into the slicker without falling off the horse. I was on the downhill side of the horses with only a few inches of trail between the horses and a long steep incline. I sometimes had to cling to a horse to keep from falling down the slope.

Two riders who did come in the morning were Mitch Miller and Michel Legrand. Miller was a band leader and LeGrand was a composer of movie music. They stayed at the hotel a week; we understood they were collaborating on a project of some kind. They wanted their horses ready at 8 a.m. every day. I would love to have ridden with such celebrities, but they wanted no guide.

———◆———

As "head wrangler," I had an extra task. After finishing my 12 hours at the stable, I was to shower, put on some colorful cowboy clothes, eat some dinner, and hang out in the hotel lobby, recruiting guests for rides the next day. I preferred waiting for guests to approach me but that didn't produce enough riders, so Earl insisted that I buttonhole people and give them a sales pitch. I detested that, but I did it for an hour or two each evening.

Music drifted into the lobby from the hotel's night club, and I soon persuaded myself that I might generate some rides by showing up there too. It was small but complete — a stage, tables surrounding a dance floor, an orchestra, and a singer. The singer was a slender blonde who wore slinky, floor-length dresses, had a throaty voice, and sang romantic, bluesy songs. Her signature number was Blue Moon, which she sang at the beginning and end of each set.

I began spending less time in the lobby and more time in the club, nursing a whiskey sour and listening to the lovely lady sing the blues. She sometimes smiled at me; in fact, before long she seemed to be singing Blue Moon specifically to me.

———◆———

One day, as I was giving a riding lesson to a six-year-old girl in an arena halfway between the hotel and the stable, I saw the singer watching us from the railing. She was wearing a cheap straw cowboy hat, blue jeans, and a plaid blouse open at the neck. The femme fatale of the night club was a perky teenager by day — slightly gangly and quite self-conscious.

She waved, I waved, and when the lesson was over she came with me to the stable. I found out her name (here I'm going to call her Suzanne). In the office I introduced her to Earl and Roberta and we all chatted a little. When the boss and his wife stepped out for a moment, Suzanne backed me up against the Coke machine and kissed me.

I had had several girlfriends, but I had never known a girl that brash. I was smitten, but it was hard to do anything about it because I worked all day and we both worked every evening. We met in the lobby during her breaks and got acquainted in fifteen-minute chunks. During the day she was a maid at the hotel. In the fall, she would be starting at a secretarial school in Denver. She hoped to make a career as a singer but feared her voice wasn't good enough. She called me "my Harvard cowboy." We both longed to go on a date, to a movie or dancing, but that was impossible. So we arranged to meet for a picnic at a cave she knew about, in the mountainside above the hotel. We went in the early evening, just before each of us began our night job.

It wasn't really a cave, just a ledge under a rock overhang, high enough to be invisible from below. It looked out over the hotel, the town and whole valley. I don't remember what we ate, or if we ate. I do remember that the next day she had a skinned-up back and I had skinned knees and elbows. Until I wrote this, I had never wondered how Suzanne knew about this rocky love nest.

After that I spent far more time in the night club than in the lobby. One night Earl paid a visit to the lobby, and the next day he scolded me for not being there.

———◆———

My employment at the stable ended after a midnight ride up a mountain to a small lake. A busload of young secretaries had come from Chicago for a week-long package vacation. Some of them came to the stable and rode, and one came several times. She insisted that I be her guide, and Earl okayed that even though parties of less than three weren't supposed to get a wrangler. Her name was Jenny; she was pretty and flirtatious, and I was delighted to be her chosen one.

The secretaries as a group booked the midnight ride. The afternoon before the ride, Jenny came to the stable and pulled me aside. "I think you should abduct me tonight," she said. I laughed off the suggestion, but it lodged in my imagination.

There was no moonlight for our moonlight ride; we could see a little in the clearings but in the trees it was so dark we had to count on the horses to see the trail. There were 20 or 30 riders, so we had three guides — Earl in front, me along the side, and Little Jimmy bringing up the rear. A short way up the trail there was a small clearing. When we reached it I rode alongside Jenny and pulled her horse off the trail. We sat on a flat rock and necked while the rest went on up the mountain, then silently rejoined the group when they came back down an hour or so later.

When I planned the gambit, I didn't think our absence would be noted. I hadn't counted on Earl's presence; he rarely rode, and I didn't think he would be able to after a long day of drinking. Even after he showed up, I thought the darkness would protect us. I was wrong.

When we arrived back at the stable, Little Jimmy whispered to me: "You're in trouble. When we got to the top Earl counted heads. You weren't there."

The next morning I went to the stable and told Earl I was quitting. "You can't quit because you're fired," he said.

"No, I quit before you fired me," I said. Little Jimmy was smiling; I knew he was happy to see me make the boss mad. Roberta took some cash out of the register and paid me off. Jenny went back to Chicago; I hope she enjoyed telling her friends of her midnight abduction.

———◆———

I now had time to spend with Suzanne. I quickly got a job as a wrangler at a boys' ranch 20 miles away. I lived in a bunkhouse at the boys' ranch ate in their mess hall. The boys were eight to twelve years old, at the ranch for a month of riding, swimming, and finding themselves. Some of them were whiney and helpless when they arrived, but by the time they left they were confident and self-reliant.

I had evenings and weekends off, but Suzanne didn't get off until her second set ended at 11 o'clock, so seeing her kept me out until the wee hours. I often picked her up after her last set at the hotel and we parked on the hotel grounds near the darkened stable. There are no warm beds or afterglows in my memories of Suzanne, only lots of shivering haste.

By the time I drove back to the ranch after my dates with Suzanne, I could only get four or five hours' sleep. The boys' rides didn't start until 9, but long before that the horses had to be rounded up, fed, groomed, and saddled.

I solved my problem — and fulfilled the dreams of a horse-crazy 12-year-old — by making him "deputy wrangler." He eagerly got up before dawn and got the horses ready. All I had to do was eat breakfast and show up at the corral in time to take a group of six or eight boys on a half-day ride.

———◆———

We had permission to ride on several ranches a few miles down the canyon. To get to them we rode on an old stagecoach road, carved into the mountainsides seventy or eighty years earlier and still used in some places by ranchers and fishermen. The stagecoach road was across the canyon from the modern highway, and between the two was a sparkling, rushing mountain river.

Sometimes we rode upriver to a swimming hole called "The Indian Bathtubs." It was a series of five or six granite depressions cascading down a steep ravine, worn smooth by eons of water, ice, and rocks. From a spring at the top, a small stream of water flowed into the highest pool and then into each of the lower ones.

We tied our horses in a nearby grove. The boys changed into shorts, slid down the polished rock into the frigid water, and then scampered out to slide into the next pool. After the last one they had an arduous climb back to the top, but they whooped and shouted as Indian boys must have done for centuries before.

———◆———

One week I took eight boys on a five-day pack trip to a high valley far back in the mountains. We reached it by riding most of the day up the rocky bed of a stream. I had never been there and had only the directions drawn in the dirt by my boss. There was a line camp in the valley, and as promised it was unlocked and well stocked with canned goods. We carried with us bed rolls and some perishables. We drank water from mountain streams after dropping purification tablets into it.

During the day we rode for miles on game trails, through woods and across meadows vibrant with wildflowers. In the evening we cooked over a camp-fire, and later the boys frightened each other with stories of bears, Indians, and mountain lions. We slept on the ground under innumerable stars and awoke shivering in the morning until I got a fire started. I don't recall that either the boss or I considered the possibility that one of the boys might get sick or hurt; the only option would have been to load him onto a horse for a long ride back down the stream.

I'd have been happy to let those days and nights repeat themselves forever if I hadn't missed Suzanne. After five days, we packed up and rode back down the rocky stream to the boys' ranch.

———◆———

The boys' summer at the ranch ended with a day of activities for their par-ents. The highlight was a "rodeo" — really just a horse show where they could show off their newly acquired horsemanship. There wasn't enough level ground at the boys' ranch so we had the rodeo a mile or so away, at the ranch of a neigh-bor who had an arena. I was in charge, and I made up a full afternoon of rid-ing events showcasing the boys' skills at reining and maneuvering their mounts. One event I recall required them to ride past a coffee can at a trot and drop a rock into the can.

At some point I needed to relieve myself so I rode my horse over a low rise out of sight of the arena. When I dismounted I spotted a large rattlesnake. I had nothing to kill it with, so I remounted and rode over to a fence line where I found a board. I rode back, doubting I would find the snake again, but it hadn't moved far. I dismounted, killed it with the board, and used my pocket knife to cut off the rattles.

Back at the arena, I held out my hand to show the boss my trophy. He angrily hissed at me, "Put that away! Don't say anything about it! You'll scare the day-lights out of everybody." I thought it would have been fitting to show the parents what perils their sons had survived, but I suppose the boss was more interested in having them send their boys back the next year.

I still have the rattles.

———◆———

The day after the rodeo, the boys all went home and my job was finished. It was just a few days before Labor Day. Suzanne's gig at the night club was over, but she worked a few more days at the hotel as a maid. Her evenings were free, so one evening I took her to a night club 30 miles down the canyon toward Denver. We drank 3.2 beer and danced until closing time. On the long drive back in my parents' 1952 Chevy, we both grew sleepy. She went to sleep with her head in my lap, and I eventually dozed off too. A serious impact woke us; she bumped her head on the steering wheel and I fought to get the car back on the highway.

The next morning I surveyed the damage: the passenger side of the car had hit something that knocked off the chrome moulding beneath the doors. I drove back down the highway and found the missing part. The car had gone off the highway and hit a low rock embankment not more than 20 feet wide. On both sides of that rock were steep, unguarded drop offs into a deep ravine. If the car had left the road a second earlier or later, we both would have been dead.

For our last night together, we planned to camp in a national forest, but it was too cold. We retreated to the car, but soon that proved too cold also, so I took her back to her dormitory at the hotel. We kissed goodbye, promised to stay in touch, and never saw each other again.

———◆———

CHAPTER 2

That Was Journalism

We learned of the robbery around midmorning. Two men had held up a bank in Sutherland, a small town in our circulation area. They fled in a 1957 Thunderbird and the highway patrol was chasing them. Keith Blackledge, the editor, tried frantically to locate our police reporter; he called the sheriff's office but they hadn't seen Bob. Bob hadn't been at the police station either. Keith summoned me. "Get over to the sheriff's office and call me when you find out anything."

I had just started working for the North Platte *Telegraph-Bulletin*, mostly rewriting obits. I barely knew where the sheriff's office was; when I got there the radio was crackling with voices from the highway patrol and the sheriff. Much of the talk was in police code, and I didn't know any of the numbers beyond "10-4," but a helpful deputy translated for me. Using a phone on the sheriff's desk, I started phoning Keith: an armada of cops were chasing the robbers in the Sandhills; a little while later the robbers smashed through a road block.

"Stay there and call me when you find out anything more. I'll hold the paper as long as I can." The *Telegraph–Bulletin* was an afternoon daily with a 12:30 news deadline, and it was already close to that time.

After half an hour or so there was a flurry of excited chatter on the radio and the deputy triumphantly announced that the robbers had been caught. A patrolman had shot out the tires of the Thunderbird and the robbers surrendered meekly.

I called in the facts, Keith rapidly pounded out the story, and the paper came out only a couple of hours late. When our readers picked up their paper that afternoon, all the essential details of the biggest news story in months were before them in black and white.

———•———

Bob eventually showed up. Somehow Keith knew he had been in a bar when the robbery story broke; I suppose he had alcohol on his breath. Lots of men like Bob worked for small newspapers in those days — older guys suffering from too much booze and too many arguments with editors. They usually had worked for some metropolitan newspaper when they were younger and now were working their way back down the ladder.

I wish I could remember Bob's last name, because I owe him something: it was his boozing that launched my journalism career. Keith fired him on the spot and I — nineteen years old and barely able to type — was the new police reporter.

You might wonder how an unknown kid could go to the sheriff's office in the midst of a major crime event and quickly get the details of the crime, the chase and the arrests. The answer is that when I walked in there, I wasn't just a kid anymore; I was the *Telegraph-Bulletin*. They knew that whatever they told me would be in the paper and everybody in town would read it.

———•———

A few weeks earlier I had walked in off the street and asked to speak to the editor; I didn't even know his name. No job application, no references, no experience. Three other Nebraska dailies had already turned me down. Keith had hired me because I was from a nearby town, Gothenburg, was on leave from Harvard, and had rudimentary typing skills. He had me do a few rewrites and then hired me at $50 a week.

Working for the newspaper was a heady experience. I covered fatal wrecks, trials, and mysterious fires — the biggest events in the lives of the people involved. I could banter with the cops and clerks as an equal. When the county attorney didn't want to show me an indictment, I could demand to see it, and he knew that I had the power of the paper behind me.

The other people in the newsroom treated me as a neophyte, but not as a kid. I didn't know anything about newspapering, but I could ask questions and I could write. It helped immeasurably that Keith liked me and supported me. He was a genius at turning greenhorns into good reporters — an essential skill at a small paper because able reporters soon moved on and had to be replaced. The alternative was to staff the paper with has-beens like Bob.

First by-line, 1958

Often after work some of us adjourned to the White Horse bar in the Pawnee Hotel, just down the street. I wasn't old enough to drink legally, but being one of the newspaper guys was credential enough for the White Horse. I drank whiskey sours — somehow I had discovered that the sourness slightly concealed the taste of the whiskey.

Keith was a superb small-town editor. He came in at five in the morning and wrote an editorial before the rest of us arrived at 7:30. His editorials were gentle, well-informed essays, rarely expressing any strong opinion, but always with a thoughtful point of view. They set an agenda for public discussion about local issues. Readers commented, complained, and argued with him, not only through letters to the editor but on the street and in restaurants. He was the conscience of the community, more of a city father than most of the elected officials.

He wasn't just an editorial writer. When 7:30 came, he became a hands-on editor, laying out pages, giving assignments, reviewing every piece of copy that went in the paper, sending some of it back for revision, and finally sending it downstairs to the composing room — all that between 7:30 and our deadline at 12:30.

The "state editor" was Ted Turpin, a wiry blond dynamo who had been a Golden Gloves fighter. He — not Harvard — introduced me to books. He lent me paperbacks that he had just finished — James Michener's "Fires of Spring," John Steinbeck's "Cannery Row," Hemingway's "Farewell to Arms," James Jones's "From Here to Eternity." I had read books before, of course, but not just for pleasure. Since I didn't know anybody and had no television set and no money for movies, there was plenty of time to read. Ted's tastes in books suited me perfectly, and we both liked talking about them.

Our "state" coverage came mostly from a network of correspondents in small towns, who mailed in their reports of minor events like school board meetings, and phoned in major stories such as fatal wrecks. They were mostly bored housewives with time on their hands. Ted supervised them, and occasionally he visited them, trips that he called "morale builders." I think Ted sometimes boosted their morale in their beds.

Even metropolitan newspapers like the Omaha *World-Herald* and the Denver *Post* used stringers to cover far-flung towns. They paid a few cents a word — the words they used, not those the stringer submitted. Ted strung for the *World-Herald* and I for the *Post*. I submitted routine stories (counties raising taxes or city councils' instituting one-way streets, for example) by mail and stories about major events like murders or especially destructive fires by placing collect phone calls to the *Post*'s state desk. It was hardly a lucrative sideline but it was satisfying to see one of my stories in the *Post*, even if it was edited down to a paragraph or two.

A newspaperman learns a lot about human vices and troubles. One night there was a fiery crash south of town; I got there just as they pulled the driver from his burning car, which apparently had flipped end-over-end several times. Months later, covering the trial that resulted from the wreck, I learned a valuable lesson about law: it is really hard to re-create reality. The testimony describing the accident scene bore little resemblance to my first-hand observations.

A man drowned in a mountain of wheat; he was walking on top when a conveyer under the pile caused a cave-in and he was swallowed up by the wheat. I was there when they found his body, after removing a few truckloads of wheat. His mouth, ears, nose, and eyes were full of wheat.

Covering police court one Monday morning, I saw that one of the drunks brought before the judge was a man named Sherm, who had once worked briefly for my dad. He was shaking violently, and the judge sent him back to jail to "dry out." I didn't realize how cruel that was, and I doubt that the judge did either. Sherm was back in police court several times over the next months; he would stay in jail a few weeks, and as soon as he got out he would get drunk and be back before the judge.

Five high school football players who had sex with a 15-year-old girl were tried for rape. The age of consent was sixteen but the statutory rape law did not apply if the girl was "previously unchaste," so the trial focused on whether the girl was a virgin. The defense attorney's questions were aimed at showing that penetration was not difficult, that she did not bleed, and possibly she had an orgasm. Those matters could not be mentioned in a family newspaper in 1959, so the coverage was very one-sided. As the boys' parents pointed out, my stories left the impression that the boys presented little in the way of defense.

The case divided the community into its usual political factions — people who worked for the Union Pacific Railroad and lived north of the tracks, and the merchant class who lived mostly south of the tracks. The boys were "railroaders" and the girl was the daughter of a small-time merchant. Keith and I both tried to explain to the boys' parents the limits that "decency" imposed on our ability to be fair, but they thought the explanation was simpler: the newspaper was once again siding with the merchant class.

The Chamber of Commerce manager appeared one week with a huge cast on his right hand. He was tight-lipped about the reason, but we soon learned the story: He suspected his friend of fooling around with his wife, so one day when the friend came to visit, he excused himself and went to a back bedroom "to take a nap." He had arranged some mirrors so he could see the living room sofa from the bedroom. In due time he saw his suspicions confirmed on the sofa. He went to the living room, pulled his friend off the sofa, and slugged him in the jaw — so hard that he broke his hand. Stories like that didn't make the paper.

I occasionally went water skiing with some young single guys who had a boat. One of them was a skinny, serious guy who managed a finance company. Another was a tall happy-go-lucky guy who never seemed to lack for girlfriends. Toward the end of summer the skinny serious guy got married to a cute girl of 18 or 19. Within a month she was sleeping with Mr. happy-go-lucky.

The newsroom was on a mezzanine above the other departments. If you followed the mezzanine all the way through its darker and grimier sections toward the back of the building, you arrived at the photographer's darkroom. The photographer, Bob, was a middle-aged man who had a weak heart.

Bob loaned me a Rolleiflex camera and tried to teach me about *f*-settings and exposure times, but all I remember learning from him was that lots of women love to be photographed nude.

I've since found that many news photographers know this secret, but at the time I was surprised to learn that even in a provincial town where newsstand copies of *Playboy* were wrapped in brown paper, there were plenty of women eager to have their lovely bodies preserved in black and white images. Bob let me see his portfolio, I suppose because he knew I wouldn't recognize the women and wouldn't jeopardize his reputation as a discreet recorder of their secret vanities.

———◆———

The Denver *Post* published a column called "Red Fenwick's West." Fenwick traveled around the West, writing folksy columns about the towns, rodeos, festivals, and colorful characters of Colorado, Wyoming, Nebraska, and Kansas. I had met him briefly when he came to North Platte to engage in a mock gunfight with Ted Turpin. To promote something — the rodeo, I suppose — the two exchanged extravagant taunts through their respective newspapers for several days, then had a "showdown" with blanks on a downtown street in North Platte. After the smoke cleared, we all repaired to the White Horse, where I, along with many others, was introduced to Fenwick.

Toward the end of that year, after I had decided to go back to college, I drove to Denver to meet Fenwick. He was by far the most famous *Post* man, at least outside Denver; in the smaller cities all the newspapermen, mayors, and rodeo committeemen knew him. I loved the way he wrote, and envied his life as a roving story-teller. I suppose I wanted to find out if I might someday have such a job.

I found Red in the middle of a huge newsroom, typing away. I told him that I was a reporter in North Platte, that I was about to go back to Harvard, and that I admired his columns.

"That's fine. Take a chair over there and wait for me if you can. I've got to finish this column."

After a while he took his copy out of the typewriter, marked it up, and delivered it to someone across the room. When he came back he said "Come on, let's wet our whistle."

We went out a back door, across an alley, and into the back door of a bar. Everybody there seemed to know Red. He introduced me to his friends, just as if I was someone they might want to know.

He had two or three drinks and I tried to keep up, though it was more than I was accustomed to drinking when I was trying to make intelligent conversation. After a while he said "I want you to meet Miss Helen. She's the publisher."

We went back across the alley and then to an upper floor of the *Post* building. The publisher's secretary greeted Red and said "Go on in, she'll be glad to see you."

Helen Bonfils was a sturdy woman in her 60s, with a bulky blonde hairdo and a warm demeanor. She seemed genuinely pleased to meet me, and quite interested in the fact that I was at Harvard and wanted to be a newspaperman. I don't remember what we talked about, but she was easy to talk to and she and Red obviously were dear friends. Before I left she told me to keep the *Post* in mind when I graduated.

Only later did I learn that she was the daughter of Frederick Bonfils, the legendary longtime owner of the newspaper, one of the most important men in early

Colorado history. She was a society woman, oft-married, a patron of the theater and the arts, and unquestioned boss of the *Post*.

Red later sent me a book called *"Timberline,"* by another *Post* man, Gene Fowler. It tells the rollicking story of Frederick Bonfils and Harry Tammen, the larger-than-life partners who built the *Post* on the philosophy that "a dog fight in a Denver street is more important than a war in Europe." They were contemporaries of Leadville Johnny and the Unsinkable Molly Brown, and their lives were almost as colorful. One target of their yellow journalism shot them both and another horse-whipped them.

After reading that book, I could see that "Red Fenwick's West" was a vestige of Bonfils's imperial ambitions. Bonfils wanted the *Post* to be the flagship of an empire that included Colorado and Wyoming, and much of Nebraska, Kansas, and New Mexico. Red's role was to plant the *Post*'s flag as widely as possible, reminding people that the *Post* was their newspaper, even if it was 200 miles away.

Writing this now, I wonder why I didn't apply to the *Post* when I graduated. I don't think I even considered it; I guess by then I was besotted with the idea of Texas.

———◆———

When I returned to Harvard, I was too busy having fun to do much to advance my journalism ambitions. I did learn a thing or two about journalistic ethics. For a few months I worked an evening shift in the morgue of the Boston *Herald-Traveler*, mostly digging through files to find photos for the news desk. One night there was an urgent request for photos of Ted Williams, the great Red Sox slugger. Williams had been involved in a fight, or at least a scene, in a bar.

I pulled a few photos from the files, including one showing Williams clenching a baseball in his upraised fist, with a pugnacious expression on his face. The staff artist selected that one, and the next morning I saw why: he had deftly painted the baseball out of the photo, so the *Herald-Traveler*'s story about the bar fight was illustrated with a photo of an angry-looking Ted Williams shaking his fist.

———◆———

In 1962 the San Angelo *Standard-Times* was the best newspaper in West Texas. It had a publisher who believed in quality journalism: Houston Harte, patriarch of the Harte branch of the Harte-Hanks chain. It published morning and evening editions, and had a news staff of 30, including an oil editor, four photographers, a religion editor, a society editor, a business editor, two city editors, a state editor, a sizeable sports staff, and half a dozen reporters. The editor was Ed Hunter, who later became editor of the Houston *Post*, and the farm editor was the acclaimed Western novelist Elmer Kelton. To cover an area the size of Ohio, we had local "correspondents" in all the towns in the area and a fleet of cars and an airplane at our disposal.

It was pure luck that I landed there after graduating from college. I had made inquiries to the New York *Times* and *Time* Magazine, but didn't apply because I learned that the *Times* would pay $65 a week and *Time* $80 a week. By that time I had a wife and a baby, and there was no way we could live in New York on those salaries.

Several of my fraternity brothers at Sigma Alpha Epsilon bragged incessantly about their state, Texas. I was swayed by that; nobody bragged about being from Illinois or Oregon or Nebraska. I had never been within 500 miles of Texas, but I researched the matter a little and decided that West Texas would be a hospitable place for a guy from western Nebraska. Early in 1962, I sent letters to papers in Amarillo, Odessa, Midland, Abilene, and San Angelo.

The *Standard-Times* was the only one that responded. They offered me a job at $95 a week, sight unseen — no interview, no resume, no references. Years later, Hunter confessed that he had misgivings after hiring me.

"You can't imagine how relieved I was when you walked into that newsroom. I had got to thinking — what if he's black? I wasn't sure San Angelo was ready for a black reporter."

Ed Hunter was no racist, but it was 1962, and Texas was the South. There were "white's only" signs over the water fountains in the Tom Green County courthouse.

———◆———

Mr. Harte had a policy that no phone in the newsroom should ring more than once; he wanted the public to know that we valued their calls. Occasionally he called with a question or a news tip at night when only three or four staffers were in the newsroom. Those calls kept us on our toes, more or less literally — there were 20 or more phones, so we learned to fly across several desks to reach a distant phone before it could ring a second time.

I think of Mr. Harte today when I call a business and get a recording that tells me that my call is important to them so please don't hang up, then makes me listen to a menu, and then tells me to please wait for the next available associate. If my call is important to you, answer the damn thing!

———◆———

My first assignment at the *Standard-Times* was the courthouse beat. I went to the office of the county judge to introduce myself. I asked his secretary if I could make an appointment. She said "He's not busy, just go on back." The judge heard that exchange and called out "Yeah, come on in and sit a spell."

After a few pleasantries, he said "What are you, Baptist or Methodist?" I thought maybe that was a preface to a joke, but after I answered "Methodist," it became clear he was serious. I soon realized that it was just a friendly let's-get-acquainted inquiry, as innocent in his mind as "Are you a Texas fan or an A&M fan?"

Apparently his manner suited his constituents just fine. He was re-elected many times, and the courthouse is now named for him: the Edd B. Keyes Courthouse.

———◆———

Ed Hunter was an editor from the same mold as Keith Blackledge. He hired young people, taught them good journalism, and watched them move on to bigger papers. One reporter who moved on during my one year in San Angelo was John Mulder, a police reporter cut from the cloth of Damon Runyon. John was around 21 years old, stocky, with dark hair worn in a duck-tail. He was the worst-dressed person on the staff: baggy pants, run-over shoes, and short-sleeved rayon shirts that smelled like they hadn't been washed. He always had a pack of cigarettes rolled up in the cuff of a sleeve.

He wasn't fastidious about grammar, but he could quickly hammer out a story about a drug raid or a wreck. He talked and thought like a cop, and they liked him. When I succeeded him on the police beat, I found out how important that was. I didn't talk or think like cop, and they didn't trust me; they were happy to slip John a rap sheet or a search warrant affidavit, but I got only what they wanted to give. John went to the Fort Worth *Press*, a paper that shared his fascination with crime, in a town that produced a lot of it.

Next door to (or maybe it was across the street from) San Angelo's only hospital was a little café that might have been the original "greasy spoon." The proprietor (I'll call him Rupert) was an aficionado of gossip which he got mostly from hospital personnel and cops who were killing time while they waited to talk to a patient about some crime or wreck.

For a time the hospital was part of my beat, and I often dropped in to the café to see if Rupert had heard any newsworthy gossip. He was a conspiracy theorist, so I quickly learned to discount most of what he reported about nefarious doings at the hospital or the police department. He was also a racist who was fond of saying things like "You want some chili today? It's extra meaty; I got that cut-up Mexican the cops brought to the hospital last night."

But once in a while he knew something useful, such as news about a crime that the hospital or the cops weren't revealing. From him I got a tip about an unruly kid whose parents locked him in the backyard fall-out shelter. They kept him imprisoned so long he became dehydrated and had to be hospitalized. The parents were prominent and apparently they had persuaded the hospital and the police to keep it quiet.

Fall-out shelters were sprouting in backyards all over town in 1962; people must have thought San Angelo was high on the Russians' list of targets. The Cuban missile crisis was the sort of thing that confirmed Rupert's pessimistic view of the world, and he listened to the radio news constantly. It was in his café that I first learned that the Russian ships had turned around and World War III had been averted. Rupert, of course, didn't believe it; he was sure that Kennedy was secretly letting the ships through so he wouldn't have to give an order to attack them.

———◆———

In towns like San Angelo, almost any visiting dignitary is worth a story in the paper. Gayle McGee, Senator from Wyoming, came to town to speak to one of the service clubs. I tracked him down and went to his hotel room to interview him. I asked how he got interested in politics. He said he had joined the local Toastmasters Club in Laramie, where he taught at the University of Wyoming, hoping to become a better public speaker. "I guess I got pretty good at it." He was asked to travel to other towns in Wyoming, speaking to their Toastmasters Clubs. "Some of the Democrats decided that wasn't much different from campaigning, so they asked me to run for the Senate."

I later learned that he actually had Washington experience with the Council on Foreign Relations and the Carnegie Foundation before his Toastmasters tours, but at the time I didn't know that journalists aren't the only ones who know the value of supplying an intriguing angle.

———◆———

My superiors at the *Standard–Times* soon realized that I wasn't much of a police reporter, so they created a new beat for me, covering federal agencies. We often enlisted elected officials to help us. Before he emerged as a star writer for *Harper's* and author of "The Best Little Whorehouse in Texas," Larry L. King was an aide to Slick Rutherford, a congressman who represented a district in our circulation area. We shamelessly used King to get information for us from federal agencies. The Freedom of Information Act had not yet been passed, so agencies weren't required to tell us anything, but they generally responded when an aide to a member of Congress called.

Our crotchety state senator in Austin, Dorsey Hardeman, was less helpful, but occasionally he could be persuaded to place a call on our behalf. When he refused our calls, we sometimes got Mr. Harte to call him. That always produced at least a grudging response, because without Mr. Harte's support Hardeman's political career would have been over.

Then as now, West Texas was obsessed with high school football. On Friday nights in the fall, the entire staff — all 30 of us — covered high school games. The sports staff covered important games in person, and the rest of us worked telephones in the newsroom. The paper had arrangements with dozens (maybe hundreds) of high school coaches. The winning coach was to phone the *Standard-Times* immediately after the game with a brief summary — the outcome, who scored the touchdowns, and maybe another detail or two, such as whether the winning team was undefeated or leading the district standings.

We had what was called a "reverse WATS" line, which meant the coaches could call the paper toll-free. Invariably, a coach or two forgot to make the call, which set off a frantic attempt to reach him, or the losing coach, or the superintendent of either school. Our goal was to have at least a three-paragraph story on every game in West Texas in Saturday morning's paper. By around midnight, we usually had all the games covered and we adjourned to someone's house for a party, with beer and snacks provided by the paper.

The paper probably should have paid us overtime, but so far as I know no one ever complained. Being part of a collegial effort that gave our subscribers football news they could get nowhere else was reward enough.

———◆———

Working for the newspapers in North Platte and San Angelo in those years was not just a job, it was a calling. Everybody in town read the paper, and if they saw an error or didn't like what they read, they let us know. The papers worked hard at identifying with their readers. The *Telegraph-Bulletin* ran a daily column of "brites" — one-paragraph notes about something funny or serendipitous that happened to somebody in our area. Each staffer was supposed to come up with one brite a day.

The *Standard-Times* had the "Red Rooster," a tradition rooted in what was most important to West Texas: rain. On those rare nights when it rained, we took dozens of calls from ranchers and residents of small towns who would report, "Got 65 hundredths here," or "Half an inch and it's still raining." If we got enough calls to confirm a substantial widespread rain, the next morning's paper carried a large rooster superimposed in red ink over the entire the front page; in that part of the country, a good rain was "something to crow about."

———◆———

In 1963 the war in Vietnam was just heating up. The notorious Madame Nhu, whose husband was the brother and chief lieutenant of South Vietnamese dictator Ngô Đình Diệm, came to Texas to drum up support for Diệm and his brother. Dudley Dougherty, right-wing scion of a wealthy ranching family, hosted a soiree for her at his South Texas ranch, aimed at introducing some of the Texas rich to the Diệm regime. I had moved by then from San Angelo to the capitol bureau of United Press International in Austin. UPI sent me to cover the event — my first assignment outside the capitol.

The Dougherty ranch house was on a hill overlooking ranch's airstrip. A dozen or more DC-3's and Convairs of the South Texas aristocracy landed there and parked on both sides of the runway. Tables with nice tablecloths and good china covered the lawn in front of the house. Japanese lanterns hung from oak trees. The hosts trotted Madame Nhu out for a news conference designed to spread her pitch for Diệm to an audience beyond the Daughertys' guests.

Like most of the other reporters, I knew nothing about Vietnam except that the U.S. had recently sent some "military advisers" there. We asked Madame Nhu questions like "How do you like Texas?" and "Is it very different from Vietnam?" But one reporter, Saul Friedman of the Houston *Chronicle*, had done his homework. He began asking her about the disappearance of critics the Diệm regime was suspected of murdering. The hosts quickly terminated the news conference and hustled us off the ranch. A few weeks later Madame Nhu's husband was assassinated.

Friedman and I ended up eating dinner together at a café on the courthouse square in Beeville. He gave me a tutorial on Vietnam, and in the process opened my eyes to the kinds of things a reporter should know. He was chafing at the *Chronicle*'s narrow-mindedness and soon left for the Detroit *Free Press*, where he shared a Pulitzer Prize for coverage of the 1967 Detroit race riots.

———◆———

In 1963, 1964, and 1965, writers from the Austin bureau covered home football games of the Texas Longhorns, Baylor Bears, and Texas A&M Aggies. The bureau chief took the UT games and I usually covered either Baylor or A&M. I wasn't much of a sportswriter, but my story on a Baylor game on Nov. 16, 1963, earned me my first shout-out from the UPI brass.

Every week the UPI managing editor in New York put out a newsletter with the highs and lows of UPI's performance during the preceding week, based mostly on our score against our main competitor, the Associated Press. Somebody in the New York bureau scoured newspapers from across the country to see which wire service they used on the major stories of the week. Each tally produced an us-vs.-them score called the "play."

The newsletter for the week of the Baylor-Kentucky game said "David Anderson had a fine angle on the Baylor-Kentucky game about Kaintuck's Nick Norton outpassing Don Trull in a 44-mph wind and took 22-8 play." That was the most lopsided UPI win of about 50 games tabulated that week.

The newsletter arrived in most bureaus on Nov. 22, 1963, and was appropriately ignored because of the assassination that day of President Kennedy. Even though nobody else paid any attention, the salute suggested to me that maybe I could succeed in this new world of wire service journalism after all. My first months at UPI had been an intimidating whirlwind, learning the geography of the capitol and state office buildings, the names and titles of many state officials, and the mysteries of wire service communication, much of which was in inscrutable code (sample: "73's" at the end of a message meant "cheers;" "ROX" was the Associated Press.)

———◆———

Speed was of the essence in covering college football games because sports editors sometimes chose whichever wire service story got to them first. That was especially true of night games, of which the Southwest Conference had many. Saturday night games often challenged the deadlines for Sunday sports pages, so a couple of minutes could make a decisive difference to a harried editor.

Wire service reporters sat in the front row of the press box, each with our own teletype machine and operator seated directly behind us connected to a direct Western Union wire. We tried to get most of our 300-word story written and in the hands of the teletype operator before the game ended, leaving only the lede — an opening paragraph or two — to be filed when the game ended. Cliff hangers were not appreciated; we liked to have the outcome decided by the third quarter, with not too much scoring in the final quarter. Trying to write the story with a lot of action going on in the fourth quarter was a nightmare.

———◆———

The assassination of President Kennedy broadened the mission of the Austin bureau markedly. I had no role in contemporaneous coverage of the event, but on the Wednesday after the shooting, UPI/New York asked us for a feature on the LBJ Ranch, to run the following Sunday. In a heavy rain I drove my trusty 1956 Ford over the two-lane road to Johnson City. (We soon saw the ability of political power to get things done: all 50 miles of that road were improved to four lanes in just a few months.)

In Johnson City I asked how to get to the ranch, and was told to "go to Hye and take the first right." There wasn't a right turn in Hye. It was still raining hard and the only sign of life in Hye was at the feed store, where some farmers were drinking beer and playing dominoes. They told me to go on up the highway another half-mile and then turn right.

I turned right on a paved road and then turned right again on a dirt road. I was soon stuck in hubcap-deep mud. I slogged through the mud to a farmhouse not far away and persuaded a farmer to bring his tractor and pull me out. He gave me better directions: proceed up the paved road another two or three miles and then cross the river on a low water crossing at the foot of a concrete dam.

I made the crossing with the rain-swollen Pedernales River crashing over the dam against the car, and pulled into the muddy yard of a handsome white ranch house. A car was parked there with the engine running, the wipers swishing, and a man seated behind the wheel. I deduced that he must be a Secret Service agent. He rolled his window down a little and motioned me to pull alongside, driver's window to driver's window.

With sheets of rain coming down between us, he asked, "What do you want?" I told him I was with UPI and wanted to do a story on the ranch, he said "Wait here" and rolled up his window. After a long wait, a tan Lincoln four-door sedan pulled into the yard and the driver motioned me to get in. He asked what I wanted to see.

It was A.W. Moursund, Johnson's business partner. He wasn't very forthcoming with information about the ranch, Johnson, or himself, but he drove me around the ranch, showing me the boundaries, the airstrip, the cattle, and the numerous buildings. I got enough details to put together a 700-word story that ran in many newspapers the following Sunday and introduced Americans to what was to be the Texas White House for the next five years.

A month later Johnson came to the ranch for the Christmas holidays and to host a visit by Ludwig Erhard, the German Chancellor. The invitation had been issued months earlier by Kennedy but Johnson seized the opportunity to show that the U.S. role in the world was undiminished. Dozens of reporters arrived from Washington, Germany, and elsewhere. The main public event was a barbeque on the grounds of the school in Stonewall, a couple of miles from the ranch.

UPI deployed half a dozen reporters, coordinated by Merriman Smith, our chief White House correspondent, who won a Pulitzer for his coverage of the Kennedy assassination. The Dallas experience had impressed on Smitty the importance of being prepared for anything, so he assigned us like a general deploying his troops: a reporter at the airport, others stationed along the route to the ranch, and Smitty in the press pool car right behind the car carrying Erhard. My station was an intersection on the road between the ranch and Stonewall. Each of us reported to Smitty by walkie-talkie.

Once the motorcade passed, I rushed to the school in Stonewall, where Johnson and Erhard both made speeches. My job was sit in the makeshift press room at the school and relay Smitty's dispatches to New York by telephone. Many others were crowded into the room making their phone calls. During a lull I heard a familiar voice dictating into a phone behind me; it was the commentator H. V. Kaltenborn; I recognized his voice from hearing him on the radio when I was a boy.

———◆———

UPI's resolve to always have a reporter as close as possible to the president didn't end when Erhard went home. For the next five years a reporter and photographer from the Austin bureau went to Stonewall whenever Johnson was at the ranch. The UPI Washington bureau would let us know when Johnson was en route and someone — usually me — would drive to Stonewall. We weren't allowed on the ranch, so we sat in our cars on a hill across the river from the ranch, where we could see when Johnson arrived and left, sometimes by helicopter and sometimes on a small jet that could land on the ranch airstrip. With binoculars or a telephoto lens, we could sometimes identify a guest whose presence might be significant. An unannounced visit by Defense Secretary Robert McNamara, for example, might presage a new development in Vietnam.

The land where we parked was on a peach farm owned by Earl and Martha

Sweeney, who welcomed us and sometimes brought us treats. Johnson hated our prying and tried to persuade the Sweeneys to ban us, but Earl resented the intervention and refused. It took several years, but Johnson's friends eventually succeeded in getting the Sweeney's farm condemned to make way for a new LBJ State Park. Many years later I confessed to Mrs. Johnson that I had been one of the spies parked on the Sweeney farm; she made it clear that she was still in no mood to forgive.

In the spring, summer, and fall, Johnson loved to go boating on Granite Shoals Lake (which was soon renamed Lake LBJ). If we saw helicopters take off late on Friday afternoon and head north, we raced to the lake. Johnson could be there in 15 minutes, but by car the trip took 45 minutes, or longer if the two-car ferry across the Llano River arm of the lake was on the opposite side when we needed it.

Interviewing LBJ

Johnson's helicopter could land right beside his boathouse, so by the time we rented a boat at Valentine's Lodges and got on the water he would have a big head start down the lake. But we cultivated friends in the houses along the lake who could tell us when Johnson had passed by and which of his boats he was in — one of them was the biggest boat on the lake and the other was the most powerful. We learned his habits well enough to guess his destination most of the time.

Johnson sometimes pulled a guest, usually one of his daughters or another young woman, on water skis and he hated to have the skier photographed or even identified. He would go into a large cove and have the Secret Service boats try to keep us out. We insisted that the waters were public and we had as much right to be there as he had, but the Secret Service wasn't interested in hearing about our rights. They had powerful jet boats and they sometimes cruised toward us, then quickly turned at the last moment and gunned their boats so the jet-propelled exhaust drove us aground.

After they won that battle, we found a wooded hillside high above Johnson's favorite cove, and a UPI photographer set up a telephoto lens the size of a cannon. After a few of those photos appeared in print, two Secret Service agents surprised us, said we were trespassing, and ordered us to leave. I was pretty sure that enforcing a private owner's property rights was not within their jurisdiction, but we were isolated in the woods and they had guns, so we meekly obeyed.

———◆———

On Sunday, Johnson almost always went to church in Johnson City or Fredericksburg. When we saw his motorcade leave the ranch we gave chase, waited outside the church during the services, and followed him home. On rare occasions Johnson invited us onto the ranch. Once early in his presidency, before he soured on the constant press attention, he invited us into the house and chatted with us. He turned to Jack Valenti, then a White House aide, and said "Dammit Jack, don't just stand there, bring these boys some beer."

Johnson invited his new running mate, Hubert Humphrey, to the ranch the weekend after the Democratic convention in 1964. The church procession was unusually large that Sunday, and Johnson allowed us all to follow him onto the ranch. A herd of cows was near the road that ran through the ranch, and Johnson and Humphrey got out and herded some of the cattle to and fro for the benefit of photographers. Humphrey stepped in a fresh cow patty and said "Mr. President, I just stepped on the Republican platform."

When the show was over I raced to the Stonewall café and parked my Smith-Corona portable on a table. For reasons I don't remember, Helen Thomas was at the café. I hammered out a story in short takes and Helen dictated it to UPI/New York. My story included Humphrey's quote, explaining that he had "stepped in some manure."

Later I got a call from our Washington bureau saying that the *New York Times* wanted to use our story but wanted to change "stepped in some manure" to "soiled his shoe" because they didn't want to use the word manure. I protested that the *Times*'s fastidious euphemism conveyed entirely the wrong connotation. The response was "Do you want the story in the *Times* or not?" I acceded and saw the story on page one the next day, but was chagrined that the *Times* didn't use my byline. I later learned that other papers carried the story with the byline of Al Spivak, one of our White House correspondents, who wasn't even present. UPI had replaced my byline with Spivak's because they wanted to burnish his reputation. Spivak sent me a kind note apologizing and praising the story.

The Sunday before the 1965 inauguration, following Johnson's landslide re-election, a long procession of reporters and photographers were following him to the LBJ ranch after church when he suddenly decided to take us on a tour of another ranch he owned. He wanted some reporters to ride with him in his station wagon. His assistant press secretary, Malcolm Kilduff, summoned an AP man and Jack Horner of the *Washington Star*. I was the only UPI staffer present so I protested loudly to Kilduff; a press pool was supposed to include both wire services. Kilduff relented and I got in the station wagon. Johnson, Lady Bird, and Horner were in the front seat and the AP man and I were in the back seat with Johnson's beagle, Him.

For the next two or three hours, Johnson drove Hill Country trails and backroads, holding forth on many subjects. It was mostly a conversation with Horner who, unlike the AP man and I, was a regular in the White House press corps. Sometimes Mrs. Johnson weighed in. They often used first names or other references I couldn't follow. It was all off the record, but I surreptitiously took notes and later tried to report the conversations to our White House reporters.

The LBJ I heard that day was far more reflective than the president we heard on television. There was little of the combative LBJ we came to know. He complained about the *Wall Street Journal*'s investigation of his financial affairs, but it sounded more like bewilderment than anger. "They never did that to Kennedy, and he had a lot more money than I have." He said Joe Kennedy "made his money on Scotch whisky and nobody made an issue about that." His tone was more plaintive than indignant.

Johnson spoke of things that were on his mind as he began his first term as president in his own right, mostly issues related to Congress and his Great Society programs. He was thoughtful, contemplative, and soft-spoken. He said very little about the Vietnam War, which had not yet become the predominant issue. The serious talk was punctuated with comments about deer and cattle that we saw along the way.

At one point he stopped at some ranch buildings and summoned Horner to join him in an outhouse. We could hear them relieving themselves and talking, but couldn't hear what they said. Cynics that we were, some of us recalled the epithet "Lyndon's curious crew," which was Barry Goldwater's unkind insinuation a few months earlier when Walter Jenkins, a longtime Johnson associate, was arrested in a Washington men's room on a morals charge.

The only thing publishable I got out of that afternoon with LBJ was a story about the dog, Him. The dog spent most of the time standing in my lap, looking out the window. When we passed a deer or a cow, Johnson delighted in inciting Him's excitement, which he expressed by vigorously hitting me in the face with his tail. I wrote a little story about that, but I guess editors around the country didn't find it as funny as I did. Or maybe they realized that I wrote it mostly to boast about riding around with the president.

———◆———

UPI was a penny-pinching outfit, but it was willing to spend money to cover big stories like space flights. Gemini 4 and Gemini 5, in the summer of 1965, were the most ambitious space missions to that date. By that time our space expert, Al Webb, had moved from Cape Kennedy to a new bureau at the Manned Space Center near Houston. For the actual flights, UPI pulled in staffers from New York, Houston, Dallas, and Austin. Jack Fallon, Southwest division manager, worked the slot, i.e., edited all the copy just before it went on the wire.

Fallon was a legend within UPI. It was his fast and flawless work in the slot that made our coverage of the Kennedy assassination the apogee of UPI's reputation. One of the many stories about him arose from a civil rights demonstration in Louisiana. A staffer in the New Orleans bureau wrote what he thought was a brilliant lead:

Bogalousa, La. (UPI) — Two Negro men strolled into the Acme Café at midmorning today, sat down at the counter and ordered pie and coffee, thus becoming the first members of their race to eat in a previously all-white establishment in this city in the last 75 years.

Before the staffer could get the second paragraph on the wire, Fallon broke in with the query, "What kind of pie?" With typical UPI indifference to the veracity of inconsequential details, the writer promptly rewrote the lead to say ". . . apple pie and coffee . . . ."

Webb wrote most of the lead stories, and even those written by others usually bore his byline. Bill Hamilton and I were the contributions from the Austin bureau. Bill spent most of the time staked out on the front lawns of the astronauts' families. I wrote a few sidebars that came out of the daily press briefings, but what I remember best are the overnight shifts when I was alone in our temporary newsroom, monitoring NASA's audio feed of communications between CAPCOM and the astronauts. I was supposed to transcribe them, or at least describe them, so Webb and the other front-line reporters could know what had happened during the night. And of course I was to call those people immediately if anything unexpected happened.

It sounds simple enough, but most of the communication was in codes, numbers, and NASA lingo that I understood only imperfectly. I worked in constant fear that a dire emergency would be mentioned in some code that I didn't understand.

⸻◆⸻

The highlight of Gemini 4 was Ed White's spacewalk. He floated around outside the spacecraft for a few minutes while James McDivitt took pictures. It was dangerous, and probably fairly pointless as a scientific matter, but it generated enormous public interest. We knew that we were being used by NASA to maintain public support for space exploration, but we participated enthusiastically because it made great copy.

The main thing I remember about Gemini 5 was that the crew, Pete Conrad and Gordon Cooper, weren't eating enough or getting enough sleep. I recall one testy exchange in which mission control badgered the astronauts to try to get more sleep and Cooper responded with something like, "Maybe we could if you would stay off the damned radio."

Gemini 4 lasted four days and Gemini 5, eight days; we worked 12 or 15 hours a day, so by the time the missions ended we felt like we had been at NASA for months. The Manned Spacecraft Center had been in operation only a year and everything seemed raw and unfinished: hastily built no-frills buildings, roads bulldozed through what had been cow pastures, barely completed restaurants and motels. After working all night, I slept most of the day. When I walked from our motel to the newsroom in the late afternoon, it always seemed like it had just rained, with steam rising from the pavement and adding to the already oppressive heat and humidity.

One day I was sent to Ed White's house to cover his wife's news conference; that seemed like a plum assignment compared to my usual imprisonment in a windowless room with clattering teletypes and static interspersed with space conversations coming over the speakers.

Pat White seemed like the pretty young housewife next door. She was proud to be part of an enterprise important to the nation's competition with the Russians, but overwhelmed by the spotlight. At her news conference she said the innocuous things that NASA had primed the astronauts' wives to say. I was just one of dozens of newsmen in her front yard, but when her husband was immolated along with two other astronauts in the explosion of Apollo 1 two years later, I grieved for her.

———◆———

After I'd been with UPI a couple of years, I made one of those mistakes you make when you try to rationally plot your future. I persuaded myself that to advance in the news business, I would have to either go to New York or Washington, or go into newspaper management. Karen and I had three small children, and trying to support a family in one of the big cities on a young reporter's salary didn't seem promising.

Keith Blackledge, my editor from my 1958-59 stint at the North Platte *Telegraph-Bulletin*, was now city editor of the *Journal Herald* in Dayton, Ohio. We had stayed in touch, and now he began urging me to join him there. When I didn't reject the idea out of hand, he got the *Journal Herald* to offer me a position as financial editor at a considerable raise in pay. I would be head of my own small department.

My better instincts told me don't do it. At UPI, I was covering state government and politics, which was my main interest, but also things like space flights and President Johnson when he was in Texas. We liked Austin and had dear friends there, such as Ernie and Mary Gayle Stromberger and Bill and Suzy Reid. But UPI/Austin was not a lifetime career, and Dayton offered an entrée into newspaper management, so I accepted. Our friends gave us a rousing going-away party and my colleagues in the capitol press corps gave me an engraved silver cigarette lighter. The *Journal Herald* paid for our move, and in February 1966 we arrived in Dayton.

———◆———

Dayton was home to a number of large manufacturers, including National Cash Register, Frigidaire, Delco-Moraine, Mead, Champion Papers, and dozens of smaller businesses, such as tool-and-die shops, that served the manufacturers. Two early experiences brought home to me the significance of being in a factory town.

As soon as we got to Dayton, I got the want ads and began calling about houses for rent. Many of the landlords said, "Sorry, it's already rented." When I mentioned this to my friend Keith, he laughed and said "They hear your accent and they think you're a briar." Briars were poor whites from Appalachia who came to Dayton to work in the factories. Many of them brought along their habit of parking junk cars and old refrigerators in their yards, and landlords in good neighborhoods didn't appreciate that habit. After that, I reined in my Texas accent and soon we rented a spacious brick house in a desirable suburb, Kettering.

The other experience that showed me what it meant to be in a factory town occurred my first week on the job. The parking lot for *Journal Herald* employees was a few blocks from the office. Between the two was an ugly brick building from which raucous music emanated when I walked to work at 9 a.m. One morning I investigated and found that it was a rollicking saloon. The place was filled with tobacco smoke and working men watching nearly naked go-go dancers perform on a small stage. The men were factory workers just off from the overnight shift, enjoying the "evening" before going home to bed.

———◆———

Soon after I arrived, the newspaper sent me to Columbia University for a two-week crash course in how to be a financial editor. It was my first stay in New York. One evening I paid a visit to my former colleague at UPI/Austin, Bill Hamilton, who had transferred to UPI/New York a few months earlier. Bill and his wife Martha lived in a fourth-floor walk-up above a jewelry store somewhere in lower Manhattan. It was the first time I had seen a steel door pulled down to completely seal off a store window at night. Beside that was a walking door covered with iron bars. I buzzed Bill and he activated the electronic lock to let me in.

The apartment was at the top of three flights of stairs, and Bill and Martha were waiting for me there. We drank some Scotch, ate a nice dinner, and had a delightful visit. At the end of the evening, as I opened the door from their apartment to the stairwell, I was looking back at Bill and Martha, full of food and drink and warm feelings. As I started to step out, Bill commanded "Stop!" When I looked down, my heart obeyed Bill's command: I was about to step on a man.

The man was obviously a wino or addict, lying curled up against the door. I was speechless, but Bill coolly said "Hey man, you can't stay here. I'll have to call the cops." After some additional warnings, the man staggered down the stairs.

Bill said, "You must not have pulled the outside door all the way shut when you came in. These guys come in looking to get out of the cold."

When I left I made sure I pulled the door tight, and I felt grateful that I had not taken a job with UPI in New York. We would have been living in a similar walk-up and most of the time Karen would have been alone there with three children. Her situation just then was bad enough: she was back in Kettering, alone in a strange city with three children who had come down with chicken pox shortly after I left. But at least she didn't have to worry about stepping on derelicts when she opened the door.

Most evenings I went to a bar near Columbia with other men attending the seminar. With one or two exceptions, we were all from the hinterlands, places like South Carolina, Minnesota or Oregon. In the bar we saw something few of us had seen at home — young men with hair as long as girls'. We made fun of them and didn't recognize that we were witnessing the beginning of a revolution.

———◆———

Back in Dayton, I soon realized that there were a few things about the job that my friend Keith had neglected to tell me (or maybe I just didn't listen). One was that my "subordinates" were twice my age and actually knew something about financial news. Brainerd had the title of business editor, had been there many years, and was known and liked by the Dayton business community. Billie, a tough, chain-smoking woman, was the copy editor who had been laying out the financial section and editing the financial news wire for years. They wouldn't have welcomed me even if I had known what I was doing, and I didn't. Their friends inside and outside the paper shared their view of me.

I can't say they undermined me, but neither did they help me out. Brainerd was proud of his sources in the business community and wasn't eager to introduce them to me. When I did something that revealed my ignorance of the mechanics of putting out a newspaper, Billie joined the composing-room people in eye-rolling indignation at my gaffe.

On the other hand, the editor in chief was unfailingly supportive, even though my stumbles gave credence to the oldtimers' opinion that he was turning the paper over to people who didn't know what they were doing. His name was Glenn Thompson, and he had recently been put in charge of the *Journal Herald* after a long career in the newsroom of the Cincinnati *Enquirer*. He believed that a smart person could be a good editor without knowing a great deal about editing a newspaper, and he implored us all to rethink the way things had been done in the past. That was a good idea, but not one to endear him (or me) to those who, like my "subordinates," rather liked the way they had been doing things.

———◆———

I learned some useful lessons from Glenn, one of which is that an editor needs to read the paper. Editors tend to get enmeshed in management matters and fail to keep track of what their paper is publishing. Glenn read every word in the paper every morning, and each departmental editor received daily tear sheets of his or her section with Glenn's marginal comments — "Confusing headline." "Nice lead." "What does this mean?" "Why no follow-up on this?" And of course, he pointed out errors — often with exclamation points, as if to say "how could anybody be so careless." But he also offered useful suggestions, such as "We ought to dig deeper and see if we can find out why these businesses are struggling."

We were expected to pass along these critiques to the reporters and sub-editors in our department. Glenn's red pencil kept us all on our toes.

The most important thing I learned was that it's hard to succeed in business, or even business journalism, unless you're interested in money — not just as a means of satisfying wants, but as an end in itself, as a measure of self-worth, as a score-keeping device, as ego-gratification. After a few months I realized I didn't have that interest. I didn't talk the same language as the CEO's and bankers I was covering. To me the difference between $10 million and $100 million was just a matter of zeros, nothing of real interest.

My interests were in public policy and politics, and compared to the intrigues of one-party politics in Texas, politics in Dayton was boring. The Republican Party was run by the business community and the Democratic Party was run by the unions. Labor-management issues spilled over into politics, and the politicians' positions were predictable.

———◆———

The summer of 1966 was a time of race riots in many of the industrial cities of the United States. The most serious was in Detroit, where 44 people died. In Dayton, our turn came on a Friday in September. In the wee hours of that morning, a black man was shot to death in the ghetto. As word of the shooting spread, the black community began to simmer, and by nightfall it erupted. Rampaging gangs overturned cars and set them on fire, smashed windows, and torched businesses. Our photographers risked their lives to get photos of looters carrying away television sets and liquor bottles.

I was the local stringer for *Newsweek*, so early on Saturday editors in New York began calling me. Their weekly deadline was Saturday night, and they were frantic to get the story into that week's magazine. I went to the police station but it was almost deserted — cops had been out all night battling the rioters and now were trying to clamp down before another night came. What the *Newsweek* editors wanted to know was what touched off the rioting. But the answer to that question was elusive. The cops either didn't know, or weren't saying. They didn't know me, so they wouldn't have been eager to share information with me anyway. I had to rely mostly on secondhand information from the paper's police reporters, who were equally desperate to be able to answer that question for our Sunday paper.

Late on Saturday the cops leaked a story to someone; it said two white men had cruised through the neighborhood and shot a black man named Lester as he was sweeping the sidewalk. They had the men in custody but gave no names or other details. Our police reporters were skeptical, and I was too. But *Newsweek* had been pressing me throughout the day for more information, and the leaked story was all I had, so I repeated it to them.

The *Newsweek* writers took it from there, and produced a lead that read something like this:

"A beat-up '62 Pontiac cruised through the silent, stifling neighborhood at 2 a.m. The ugly snout of a 12-gauge shotgun poked out the passenger window. Inside were two angry white men, seeking a target for their wrath. They found one, when they came upon Lester sweeping the sidewalk in front of his business. A blast shattered the stillness, and Lester lay in a pool of blood on the sidewalk, dying."

Late Saturday night they read me the proposed story. I objected: "We don't know what kind of car it was." They said a television station had found a witness who described the car. "We don't know anything about the men in the car," I said. "Well, didn't the cops say they were white men? Didn't they have to be pretty angry to shoot a black man in the back in cold blood?"

When the magazine came out on Tuesday, it was clear I should have objected more strenuously. By then it was clear there was no beat up car and no shotgun sticking out a car window. The police had arrested no white men. Lester was a pimp gunned down by a rival in a territorial dispute. The cops probably leaked the fabricated story in hopes that it would prevent more rioting.

I was the laughing stock of the *Journal Herald* newsroom. Nevermind that the story was written by the big-time journalists in New York; I was the face of *Newsweek* in our newsroom, and there was egg on that face.

One day Fallon, the UPI Southwest Division manager, called me to talk about a libel suit that had arisen from a story I had written for UPI/Austin. At the end of the conversation he said "We'd sure like to have you back." He said there was about to be an opening in Austin and I could have the job if I wanted it. I made up my mind in an instant; until then, I hadn't realized how miserable I was. So after less than a year in Dayton, we were driving a U-Haul truck back to Texas. I returned to my old job as if I had never been gone.

Back in Austin, one of my first assignments was to cover John Nance Garner's 98th birthday celebration in Uvalde. It was one of those crisp, sunny November days that make Texans forget how miserable the summer can be. I drove to San Antonio and turned west to Uvalde, a long glorious open road. I'd forgotten how much I loved the vastness of land and sky; in Ohio I always felt hemmed in — by buildings in the city and by trees and cornfields in the country. I felt as if I had been let out of a dungeon into the brightness of day.

Soon the legislature was in session and we were busy covering committee hearings and floor debates. We tried to focus on stories of statewide, or occasionally national, interest, but our newspaper or television clients often asked us to cover matters of local interest to them. At the height of the session our four-man bureau was filing 50 or 60 stories a day. It was my second session so I sometimes got to write the main roundup story, which usually revolved around the state budget, a tax bill, or some controversy like legalizing gambling or liquor by the drink.

Lieutenant Governor Preston Smith, who presided over the senate, and the house speaker, Ben Barnes, were rivals with ambitions for higher office. Once when they were at odds over some major legislation, I wrote a Sunday interpretive piece (we called them thumbsuckers) saying they were engaged in a high stakes poker game in which Barnes appeared to hold the high cards. A week or so later Smith won. My friend Ernie Stromberger lured me to the lieutenant governor's podium in the senate and laid out a hand of cards — king, queen, jack, and joker, with Smith's photo pasted on the joker. Smith loved it.

The Senate was a girl-watcher's paradise. Many of the senators had attractive college-age women working part time on their staff. They seemed to have no trouble hiring beauties; the girls had at least the illusion of being where important things were happening, and there was a party most every night. The girls sat in chairs on the senate floor, outside the railing but within hailing distance of the senator. They were visions of loveliness; the mini-skirt was the fashion of the day, and the hippie the era had not yet arrived, at least in the Texas senate.

Ralph Hall and Charlie Wilson each had six or eight women working for them part time, and they often had a friendly competition to see which one could amass the most beauties at one time. The press table was inside the railing and while the business of lawmaking droned on, we egged on the competition. If we noticed that six of Hall's girls were on the floor and only four of Wilson's, we would point out to Charlie that he was being outdone. He would phone upstairs to his office and ask to have some more of his girls sent down.

Most of the nightly parties were thrown by one or another lobby group and sometimes there were impromptu parties in a senator's office. Usually the wretches of the press weren't invited. But occasionally we were, so even we were a peripheral part of the continuous party that began the weekend before the opening of the legislative session and lasted until sine die.

On House Floor, 1969, Photo and Inscription by Bob Armstrong

Members of the legislature were pretty unrestrained, accustomed to saying whatever popped into their heads and doing as they pleased.

Senator Dorsey Hardeman of San Angelo was famous for saying, on the senate floor, "I don't know which is worse, socialism, communism, or journalism."

Senator Bill Moore of Bryan was called "The Bull of the Brazos," a nickname he seemed to cultivate. As committee chairman, he sometimes killed bills he didn't like by putting them in his pocket and walking out. After a hearing at which women testified about the need for an equal rights amendment, Moore said "I don't know what they're complaining about. They've already got half the property and all the pussy."

Senator Doc Blanchard of Lubbock once told reporters about an escapade in which he and another senator left a party with a couple of women who were ready and willing. Blanchard lamented that he was willing but not ready: "My dick was limp as a cotton rope."

Senator Grady Hazelwood was a staid, elderly gentleman from Amarillo. During one session he invited a few senators and wives on a boating excursion on Lake Austin. One of the wives needed to relieve herself when the boat was far from a facility, so she maneuvered her derriere over the side of the boat and discharged her water into the water.

Representative DeWitt Hale of Corpus Christi was a respected veteran legislator. For several sessions he had obtained funding for an interim committee to codify some branch of Texas law. He chaired the committee and was noted for his expertise on the law and the judiciary, so his requests were rarely opposed, but one session a member said "Mr. Hale, isn't this the same interim study we've funded several times before? I thought last time you said it was almost finished."

Hale responded, "Yes sir. It was 95 per cent done last summer. A stack of pages this thick (he held his hands half a foot apart) was on the window sill in my office back home. When Hurricane Beulah came it blew out the window and scattered the pages all over town. We're gonna have to start over."

Governor Connally was immensely popular after he was wounded in the Kennedy assassination, but organized labor was not among his fans. Most of the capitol press corps was as hostile to the AFL-CIO as Connally was, but I had always had good relations with the labor leadership. At one news conference Connally answered questions about a variety of issues, then was asked something about the AFL-CIO. He answered the question, but then said "I want to tell you something about Hank Brown (AFL-CIO president), off the record. He can't keep his pants zipped, and I can tell you some interesting things about that, but you have to promise not to print anything."

I walked out, mainly because I didn't want to waste time listening to something I couldn't print. But Connally's people interpreted it as an act of indignation, and it solidified their belief that I was their enemy.

———◆———

In the halcyon days of UT football in the late 1960s, Coach Darrell Royal held a press conference every Monday during the season. The bureau chief usually took that assignment himself, but once in a while I got to do it, and I remember a couple of Royal's choice quotes.

The week before the Longhorns were to play a hapless TCU team in a season in which Texas seemed to be marching toward at least a Southwest Conference championship, somebody asked Royal about the upcoming game. "TCU is like cockroaches," he said, "it's not so much what they carry off, it's what they fall into and mess up."

Texas had a place kicker whose extra points barely cleared the crossbar but were almost always good. Demonstrating with one index finger extended to represent the crossbar and the other crooked downward over it, Royal said "His kicks look like a limp prick."

Press conferences were more fun before they were televised.

———◆———

The Southern Governors Conference met in 1967 at The Grove, a famous old resort in Asheville, North Carolina. I was assigned to cover it. Two memories stand out. One is of the homespun wife of Lester Maddox, governor of Georgia, enduring the supercilious scrutiny of the other governors' wives.

Maddox was a staunch segregationist who had gained fame by equipping supporters with ax handles to help him prevent civil rights activists from entering his cafe. He had just parlayed that notoriety into success at the polls. His wife was a plain woman whose manners, carriage, and dress clearly showed that she had not been raised as a Southern lady. She was embarrassed, and I shared her pain.

The other memory is of an interview I had with Winthrop Rockefeller, who had just been elected governor of Arkansas, the first Republican to hold that office since Reconstruction. It was a one-on-one interview, with not even a press secretary present. Rockefeller acknowledged that he was something of a black sheep in his family (one brother, Nelson, was governor of New York and later Vice President of the United States; brother David was chairman of Chase Manhattan Bank; brothers John D. III and Laurance were major philanthropists). He went on at some length about how grateful he was to the people of Arkansas to give him a chance to do something useful. He was probably thinking about what would sound good back home, but I prefer to see it as evidence that even the very rich feel a need to accomplish something.

———◆———

Our bureau manager, Kyle Thompson, quit to become press aide to a gubernatorial candidate in late 1967 or early 1968, and I succeeded him. It wasn't a big change, because Kyle had not been a controlling bureau manager so I was already pretty self-directed. The major difference was that I was now ineligible for overtime and had to submit various reports.

One of my new duties was recruiting. With major journalism schools at UT, A&M and Trinity University in San Antonio, there were a lot of prospects to choose from. I recommended the hiring of several people, including Daily Texan editor Karen Elliott House, who didn't accept UPI's offer but later won a Pulitzer Prize for the Wall Street Journal, and Ann Arnold, who succeeded me as bureau chief, later became press secretary to Governor Mark White, and eventually executive director of the Texas Association of Broadcasters.

Another of my recruits was an African-American woman from UT. I'll call her Lakisha. My recruits went to bureaus throughout the Southwest, but Dallas bureau chief (my boss) and I agreed that Austin was more likely to be hospitable to Lakisha than other bureaus. UPI had a few black reporters in the North but none in the South. There were none in the Capitol Press Corps but I believed Lakisha would encounter no hostility from those people and little from news sources in state government. Nevertheless, everybody in the UPI hierarchy was holding their breath to see how Lakisha would work out.

About midmorning of what was to be Lakisha's first day, the Dallas bureau chief called and asked how she was doing. I didn't want to tell him that she had failed to show up, so I lied: I told him she was ill, but expected to be in tomorrow. When tomorrow came and she still didn't show, I phoned her mother. "She's not feeling well," her mother said. When she still didn't show on the third day, I cross-examined mom a bit: "What's her ailment? Has she seen a doctor?"

Mom confessed: Lakisha was in jail, and didn't want anybody to know. She and several other young black people had been arrested for picketing a service station near the UT campus, whose owner refused to sell gasoline to black people. After telling that to the Dallas bureau chief, I went to the county jail prepared to bail her out. When I told the district attorney that Lakisha had a job with UPI and might lose it if she wasn't freed, he told the jailer to release her to me.

Lakisha was in a cell with several other women. She said she didn't want to leave. She was angry with her mother for telling. She was sure the job was already lost. When she finally agreed to leave, I took her home and scolded her for not being truthful.

After a high-level pow-wow, UPI executives in New York decided to send her to the Denver bureau in the belief that she would encounter less prejudice there and would be away from the influence of her collaborators in Austin. I never heard what happened to her after that.

———◆———

The year 1968 would have been a major election year even if Lyndon Johnson hadn't shocked us all by announcing he would not run for re-election. Connally had announced he wouldn't seek re-election, which set off an eight-candidate free for all in the Democratic primary for governor. I decided I should travel a day or two with each of the four or five serious candidates.

That led to some adventures. The candidates were hopping from city to city on private planes furnished by their supporters, and hitching a ride was the only way to travel with them. We usually didn't know who owned the plane, when it had last been serviced, or when the pilot had last slept.

To get to Dolph Briscoe's campaign kick-off in Uvalde, two or three reporters showed up at dawn at the general aviation terminal in Austin and boarded a four-passenger plane. It was foggy and we weren't sure we would be able to fly, but the pilot said "Don't worry, I'll just fly down I-35 to San Antonio and turn right." He did, and I remember seeing big highway signs for San Marcos and New Braunfels not far below us.

When we got to Uvalde the airport was socked in. The pilot locked onto the signal of a commercial radio station and circled, trying to reach the local fixed-base operator on the plane's radio. We circled for 10 or 15 minutes, and the pilot said "If he doesn't answer in the next couple of minutes, we're going to have to head to Corpus Christi while we've still got enough fuel to get there."

Just then the airport man finally answered, saying "Sorry, I had to take my daughter to school this morning so I'm a little late."

The pilot asked what the cloud ceiling was. "It's pretty low, but you can just go out east and come on down till you see the ground. There's nothing out there to hit."

We started down through the clouds, and kept going down and down. Jerry Hall, reporter for the Austin *American-Statesman*, was riding shotgun. Suddenly Hall said "I see the ground and it's coming up fast!"

For a campaign event for Eugene Locke in Dallas, reporters were loaded onto a bigger plane, eight or nine passengers. But the pressurization didn't work properly and as we descended to Love Field my ears began crying for mercy. I covered the rally without being able to hear much, and endured further agony on the trip home.

Waggoner Carr had a low-budget strategy: He would charter a small helicopter, hover over a shopping center long enough to draw a crowd, then land in the parking lot and give his stump speech. I rode with him for two or three stops, then Carr and I both got off and the pilot took off again. I didn't know it until the next day, but the helicopter crashed on the way back to its base and killed the pilot.

Preston Smith's campaign was sufficiently well funded to have a plane big enough to carry the press with the candidate. On one trip we stayed overnight in El Paso, and half a dozen reporters walked across the bridge to Juarez. We were looking for a bar called La Cucaracha, which somebody (I think it was Bo Byers of the Houston *Chronicle*) remembered fondly. A few blocks past the bridge we turned right and walked two or three blocks on a side street, but didn't find it.

"I guess it must be the other way," Bo said, so we retraced our steps and walked a few blocks in the other direction, still without finding La Cucaracha. None of us spoke Spanish, but we asked several people on the street, "La Cucaracha?" They just looked bewildered; I suppose they wondered why we were asking about a cockroach.

Finally Bo said, "Oh, you know what? La Cucaracha is in Matamoros."

—◆—

UPI had two distinct operations at the 1968 Democratic National Convention in Chicago. One was inside the International Amphitheater, covering the actual convention. That was run by our Washington people, with help from political reporters pulled in from bureaus around the country. The other was outside on the streets, covering the 10,000 demonstrators and what turned out to be a police riot. That was staffed by the Chicago bureau, and, mercifully, those of us brought in to cover the convention didn't have to deal with the mayhem outside.

The Texas delegates and the Texas press traveled to Chicago on a special train. Soon after we arrived at our hotel, the Conrad Hilton, Governor Connally held a news conference. The delegation he headed was for Humphrey, but Connally's disdain for Humphrey and his increasing dislike of President Johnson's policies were well known. There was much speculation about what he might do — endorse Humphrey, disapprove him, bolt the convention, or spring some other surprise.

Connally had most of the Texas press eating out of his hand, but I thought the big-time press at the Chicago news conference would cut him down to size. I was wrong; Connally charmed, humored, and scolded them and by the end of the session they were as impressed by him as we in Texas were.

The Texas delegation had a choice position in the center of the convention floor and Connally sat in the front row. Most of the time singer Anita Bryant sat beside him. She wasn't a delegate; I think she may have sung the national anthem. She was flamboyant, beautiful, and flirtatious, and Connally plainly enjoyed the attention the two of them attracted, if not the speculation about a possible affair.

Our teletype machines and the main editors were in a press room in the bowels of the amphitheater. Another group of staffers were on the stage, or in the wings of the stage, reporting what was happening at the podium. I was one of four or five UPI reporters who had floor passes and were allowed to roam the hall talking to delegates. We used walkie-talkies to report to the editors in the press room.

———◆———

Access to the amphitheater appeared to be tightly controlled. Delegates, alternates, and press each had a different color of pass, a heavy plastic card on a lanyard around the neck. At each door was a box with a slot and a light on top. We were told that the boxes read the passes and gave a green light only to the type of pass that was right for that door. The very first day someone discovered that a credit card or any other hard plastic rectangle worked just as well as any of the passes.

I was assigned to cover the California, Connecticut, and South Dakota delegations, and a few others that I don't remember. I spent most of my time with the California delegation, which was bitterly divided. A slim plurality were for Hubert Humphrey. The Robert Kennedy delegates had been selected on the day he was assassinated just weeks earlier, and they were grieving and angry. Another sizeable group supported Eugene McCarthy. Among the factions there were shifting alliances, deals that fell through, and threats to walk out. I was constantly informing our editors of the latest rumors and schisms.

Actress Shirley MacLaine and football star Roosevelt Greer were Kennedy delegates from California. I made my way through the delegation to interview them, but as soon as I spoke, MacLaine shushed me; she was watching a tiny portable television set, the first one I had ever seen. Looking over her shoulder I saw footage of cops beating demonstrators with billy clubs as they pushed them into paddy wagons.

At that time most of the people inside the hall were unaware of what was happening outside, but word soon spread and anger rippled through the convention.

Eventually Governor Ribicoff of Connecticut gave voice to the anger from the podium, shaking his finger at Chicago Mayor Daley, who was seated front and center, and saying "Shame, shame on you." I was far back from Daley and couldn't hear his response, but later learned that it was "Fuck you."

Another reporter with a floor pass was Dan Rather of CBS. For reasons that were unclear, security guards hustled him out of the hall while he was on the air live. I happened to be near him and followed him and the guards out of the hall, still on live TV. My recollection is that he signed off saying "This is Dan Rather, somewhere in custody . . . ." But that comment is not in CBS's account of the incident, and it's possible my memory is colored by my belief that Rather was a grandstander.

———•———

Going back to the Conrad Hilton at 2 or 3 a.m., we encountered shocking sights. Parked around Grant Park were dozens of National Guard trucks and jeeps, some with barbed wire people-pushers attached to the front. Near the hotel I saw a young man lying in the gutter, bleeding from one ear. Two medical students who had volunteered to help the wounded approached him but a cop raised his club at them and said "Leave him alone."

At the hotel a large plate glass window had been broken out and the lobby was full of tear gas and the smell of stink bombs. The furniture was in disarray, as if a battle had been fought there. People were mobbing the elevators, trying to get to their rooms and out of the tear gas.

In the days leading up to the convention there had been dire reports from Chicago: Yippies were planning to put LSD in the Chicago water supply; antiwar demonstrators would shut down the city; Humphrey delegates would be attacked. So when we arrived in Chicago it was reassuring to see police everywhere. But that illusion of safety was soon shattered; the police were a lawless mob more dangerous than the demonstrators. It was a taste of a world without law.

When I finally reached my room I saw on television the scope of the police rampages: cops wading into crowds, swinging their billy clubs indiscriminately; people clubbed on the head as they meekly climbed into paddy wagons; menacing cops snarling at the television cameras. I could never again trust police unquestioningly. Only much later did I learn the most discouraging fact: polls conducted after the convention showed that the public overwhelmingly supported the Chicago police.

———◆———

The biggest news stories of the 1960s were the assassination of President Kennedy and the antiwar movement. My engagement with both was peripheral. As I've already mentioned, the assassination dramatically changed the mission of the UPI Austin bureau, but I had no role in the coverage of the event itself. The 1968 Democratic convention was one of the signature events of the antiwar movement, but I was inside covering the convention itself, not outside covering the protests.

One of the earliest antiwar demonstrations aimed at Lyndon Johnson personally was the "Easter vigil" of 1965. A loose coalition of Quakers, draft resisters, student activists, and Texas liberals who had always despised Johnson, organized the demonstration. Knowing that Johnson was likely to spend the holiday at the LBJ Ranch, the antiwar activists planned to stand silently, a few feet apart, beside the two-lane road leading to the ranch. The idea was that Johnson could not ignore them if hundreds of them lined the road for several miles along the route he would take to and from church on Easter morning.

I heard that the staging area was to be a picnic area beside the highway from Austin to Johnson City, so I went there early to talk to some of the demonstrators. Only one person was there — a short-haired, middle-aged man in a gabardine suit and boots. He was not the kind of protester I expected, but I thought, "Well, I know there are supposed to be some Quakers so maybe he's one of those."

I questioned him about plans for the demonstration, but he seemed ill-informed and was tight-lipped about his role. After half an hour in which no one else showed up, it dawned on me that he was an undercover agent for the Department of Public Safety. I wasn't sure who was more foolish: I for thinking he was a demonstrator, or he for thinking that a man who looked like a Texas Ranger could be undercover at an antiwar demonstration. He and I both had bad information about the demonstrators' plan.

I drove a few miles farther and found the vigil in full swing on Ranch Road 1: hundreds of demonstrators standing about 20 feet apart, some carrying antiwar signs, some with peace symbols painted on their bodies or clothing, and some chanting antiwar slogans like "Hey, hey, LBJ, how many kids have you killed today?"

Later we learned that Johnson had traveled to church by a back way and never saw the demonstration.

———————

One of the most active chapters of Students for a Democratic Society was at the University of Texas. I was occasionally able to get information from them until one of their number, a young man named George Vizard, was murdered while working in a convenience store. The police said he was killed in a holdup but his wife and other members of SDS were convinced he had been assassinated by the police or someone they were protecting.

At the funeral his friends' emotions were raw. The large police presence turned their pain to fury. Ted Powers, an AP photographer, was taking photos. SDS members approached him menacingly, accusing him of being a police photographer. Powers stood his ground and police intervened in time to prevent mayhem, but the episode convinced them that all of us in the press were the enemy. After that I lost my sources in SDS just at the time the Texas chapter was becoming influential in the national organization.

Many Texans, including some of my colleagues in the press, called SDS members Communists. I thought that was just hysteria, but much later it emerged that some of them, including Vizard's wife, had joined the Communist Party.

———————

In the run-up to the general election that fall, Hubert Humphrey ran the last old-fashioned presidential campaign and Richard Nixon the first modern one. I traveled for a few days with each.

Humphrey packed as many appearances into each day as possible, and invariably ran behind schedule. Sometimes his crowds had been waiting for hours by the time he showed up, and sometimes people had already begun drifting away.

He was accessible to the press at almost every stop; we could just walk up to him and ask our questions. That of course made it impossible for him to control the message. But his interaction with the crowds was warm and genuine; people loved him, and they energized him. After the election, all of us who had traveled with him got a warm but wistful letter from him, revealing the pain of having lost, but gratitude for the good times.

Nixon's campaign, by contrast, was tightly scripted. He usually made only one appearance each day, generally an evening rally in a large auditorium. In most instances he flew into military bases, where access could be limited to families of military personnel. His plane landed ahead of the press plane, so he would have walked the airport fence shaking hands and decamped for his hotel before the press plane landed. We never had a chance to question him except in news conferences, which were rare.

At one stop, in San Antonio, his campaign had arranged for flirtatious wives of young Republicans to serve drinks to the reporters and chat with us while we waited for the evening event — an effective way to keep us from venturing out to talk to voters.

A plane carrying dozens of college-age girls in miniskirts, boater hats, and red, white and blue jackets accompanied Nixon's party. They sat front and center at the Nixon rallies, giving the television cameras a wholesome and photogenic image to contrast with the anti-war activists who heckled at Humphrey's events.

At the evening rally, Nixon would deliver a speech tailored to the place and the message that he wanted to present that day. We were given the text well in advance and he rarely deviated, so our stories could be filed in plenty of time for evening newscasts and morning papers. Humphrey's speeches were largely extemporaneous, which often meant we were trying frantically to find a phone to call in a story before our plane took off.

Not surprisingly, the image the Humphrey campaign conveyed to voters was one of dissention and chaos, while Nixon's was of orderly calm. The only surprise is that Nixon didn't win by a larger margin than he did.

———◆———

Peter O'Donnell was chairman of the Texas Republican Party. John Knaggs, who had briefly been my colleague when I started at UPI, was public relations man for the state GOP. One day during the fall, when Richard Nixon and Hubert

Humphrey were both courting Texas voters feverishly, Knaggs invited me to join him and O'Donnell for coffee. We went to the dingy, smelly coffee shop run by the Commission for the Blind in the basement of the capitol. They soon got to the point: O'Donnell said Governor Connally was supporting Richard Nixon.

That was a bombshell, although knowing what we know now, it does not seem so surprising: a few years later Connally switched parties, became Nixon's Treasury Secretary, and ran for president himself as a Republican. But in 1968 it looked very different. Connally had been Lyndon Johnson's protégé and President Kennedy's Secretary of the Navy. He had been in the car with Kennedy when he was shot.

Connally despised Humphrey and had not campaigned for him, but he was still a Democrat. News that he was supporting Nixon would be a big story. It would make Connally out to be disloyal to his party; it is one thing to not support the party's nominee, but quite another to support the opponent. And it would fuel speculation that Johnson must have at least tacitly authorized his old friend to turn against the Democratic ticket.

I asked O'Donnell how he knew. "Can't tell you," he said.

"Okay, tell me how I can confirm it."

"Can't do that either."

I turned to Knaggs. "John, you know I can't run a story like that without a source." But Knaggs said he couldn't help me either. I think eventually they did hint that the evidence had to do with conversations Connally had with some of his supporters in Dallas, but they gave nothing more specific than that.

I knew that neither O'Donnell nor Knaggs would peddle that story if it had no basis. And it was inherently credible: Connally regarded Humphrey with contempt and had conspicuously failed to campaign for the ticket. But unless I could find some proof or a responsible source to whom I could attribute the story, I couldn't do anything with it. The Connally camp and the Humphrey people would deny it, and without any evidence, UPI would look foolish.

In fact, it would never get that far. As chief of the Austin bureau, I normally didn't have to clear stories with anyone, but I would have to give the UPI editors in New York a heads-up about this story because of the sensation it would cause. And I knew what they would say: "Get some proof first."

I had no sources among Dallas Republicans or in the Nixon camp, and the

Connally camp wasn't going to confirm the story, so I just gnashed my teeth and let the story die.

Eventually the details came out: Connally in fact *had* convened a meeting with his big donors in Dallas and encouraged them to support to Nixon. Ernie Stromberger and Jim Lehrer of the Dallas *Times Herald* got confirmation of the story from Bill Clements, a prominent Dallas Republican who later became governor. But their editors watered down the story and didn't give it prominent treatment in the paper. It ran the Sunday before the Tuesday election, and by then it was more or less lost in the flurry of last-minute election news. The story would have had far greater impact if UPI had been able to confirm it earlier and give it national distribution.

Timely news of Connally's support wouldn't have necessarily tipped Texas to Nixon, and Nixon won the election without Texas's electoral votes anyway. But it surely would have at least diminished the 40,000-vote margin by which Humphrey carried Texas.

———◆———

Bill Heatly was the tough-talking, barrel-chested, square-faced chairman of the House Appropriations Committee. Agency heads and legislative colleagues feared him; he knew more about the state budget than anybody and was quick to use his knowledge and the power of his position to punish anyone who crossed him.

In the course of covering a scandal at the state facility for juvenile delinquents, I came across someone named Heatly who was on the state payroll as state psychiatrist. He wasn't connected with any state mental health facility and didn't seem to have any regular role with the state.

I determined that he was Bill Heatly's brother, and wrote a story questioning his presence on the payroll. That story brought a flurry of tips about other Heatly arrangements with the state. The Texas Employment Commission rented a building from Bill Heatly in his hometown of Paducah — a West Texas burg not big enough to have much need for an unemployment office. He was profiting from other dealings with the state as well. Enough people with festering resentments of Heatly came forward to give me a series of stories that went on for weeks. Newspapers criticized him editorially.

Eventually Heatly asked me to come to his office. "Why are you doing this to me?" he asked. I replied (too self-righteously, in retrospect) that I wasn't doing anything to him, just reporting what he was doing. To my amazement, he broke down in tears, though his anger didn't diminish. "You're worse than a rattlesnake. A rattler at least gives warning."

The furor eventually cost Heatly his chairmanship but he still had power, and when plans for a remodeling of the capitol were revealed, they included a new elevator that obliterated my office. By the time it was installed I had left and gone to law school, but my former colleagues in the capitol press corps enjoyed calling the elevator Heatly's revenge.

When I graduated from law school, Supreme Court Justice Tom Reavley hired me as chief counsel for the state judicial council. Much later Judge Reavley asked me, "What did you do to Bill Heatly? He got Governor Smith to call me and tell me not to hire you."

A lesser man would have heeded the warning, because the judicial council existed at the sufferance of the legislature and the governor. But Judge Reavley was a man of courage and integrity, and he didn't withdraw the offer. And he spared me anxiety by waiting to tell me about the threat until after I had left the job.

———◆———

When Preston Smith was inaugurated as governor and Ben Barnes as lieutenant governor, they had five or six inaugural balls at different venues around Austin, each with a different genre of music and a different crowd. Smith and Barnes went from one to another and some reporters accompanied them, on the rather transparent pretext that we were covering the inauguration.

The last stop was at the Stephen F. Austin Hotel. After that ball ended, Barnes and his wife headed upstairs to the elegant, private Austin Club for an after-party. Karen and I and Ernie and Mary Gayle Stromberger followed. We were met at the door by Frank Erwin, a powerful political figure and longtime Barnes backer. Erwin said "Sorry, this is a private party."

Ernie and Mary Gayle had the good sense to go home, but I, full of alcohol and indignation, went down to the lobby and phoned up to the Austin Club. I asked to speak to Barnes and when he answered I said "Your buddy Erwin is keeping us out of your party."

"Come on up," Barnes said, "I'm sure you're welcome."

Erwin was at the door again, and with exaggerated courtesy, he invited us in.

It was soon plain that we didn't belong. The guests were the rich and powerful; the atmosphere was hushed and sedate, not exuberant like the evening's previous events. There were no other press people. Karen and I managed to find a few people to talk to but mostly we were ignored. Karen wanted to leave immediately but I was stubbornly determined to exercise my "right to cover all the festivities."

After an hour or so a breakfast buffet was served. When we reached end of the buffet table a waiter took our plates and led us to a side room. We sat down, waiting for others to join us, but no one did; Erwin may have had to admit us, but he didn't have to let us mingle with his guests. When we got ready to leave, Erwin had a highway patrolman drive us home.

———◆———

When I left UPI and enrolled in law school in the fall of 1969, I thought my journalism days were over. But that was not quite true.

In 1974 Texas had a constitutional convention. KLRU and KLRN, the public television stations in Austin and San Antonio, decided to broadcast a weekly interview program with various convention delegates, and they asked me to host it. By then I was teaching at the law school, but I had drafted a proposed judiciary article during my time with the state judicial council just after law school, and I had worked on a broader constitutional revision project after that. Delegates to the convention were members of the legislature, and I knew many of them from my days in the capitol press corps. I agreed to do the program on the condition that someone else book the guests and choose the topics.

The show was called Capitol Gallery. Initially it was an hour long and was broadcast live by KLRN and KLRU and on tape by other public stations in Texas. Each show consisted of three 20-minute segments, each with three or four different guests and each on a different issue currently before the convention.

I arrived at the studio half an hour early for makeup and to be briefed on the guests. I was generally familiar with the issues and most of the guests, but the logistics of live television were all new to me. At the beginning of the show the first group of guests would be seated on the platform with me; we would all be miked up and ready for the cameras to roll. The producer would hold up large cards showing how many seconds were left before air time, and then, at zero, signal me to introduce the show and the guests. For the next 20 minutes I asked questions and moderated the discussion.

That was the easy part. At the end of the first segment, I was to fill the air for a minute or two while off-camera the staff quickly swapped the first group of guests for the second. Frequently one of the first group would forget the microphone attached to his lapel or walk between the camera and me. If there was any delay in getting the second group seated and miked up, I was likely to run out of things to say. The producer would frantically signal me to keep talking, but his panic only made it harder for me to think. There were some awkward silences. The stressful transition repeated itself between the second and third segments.

Guests sometimes failed to understand the need to switch places quickly. I remember one occasion when Harry Whitworth, lobbyist for the chemical industry, was a guest, voicing the business community's views on some subject. Just as his segment ended, he dropped a large file folder, scattering papers all over the platform. He tried to retrieve the papers; the producer and I were trying to signal him to leave them so the next guest could come on, but he didn't understand our frantic gestures.

———◆———

We did the show from 6:30 to 7:30, and sometimes the guests didn't let it interfere with their cocktail hour. Senator Oscar Mauzy showed up once with a tumbler full of Scotch in hand and apparently another glass or two in his bloodstream. He refused to surrender the drink to the staff, so during his segment the camera showed him with drink in hand. Charles, the producer, said later "I wish they would drink vodka. Viewers might think that was water."

The convention ended in failure when a stalemate over a right-to-work clause blocked approval of the new constitution. Post-mortems and recriminations over the defeat of the constitution furnished good material for a few weeks, but after that we were reduced to interviewing bureaucrats about the doings of their agencies. Capitol Gallery shrank to half an hour after that, and often covered only one subject with one set of guests. Surprisingly, the show survived for another year or two, which seemed to me to be a year or two too long, but we continued to hear (occasional) favorable comments from a few viewers.

I lacked enthusiasm for the show even in its best days. I was too old-school; I didn't appreciate that television had become the most influential source of news. I hadn't overcome the impression formed in my early days in journalism: television was for entertainment and newspapers were for news.

About the same time I was doing Capitol Gallery, Jim Lehrer and Laura Miller were doing a news discussion show on the Dallas public television station, KERA. Lehrer had been a fine reporter for the Dallas *Times Herald* during my years with UPI, and he could have been as disdainful of television as I was, but he embraced it and the KERA show became a huge success. I have often wondered whether I could have made something of the opportunity Capitol Gallery provided if I had only been more open minded about television, spent some time preparing for each show, and got some coaching to make my on-air presence a little less awkward. But in more sober moments, I recognize that Lehrer was just a lot more talented.

CHAPTER 3

An Ode to Honky Tonks

There are two things that always make me feel at home. One is a high plains breeze. If I get off a plane in Amarillo or Denver, or get out of an air conditioned car in Ogallala, Nebraska, or Casper, Wyoming, the breeze dries the sweat on my back and sends a little shiver up my spine. I instantly feel better, spiritually as well as physically. I can breathe better, see farther, and sleep sounder. It tells me I'm at the longitude of my birth.

The other place where I feel at home is a honky-tonk. The twanging guitars and the endless laments for lost love; the boots, jeans, and snap-button shirts shuffling counterclockwise around the dance floor; the clank of pool cues in a corner; the jaded waitresses who call everybody honey — these all tell me I'm among my own kind.

It's getting harder, of course, to find my kind of honky tonk, and I'm long past my honky-tonking days. That's probably why I feel the urge to describe some of the ones in which I've spent memorable bits of my life. I should probably be ashamed (but I'm not) to admit that this is just a sampling of the many joints I've patronized, from Uvalde, Texas, to Idaho Falls, Idaho.

I wet my first whiskers at Joe's Dine and Dance in North Platte, Nebraska. I may have sneaked in there a time or two as a high school student from a small town 35 miles down the road, but my real memories of Joe's begin when I was nineteen. I was still two years shy of legal drinking age, but I was on my own, working as a reporter at the North Platte *Telegraph-Bulletin*, and I don't recall that anyone ever questioned my right to go where other free-spirited young men went for their entertainment.

Joe's Dine and Dance has been gone for many years now, but it is still the model against which I measure all other honky tonks. It sat beside Highway 30 at the west edge of town, at the turn-off to the rodeo grounds. The low building squatted in the middle of a huge gravel parking lot. It had a hard-wood dance floor, slightly elevated, with a bandstand on one side and tables on the other three sides. At the far end of the room was a long bar with a row of stools.

Even in the afternoon, you might find a wayward housewife dancing to the juke box with an out-of-work cowboy or a guy who works the night shift on the railroad. Weekday evenings, traveling salesmen and a few couples might go there for a steak. For its clientele Joe's was "the scene" in North Platte, the way the drive-in is for small-town teenagers. They kept tabs on each other by stopping by Joe's to see who was out with whom, who was out of work, what wife or husband might be about to become unmarried.

Most Saturday nights Joe's had a band. The best was Hadley Barrett and the Westerners, but they played dances all over western Nebraska, eastern Colorado, and western Kansas, so they weren't always available. When they weren't, the quality of music dropped to the universal honky tonk minimum: a drummer who can bang out a strong two-step beat, a fiddler, and a guy who can play the guitar and sing recognizable versions of honky tonk standards. When Hadley played, the place was packed, but even a lesser band brought out a good crowd; people don't go to a honky tonk for the excellence of the music.

Why *do* people go to honky tonks? I suppose it's for some of the same reasons they go to taverns and pubs — for the society of other humans, to play pool or darts, for some conversation, to avoid drinking alone. What sets honky tonks apart is the dancing — if there isn't dancing, it isn't a honky tonk. Because they are necessarily co-ed, the atmosphere is always charged — slightly or highly — with sexual dynamics and the prospect of jealous vio-lence. Honky tonks aren't pick-up bars; most people go there to dance and that's all. But dancing can also be romancing, and the difference isn't always clear to all parties. Opportunities for misunderstanding — or deliberate mis-chief — are numerous.

Honky tonks have their own rules of engagement, and if you pay attention to them you can usually stay out of trouble. The key principle is that dancing is not necessarily a prelude to something more. That means you don't have to take umbrage if someone asks your partner to dance. If you're with your spouse and another couple, you should offer to switch partners once or twice, but only often enough to be sociable. If you go with someone you're not married to, honky tonk etiquette says it's okay for a stranger to ask your date to dance, and it's up to her to decide whether she wants to do so. If the circumstances are right, it may even be okay to ask a married woman to dance.

But dancing is a multi-layered interaction, and sometimes the layers get jumbled. Asking the wrong woman to dance (or the right woman if she's attached to the wrong man), asking her to dance one too many times, holding her too tight, or extending a friendly flirtation a little too long can trigger an alcohol-fueled eruption, and often does.

Fortunately, the kind of violence that erupts in honky tonks is usually of the fair-fist-fight variety. You're not likely to get stabbed or shot, as you might in a bar or strip club, but you may get a black eye or a bloody nose.

My only honky tonk fight was at Joe's. I had double-dated with an acquaintance who for some reason began to disparage the virtue of my date, a girl named Dixie. If I hadn't drunk so much I might have realized that Dixie had little virtue worth defending, or I might have put up a better fight. As it was, I lost the fight, ended up with a permanent scar over my eye, and Dixie took up with the victor.

The best fight I ever saw was at Joe's, during the Buffalo Bill Rodeo. Two farmers from the nearby town of Maxwell were at Joe's and weren't dancing with their young attractive wives. Two steer ropers from Wyoming, Hyde Merritt and John Dalton, came to the women's rescue, dancing most every dance with them. The women reveled in the attention of the cowboys while the farmers sulked. Just before closing time, the farmers charged onto the dance floor and went after the ropers. The smaller of the farmers took on Dalton, who was at least a head taller. The other farmer, big and barrel-chested, took on Merritt, who was as small as the little farmer.

The fighters had the dance floor to themselves and the rest of us had ringside seats. All four were good fighters. Merritt and the little farmer had a hard time reaching their opponents' heads, but they did a lot of damage to the midsection. Merritt was wearing a ring that eventually shredded the big farmer's shirt and bloodied his chest.

The manager eventually was able to move the fight outside but by that time the combatants had pretty well worn themselves out. The next day at the rodeo Dalton roped and tied his steer, but walking back to his horse he could barely move.

I should make clear that not everyone in North Platte patronized Joe's. Most of the respectable church-going population never darkened its doors. Others, like me, went there only for an occasional escape. In a small town it's easy to feel suffocated by other people's expectations; the honky tonk is a place where you can do what *you* want, at least for one night. Honky tonks are mildly disreputable, and that's part of their allure — they're a bit of a walk on the wild side, a small departure from the straight and narrow. For a woman, of course, it's a more serious departure, but in honky tonk circles, not necessarily ruinous.

As the song lyrics suggest, honky tonks have a complicated relationship with love and marriage. I suppose love is sometimes born in a honky tonk, but more often that's where it is tested, betrayed, or lost. The honky tonk plays a crucial role in marital communication. Nothing says "I'm fed up" quite as emphatically as storming out of the house and not coming home until closing time. Not coming home until two hours after closing time says "We have a serious problem." Not coming home until morning says "It's over."

A student of mine once mentioned that she was from Hico, Texas. I said "Then you must know Cody Ohl." He's possibly the greatest calf roper of all time, world champion several times, and he lives in Hico. But she said "No, who's he?" When I explained, she said "Oh, one of those rodeo people. We don't have much to do with them. They're kind of trashy."

I was stunned. In the rodeo world, Cody Ohl is royalty — revered and respected. But that's rodeo, where drinking, carousing, and fighting are normal. Until that moment, I hadn't realized that the honky tonk world I'm so fond of seems trashy to some people.

———◆———

Until the citizenry got fed up with it, downtown Cheyenne was one wild party for the entire week of Frontier Days. The partying moved seamlessly from the bars into the streets, and so did the fighting and drunkenness. I went to Frontier Days many times in the 1960s and 1970s, but I only remember one honky tonk experience.

It was in a joint called the Manhattan, or maybe the Mayflower, on one of the main streets in downtown Cheyenne. It was overflowing with cowboys and women.

The crowd parted like the Red Sea when a tall, shapely blonde wearing a skin-tight silver lamé pantsuit walked in. She danced with a few cowboys and soon left with one of them. We were all disappointed to see her go; she looked like an actress portraying a beautiful alien in a science fiction movie.

To everybody's surprise — or at least mine — she returned in a short while, by herself, now wearing a *gold* lamé pantsuit, just as tight and just as glamorous as the silver one. Once again, she danced with a few cowboys. I regret that I didn't stay long enough to see if she again left with one. I've wondered ever since: was she a hooker with a spectacular wardrobe? An actress out to have a rollicking good time in Cheyenne? A wealthy ranch girl or rodeo queen? Maybe she really was an alien, amusing herself by mesmerizing the yokels in a rodeo honky tonk.

I was disappointed when I went to Frontier Days again in the 1990s. It was still a great rodeo, but the powers-that-be had succeeded in making it family-friendly. I was told the citizens got tired of people urinating in public, throwing beer bottles through windows, and fighting in the streets. They tolerated the wildness when it was just cowboys come to town to raise a little hell, but not when it became a magnet for hooligans in search of lawlessness.

When I returned there in the 1990s, I sought out the place where the cowboys went to drink and dance. Some rodeo stars (Cody Ohl among them) were there, but the place was as demure as a small town Elks Club. Sic transit gloria.

———◆———

Many years ago I was a visiting professor in the law school at the College of William and Mary in Virginia. Visiting there at the same time was Gene Nichol, a law professor who grew up in Mesquite, Texas. Eventually we both got bored with the propriety of Tidewater Virginia, so we found a honky tonk called Fred's Place, in the woods a few miles from Williamsburg. It had a dance floor and a band on Saturday nights but Gene and I only went on Wednesdays; we treated it as boys' night out. The clientele were local rustics, not as friendly as the locals we were used to in Texas, so we were careful not to give offense. Mostly we drank beer and listened to jukebox music from home.

It was innocent fun, two Texas boys doing what came naturally. But when our outings became known around the law school, they created a stir. I think most of the faculty and students were merely amused by the idea of two professors going to a place they wouldn't dream of going themselves, but no doubt there were some who disapproved.

Gene had a class that met at 8 a.m. on Thursdays, and one morning after a night at Fred's Place he must have joked about having a hard time keeping his eyes open. A couple of years later a disgruntled professor who had been denied tenure sued the law school. As evidence that he was being discriminated against, he alleged that William and Mary had granted tenure to Nichol even though he had come to class drunk.

It was untrue, but our patronage of Fred's Place got a lot of publicity, and it didn't seem as innocent in the glare of litigation. We probably should have realized that Virginians might not understand our need for a honky tonk fix. But Gene went on to become a distinguished constitutional law scholar, dean of the law schools at Colorado and North Carolina, and, eventually president of William and Mary, so it's clear Fred's Place didn't permanently damage his reputation.

A few years later, when I returned to William and Mary for a conference, my wife wanted to visit the infamous Fred's Place. The night we went most of the customers were members of a wedding party. The bride, still in her wedding dress, looked to be no more than 17 or 18. The groom and the rest of the party weren't much older, but they were all being served liquor, possibly in accordance with the principle that anyone old enough to get married is surely old enough to drink. A band was playing but the wedding party all sat at one long table and didn't dance.

From the beginning, there appeared to be more tension than joy in the celebration. After a while there was a commotion and two of the groomsmen were throwing fists. I didn't see what started the trouble; the thought that came to mind was that somebody probably disparaged the virtue of somebody else's girl. The long table got knocked over, the bride fled, more people joined the fray, and the fight moved out to the parking lot.

Karen had a hard time believing that the evenings Gene and I spent at Fred's Place were as uneventful as I had described.

When I was a freshman at Harvard, my friends and I spent many evenings walking the streets of Boston. The big-city sights were free entertainment. One night I was amazed to hear the sounds of a honky-tonk band coming from somewhere nearby. We followed the sound around a corner, and there, in the very heart of Boston, was a real honky tonk, a place called the Hillbilly Ranch. It had a hardwood dance floor surrounded by tables and a five- or six-piece country band that played the same songs you would hear at Joe's Dine and Dance. Several doors opened onto the street, so we stood on the sidewalk and listened a while. But my friends weren't interested in spending money to hear honky-tonk music, so we moved on.

A few nights later I was back at the Hillbilly Ranch, using my phony ID to get in and drink beer. The clientele were mostly sailors, and they were a rowdy lot. Many of them were seriously drunk. A couple of fights broke out. There was a serious shortage of women, and with all those belligerent sailors around, I wasn't about to ask anyone to dance.

The women in honky tonks are rarely prostitutes; they're just girls out to have some fun. But I suspect some of those women at the Hillbilly Ranch were there for business reasons. There were a lot of prostitutes in Boston at that time; if you walked down Columbus Avenue you would encounter a hooker every few feet. A honky tonk full of liquored-up homesick country boys would have offered too many business opportunities to be ignored.

I didn't go back to the Hillbilly Ranch; not being able to dance was disappointing, and the place felt a little too raunchy. Honky tonks in the West have a semblance of etiquette — you don't get falling-down drunk and you're expected to remember that there are ladies present. That part of the honky tonk ethos didn't seem to make it to Boston. Still, just knowing that all the honky tonks weren't two thousand miles away was comforting.

Years later I encountered honky tonk sounds in an even more improbable locale. Karen and I were living in London and had rented a car for a weekend in Kent. We stopped at Faversham, a town that has carefully preserved its Tudor heritage of crooked narrow streets lined with half-timbered buildings. The town is the capital of the hops-growing region and was having its annual festival celebrating the hops harvest. We watched locals wearing crowns of hops doing wild dances in the street, punctuated with eerie cries that seemed like they must have been descended from ancient pagan rites.

After the festivities, as we walked down one of those quaint sixteenth century streets, I heard an alien sound: it was Billy Ray Cyrus singing "Achy Breaky Heart." We found the source: a low-ceilinged pub in one of those ancient half-timbered buildings, with a juke box belting out the song that was then a big C&W hit in the U.S. Two English girls were practicing the distinctive line-dancing moves depicted in the video that propelled "Achy Breaky Heart" to the top of charts all over the world. It wasn't a honky tonk, but it was a welcome jolt of back-home feeling.

———◆———

Karen and I were once stranded overnight in Cobar, a small Australian mining town in the outback 440 miles west of Sydney. We were planning a weekend visit to a remote sheep station but a rare rainstorm had flooded the road so were forced to spend the night in town. At dinner I asked the waitress where we might go for some entertainment. She recommended a club she described as "a nice quiet place with a piano bar." I asked if there might be someplace livelier.

"Well, there's the Ox. The Occidental. That's where the miners go." She gave us directions and we found the place along the main highway. It was a big homely cube of a building with few embellishments. There was a big square bar in the center with men standing two or three deep all around. A juke box was blaring out music by the likes of Slim Dusty, Australia's most popular singer of "bush ballads," which include some songs that we would call honky tonk and some that are more like Don Edwards's cowboy ballads. The music and the raucous crowd were both loud.

I made my way to the bar and ordered two beers. The bartender looked at me like I had just set off a bomb. "Sye wot?" he said. "Sye agin?" I tried to look friendly and repeated my request.

The bartender shouted loud enough to be heard over the din, "Hye, mates, lis'en t' 'is bloke. 'E talks funny." The crowd quieted and the bartender asked me to speak again. When I did, there were enough laughs and exclamations to make clear that the bartender wasn't the only one who had never heard an American accent.

After I got the beers, a young man made his way through the crowd and introduced himself. He was head of a shearer's union, in Cobar to organize miners. His union was a breakaway group from the dominant Australian Workers Union and was considered dangerously radical by some. It had been created by shearers who were dissatisfied with their representation by the AWU, and its leaders believed similar dissatisfaction among the Cobar miners would enable it to get a foothold in the mining industry.

A local Cobar mine — I wasn't clear whether it mined copper, gold, or zinc — had been bought by a subsidiary of an international mining company, and the subsidiary declared bankruptcy, owing $10 million in back wages and other benefits to miners. According to our new friend, the AWU had failed to protect the miners' interests and the shearer's union had moved in, promising to deal more aggressively with the company. Some of the men in the Ox were shearers, he said, but most were out-of-work miners.

The young man was articulate and passionate for the cause of the miners. He had started as a shearer himself but was now a full-time union official. But that too was about to end: he had been admitted to the University of Melbourne Law School and was planning to enroll there the following term.

I don't know if the Ox can be considered a honky tonk. I can't remember whether there was a dance floor, but it didn't matter — Karen was the only woman in the place. But if it wasn't a honky tonk, it certainly gave us a more memorable evening than we would have had at the piano bar.

———◆———

In the mid-1980s I went to the Calgary Stampede with my wife and daughter Elizabeth. Like Cheyenne, Calgary once tolerated some remnants of the wild West. In the mid-1980s, prostitution and gambling were legal in Calgary for the duration of the Stampede. Hookers lined some of the downtown streets and a casino or two set up operation.

Elizabeth was about 20, had never gambled, and wanted to try it. I gave her a twenty-dollar bill and sent her off to the casino. She returned in a few minutes, ashen-faced. "I lost it all," she said. She had played roulette and was shocked to see how quickly the spinning wheel can take your money.

After a few days Karen and Elizabeth had to return home, but I stayed a little longer. One day after the rodeo, I headed for the place I had been told was the liveliest spot in Calgary. I don't remember the name, but it was a huge place, completely full. I managed to find a seat at a table with half a dozen Canadian cowboys. I didn't recognize any of the names, but I gathered from the conversation that they were all steer wrestlers and at least some of them were competing at the Stampede. They were big rugged guys, as steer wrestlers normally are. They made a few good-natured jokes about Texas but they were friendly and expansive.

We drank beer and they swapped stories. It was like locker room talk — lots of joshing and needling and challenging. At one point, the repartee between two of them got overheated. There wasn't a lot of arguing, just "You're a lying son of a bitch" from one and "Come outside and say that" from the other. They got up and disappeared.

The others stayed put and went on drinking and joshing. One explained to me, "Those guys just like to fight. They're cousins, been fighting all their lives I imagine."

After a few minutes the cousins returned, one of them with a fat lip and the other with a cut under his eye. Somebody asked, "Get it settled?" and one of the combatants answered with a cheerful "You bet." They sat back down and joined the merriment as if nothing had happened.

———◆———

The biggest threat to a good honky tonk is fame. Once it becomes a tourist destination, it isn't really a honky tonk anymore. It's an "attraction," its name emblazoned on souvenir T-shirts, listed in guide books as "an authentic slice of the local life."

My favorite honky tonk (after Joe's Dine and Dance, of course) used to be the White Elephant in the stockyards district in Fort Worth. I first started going there in the 1970s. It had a long bar along one wall, a dance floor, and some tables in the back.

Many nights the standard honky tonk band was fronted by Don Edwards; occasionally, it was Don alone, adding his vocals to recordings of the honky tonk standards and popular C&W hits of the moment. Later Edwards became the world's premier singer of real cowboy songs — not country western or honky tonk music, but western ballads, old and new. But then he was just everybody's favorite at the White Elephant.

The clientele were cowboys competing at the weekly rodeo at the nearby Northside Coliseum, West Texans in town to shop or sell livestock, and Fort Worth residents with country roots. One night Don introduced a couple sitting at a table near the dance floor — Mr. and Mrs. Harry Thompkins of Dublin, Texas. The crowd knew without being told that Thompkins was a former world champion bull rider.

The tiny, primitive men's room at the White Elephant was no match for the quantities of beer consumed. The de facto toilet facility was an unlighted loading dock or balcony of some kind out the back door, where men stood and peed into a weedy ravine below.

I went to the White Elephant many times in the 1970s and 1980s, sometimes with Karen, sometimes with friends, and sometimes by myself. The music was always danceable, and there were local salesgirls and secretaries knew how to dance and weren't afraid to dance with a stranger who wasn't going to try to go home with them. If you danced enough, you could drink prodigious amounts of beer without getting drunk. I never saw a fight at the White Elephant.

Eventually, success spoiled the White Elephant. The city promoted the stockyards area as an entertainment district, the smell of the stockyards disappeared, and shops selling kitschy western goods opened. Tourists and conventioneers poured into the area; they were attracted at first by the huge Billy Bob's emporium nearby, but then word got out that if they wanted to see a *real* honky tonk they should go to the White Elephant instead. Esquire magazine named the White Elephant one of the country's 100 best bars.

The Elephant expanded into an adjoining building and added so many pool tables that it began to look more like a pool hall than a honky tonk. They began selling White Elephant T-shirts. The single women were now visitors from Wisconsin or New Jersey who wouldn't dance with a man they didn't know.

Mourning the transformation of the White Elephant, I set out one night in search of a real honky tonk. A block or two away, I found a place that I think was called The Cowboy. It had 1930s style glass blocks around the entrance. The inside appeared to be unchanged from some earlier life as a butcher shop or a laundry. Lighting consisted of glaring bulbs hanging from the ceiling. The walls were a dingy yellow. There was a raised band platform at the rear and in front of that a dance floor of well-worn boards. Most of the people looked like the kind that spend all day in a beer joint, not the kind that come out for an evening of fun.

I took a seat at the bar and ordered a beer, thinking I shouldn't be too quick to condemn the place; many good honky tonks are pretty sorry looking places. At the other end of the bar sat a bleached blonde who looked like she had been sitting there most of her life. After a few minutes she moved to the seat beside me and asked if I would buy her a drink. I said, "Sorry, no thanks."

She immediately grew angry, and said loudly, "What's the matter, ain't I good enough for you?"

I said "I'm just about to leave. I just stopped in for a quick beer."

A middle-aged man with several missing teeth staggered over and said "What's the matter, Mabel?"

"This bastard thinks he's too good for me. Won't buy me a drink."

"Buy the lady a drink," the toothless one said.

I laid a few bills on the bar and eased out the door, with Mabel and her friend spouting insults after me. I thought, I hate what's happened to the White Elephant, but maybe the real thing isn't right for me either.

———◆———

Another great honky tonk threatened by fame is the Broken Spoke in Austin. It's been intertwined with the good times and bad times of my life over the past 40 years, but now it has become one of those must-see attractions for visitors to Austin, like the bats under the Congress Avenue bridge.

I don't begrudge the Spoke its success. The proprietor, James White, and his wife Annetta, have spent their lives giving their customers a world-class honky tonk. For almost 50 years they've dealt with unreliable musicians, rowdy patrons, developers who covet the site, picky fire marshals, nosy city inspectors, and thieves who once stole James's prized silver saddle.

Dancing at the Broken Spoke

James looks and sounds a little like Gene Autry, and every weekend night about 10:30, he goes to the bandstand and sings a few bars of "Back In The Saddle Again." Then he delivers an unchanging spiel about "the last of the true Texas honky tonks," where "you won't find no ferns, no grey poupon, just good food, cold beer, and great country music."

I'm happy to see James and Annetta rewarded, but their success comes with a price. The Broken Spoke is not as far gone as the White Elephant. It sells Broken Spoke T-shirts and bumper stickers, and the place has made the guide books, but James has refused to gussy up the ramshackle building or substitute pool tables for dancing space. But the people who own the land that was the Spoke's parking lot sold it, and now a monster condo development dwarfs the dance hall, making it look like what it is — a relic of something that was once authentic.

Now you have to arrive early to get a table. The dance floor is often too crowded, partly with people who can't dance and partly with people who seem to think they're auditioning for Dancing with the Stars. Honky tonk regulars were courteous because they knew that if you're rude you might get your butt kicked; the fraternity boys and software designers who now show up at the Spoke don't know that. If you ask a woman you don't know to dance, she might call 911.

I suppose these changes are just inevitable consequences of "reaching out to new markets," and "adapting to changing demographics."

———◆———

The poster child for reaching out to new markets and adapting to changing demographics is Billy Bob's Texas in Fort Worth. It calls itself "The World's Largest Honky Tonk," but it is really a honky tonk theme park. It has 20 bars, an indoor rodeo arena with live bull riding, numerous shops, acres of pool tables and video arcades, and room for 6,000 people. It has several dance floors, but it is more notable as a concert venue for big-name sit-and-listen acts like Dwight Yoakum and Hank Williams Jr.

My wife and I once went there to hear George Jones. He was so far away we could barely see him, and there were so many rows of people between us and the dance floor that dancing was out of the question. Not my idea of a honky tonk. It made me think wistfully of a time when I saw Jones play at Gil's Club on South Congress in Austin. It was the mid-1960s and Jones's big hit was "The Race is On." We were all there to hear that song, but he was drunk and left the bandstand before playing it.

I've gone to Billy Bob's on a week night a few times, and on those occasions I could find something resembling a honky tonk — an area with a bar, a dance floor, and a juke box. But too many different things were going on around it. A honky tonk needs to feel like a self-contained universe. This felt like one attraction in a three-ring circus.

———◆———

I'm reluctant to describe my kind of honky tonks in the past tense, but present tense doesn't seem quite right either. The two-step is no longer something kids learn by the time they're in junior high. I was bemused to learn that adults pay good money today for private lessons to learn to two-step. We learned it the way we learned to swim or ride bicycles. Among country people, dancing was once a nearly universal skill, though skill may be the wrong word: if a man could pick out the beat and a woman could follow, they could dance. And of course there aren't many country people anymore, only people who long for the country life they imagine.

The blossoming of line dancing must have been a godsend to single women who just want to dance. No more waiting to be asked, no more humiliation of being ignored, and no more need to accept the embrace of mashers or inept dancers. At first, line dancing tended to divide honky tonks into two camps: those where women dance in the arms of men, with all the pleasures and perils that entails, and those where dancers form a unisex line and the sexual dynamics aren't much different from those in a bar.

The line dancing craze passed, but its influence continues. Now you can sometimes find both styles of dancing in the same place. But honky tonks are no longer full of women eagerly waiting to be asked to dance; women who want the primordial pleasure of moving to the sounds of music without the complications of male-female interaction have other places to go.

I don't know this from personal experience, but I suspect the era of the fair fight has passed, too. If I got in a fight at a honky tonk today, I wouldn't be confident that the only weapons would be fists. The latent prospect of non-lethal violence made most of us careful about who we offended, and it gave honky tonks an aura of excitement. That, like the presence of women willing to dance, was what made a honky tonk a more stimulating place than a bar. But if offending the wrong person is likely to get you shot, that's not just healthy excitement.

———◆———

CHAPTER 4

Forty-seven Years at UT Law, Man and Boy

In July 1969, I decided to go to law school. I phoned the University of Texas Law School to inquire about enrolling that fall, and was transferred to T.J. Gibson, an associate dean. I suppose I told him I had been a journalist for seven years and was currently a UPI bureau chief.

I remember him asking, "Have you taken the LSAT?" I said yes, but it was years ago, before I graduated from Harvard.

"Do you remember what your score was?"

"I don't remember the number, but I know that it was in the 95th percentile."

"Okay, come on out here," Gibson said.

I'm sure I eventually had to provide evidence of the LSAT score and a transcript from college, but with nothing more than Gibson's invitation, I gave notice to UPI and got a part-time job writing speeches for Ben Barnes, then a candidate for governor. Karen got a job in the UT audio library and we arranged for our children, then 8, 6, and 5, to go after school to a neighborhood woman who provided day care in her home.

Tuition was $100 a year. My part-time job paid $300 a month and Karen earned about the same. When I graduated I owed about $1,500.

It wouldn't be possible today. The UT Law School now receives more than 5,000 applications each year for about 300 places in the entering class. Applicants for the fall class must take the Law School Admission Test no later than the preceding January, and the deadline to apply is March 1. A resume and two letters of recommendation are required. Tuition is $36,000 a year, or $54,000 for nonresidents. The average student debt on graduation is $67,000.

I don't recall that I ever had second thoughts about leaving journalism, even at the least pleasant moments in law school. I fact, I can think of only one time when I had second thoughts about any career move. That was when I realized that leaving UPI for the Dayton *Journal Herald* had been a mistake. I loved journalism, but I couldn't envision a lifetime in it. Maybe I unconsciously recognized that I didn't have the single-minded news instincts that I saw in the best journalists — people like David Halberstam and Theodore H. White.

———◆———

The class that entered in the fall of 1969 — my class — was reputed to be the largest ever, around 700 students. The Vietnam War was reaching a peak and so was resistance to it. The draft lottery had not yet begun, so able-bodied young men who did not enlist voluntarily were at risk of being drafted. The best protection against that was a student deferment, so a lot of men graduating from college around that time developed a sudden passion for law school. The faculty members who made up the law school admissions committee knew that denying an application might be tantamount to sending the applicant to Vietnam, where casualties were near their peak, so they dealt generously with borderline cases. The size of the class required an extra first-year section.

Many of us had more book learning than sophistication. My criminal law teacher was a visiting professor named Heathcote Wales. One day he asked whether there was any justification for different sentences for the same crime. I suggested that sometimes the circumstances might be more egregious. Because I knew the word only from reading and had never heard it spoken, I pronounced it e-*gregg*-e-ous. Wales said nothing, but a fleeting smile that crossed his face told me I had better look up the pronunciation. I'm still grateful to him for sparing me the humiliation of being corrected in front of my peers, none of whom seemed to recognize my gaff.

Getting admitted to the law school was easy, but so was flunking out. Bill Fritz was the champion quality-control officer; he taught first-year property and normally flunked at least one-third of his class. He died in the spring semester of 1972, creating the faculty vacancy that I was appointed to. I didn't have to fill his shoes as enrollment-manager because admissions standards rose and flunking out became rare.

The most memorable of my teachers was Leon Green — universally known as Dean Green because he had been dean of the Northwestern University law school for eighteen years before joining the Texas faculty. He was eighty years old when he taught me torts in 1969-70. By then he was hard of hearing and his eyesight was failing. He dealt with these physical limitations in an unusual way. He didn't just ask students to stand; when he called on someone, the student was to come forward and sit beside him. That student's job was not only to answer Dean Green's questions about the day's reading, but also to serve as Dean Green's eyes and ears.

When someone out in the room raised a hand, Dean Green's surrogate was expected to alert him. Dean Green would say "OK, what is it?" The student would then ask the question, the surrogate would repeat it to Dean Green, and Dean Green would answer. If your friend in the hot seat beside Dean Green began to stumble, you could buy him a little time by raising your hand — drawing fire while your buddy looked for cover, as it were. Dean Green continued to teach, using the surrogate strategy, until he was almost 90.

He and Dean Keeton were among the most famous torts scholars in the country, and they were rivals. Dean Green would say "Mr. Keeton is a good man, he just has some mistaken ideas." Students in Keeton's course spent weeks on the concept of proximate cause, but uttering those words in Green's presence would unleash a tirade. "There is only cause. Proximate cause, superseding cause, producing cause, intervening cause, remote cause, and all those other 'causes,' they're phony, just weasel words."

At first I thought the Green-Keeton disagreement was a friendly rivalry, but I later realized that each man thought the other was dangerously misguided, sowing confusion and misunderstanding with his teaching and writing.

Dean Green was blunt. During law school I quit smoking and gained some weight. When Dean Green saw me, he said "You need to look after yourself. You're getting pudgy."

One of my classmates remembers an incident I had forgotten. There were three Andersons in Dean Green's torts class — Don, John, and me. One day Dean Green was eager to make one more point quickly before the class ended. He called on "Mr. Anderson." Don thought Dean Green was looking at him and began to answer. "Not you," Dean Green said, "The smart one."

It was Don, not me, who remembered that incident — proof I suppose that an insult has a longer afterlife than a compliment.

Ed Cohen, my property teacher, was the last UT professor to insist that the student he called on stand. A number of my classmates were in ROTC units and wore their uniforms to class on the days when ROTC met. When the student called on stood and Cohen saw that he was in uniform, he often made some unkind crack, like "Ah, General Smith, how's the war going today?"

One day Hugh Rice Kelly brought his rather spectacularly dressed girlfriend to class. Cohen said, "Mr, Kelly, I see you've brought your mother today. How nice."

Today the Law School conducts training sessions to teach faculty how to avoid making students feel uncomfortable. Sample: "Don't call students Mr. or Ms. Call them something like Counsellor."

The 1960s didn't really arrive at the Law School until the 1970s, and then it was not terribly tumultuous. The activism that swept college campuses in the 1960s was never as intense at the Law School, but we did have our moments. In 1971, law students helped orchestrate the largest anti-war demonstration in Austin history. Students applied for a permit to march through downtown Austin to the Capitol, but the city council turned them down. A group of law students, many of them law review editors, filed a petition with U.S. District Judge Jack Roberts, who ordered the council to grant the permit. About 25,000 protesters, led by recent law school graduate Jeff Friedman, among others, marched down Congress Avenue. That event galvanized liberal activism in Austin and Friedman was soon elected mayor.

I don't recall much drug use when I was a student, at least not in my circles. But when I began teaching in the early 1970s a lot of students, and even a few of the younger faculty, smoked dope. One of my students in 1973-74 (later a notable public interest lawyer) supplied many of his classmates and occasionally, me. He would let us know when he had a new supply and we could buy a "lid," maybe an ounce or so in a plastic sandwich bag, for $10. It was full of seeds and stems which required a lot of meticulous removal so only the leafy stuff was left to smoke. My impression was that it was usually more trouble than it was worth, but on one occasion at a faculty party a woman had some she called something like "Columbian Gold" or "Acapulco Gold." Smoking that was an experience of an entirely different order, but even then the experience wasn't transcendent enough to make me a regular smoker.

I didn't encounter cocaine until around 1980. I was at a party at a student's house when a young woman took my hand and led me into a bathroom. There, with a small mirror and a razor blade, she laid out two lines of white powder. She produced two short straws, used one of them to inhale one of the lines herself, and showed me how to do it with the other. That young lady is now a highly respected lawyer with a major law firm.

I liked the feeling of well-being I got, and later one of the Law School secretaries gave me a bit of cocaine on a couple of occasions, but I never became an enthusiastic user. I suspect that it was more widespread than I knew, because cocaine use was more easily concealed than use of dope. Once a carload of students rode with me to a charity event and the next day I found several tiny vials discarded in my car. Presumably they snorted the contents of the vials while I drove, but I was totally oblivious.

———◆———

In the summer of 1971, the entire editorial board of the law review decamped to Washington to work on public interest projects. Inspired by Ralph Nader, they dispersed into federal agencies investigating environmental, consumer, and poverty issues. When they returned in the fall, an entire issue of the law review was devoted to their reports.

———◆———

The top students in my class entered into a pact: we would refuse to go to work for big law firms. The first to cave was Hugh Rice Kelly, editor in chief of the law review, who signed with Baker Botts during our second year. Others soon followed suit, and the pact dissolved.

I saw first-hand why it was hard to resist. When Vinson & Elkins came to the Law School to recruit in the fall of 1970, I didn't sign up to interview because I wasn't interested in working for a big corporate law firm. An announcement came over the loudspeakers in the hallways: "David Anderson, please come to the placement office."

When I did so, I was told "Mr. Reasoner wants to see you. He's in room xxx." I entered that room with a chip on my shoulder the size of a boulder, but it was quickly eased off by Harry Reasoner, then a young associate at V&E. He said something to the effect of "I know you're probably not interested in joining a big firm, but I just want you to know that if there is ever anything we can do for you, please let us know."

He went on to talk genially about my law school record, my journalism experience, and other ex-journalists who worked at V&E. My resolve began to weaken. It weakened further when V&E invited Karen and me to hear Beverly Sills at the Houston Opera. Later they invited us to bring our children for a weekend that included seats behind home plate for a ball game in at the Astrodome, then new and considered one of the wonders of the world. That made our Little Leaguers enthusiastic advocates for V&E.

V&E was the first big Texas firm to turn recruiting over to its youngest and most sociable associates, giving the impression that life at V&E would be an extended party among fun-loving colleagues like Joe Bill Watkins and Charles Berry and their lovely and vivacious wives. If I hadn't got an offer to teach, I probably would have gone to Houston with V&E.

———◆———

In the early 1970s the small cadre of women in the Law School challenged the faculty to a flag football game. It was a popular annual event, played on a makeshift gridiron in Eastwoods Park, with a few kegs of beer on the sidelines. Most of the women were unathletic and so were most of the faculty, but each side usually had someone who could pass and at least one fast runner. The rest were mainly blockers. It was ostensibly a no-contact game, but of course you couldn't block without interposing your body between the defender and the ball carrier, and it was hard to grab one of the streamers dangling from the player's waist without brushing against a leg or torso.

Eastwoods Park, Class of 1999, and Bill Powers

Occasionally a faculty member used a bear hug to restrain a runner long enough to grab a flag, and women sometimes did the same. I can't say there was any groping, but the male students who lined the sidelines thought there was and often shouted semi-lewd encouragement.

I never heard complaints from any of the women, whether participants or spectators. The best female passer I remember was a woman who became a prominent feminist lawyer and public official. The tradition died out after a few years; I suspect peer pressure dissuaded women from participating. Or maybe when they were no longer an insular minority, they no longer felt the need to prove that they were good sports.

I once had a student who arrived at law school at age 19 — through lots of advanced placement, I suppose. I'll call her Gloria. She also arrived with her virginity intact, a condition she apparently considered lamentable if not deplorable. (It was a different time, folks.)

Gloria confided in a couple of close friends, who of course confided in a few of their close friends, etc. By the time the secret reached my ears, solving Gloria's problem had become something of a class project. She of course was not to know of the intervention, and neither was the classmate who they would select to be the instrument of her deliverance. The idea was merely to fix them up and let nature take its course.

After a false start or two, they found a candidate who clicked with Gloria. Nature did its job, and Gloria let her friends know it. The news led to a party at which everyone but Gloria and her new boyfriend knew what was being celebrated.

<hr/>

The Student-Faculty Relations Committee encouraged faculty to fraternize with students. Faculty were urged to attend (and participate in) some student events, such as the Fall Drunk (yes, that was its official name) and Assault and Flattery. When students had a party, they often invited their professors, and professors occasionally gave parties for their students. In my first year of teaching I went to lunch with a small group of students once a week. I quit that when I saw what it was doing to my waistline.

Karen and I gave a party every year for my first-year students, and Karen was more than a good sport about them. We had the food catered but often she made desserts. Usually she played the piano, and students sought her out for conversations about our family and her life before and after she met me. She didn't take offense when attractive young women gave me a hug as they departed at the end of the party.

<hr/>

Many law professors married their former students: Page Keeton, Jerre Williams, Ernest Smith, Ed Cohen, Bob Dawson, Steve Goode, Bill Powers, Guy Wellborn, George Dix, Philip Bobbitt, David Robertson. Very few of those marriages ended in divorce. Today, before a professor and student can so much as hold hands, the faculty member is required to report the relationship to the dean and the Provost and file a Mitigation Plan, in writing and signed by both parties. Unless the university approves this plan, the couple is required to cease and desist.

There were two faculty restrooms in the 1970s, one for each floor of faculty offices. The signs on the doors said simply "Faculty." Saying "Faculty Women" would have been fanciful and saying "Faculty Men" would have been redundant.

———◆———

When I joined the faculty in 1972, the Law School was an up-and-coming state school — not among the nation's elite, but well-regarded in the law school world and powerful in Texas. UT Law grads were the dominant power in the Texas legislature, the bar, and the judiciary, largely because of the Texas-educated and practice-oriented faculty. Albert Jones had just finished a stint as first assistant attorney general of Texas after a long career as a successful trial lawyer. Woodfin Butte had been Latin American counsel of Humble Oil and Refining Company, predecessor of Exxon Mobil. John Sutton, son of a West Texas district judge, had drafted the Model Rules of Professional Responsibility. Gus Hodges was the prime authority on the then arcane Texas Rules of Civil Procedure. Charles Alan Wright was a leading authority on federal courts. Jerre Williams had been head of the Administrative Conference of the U.S. and later became a judge of the Fifth Circuit U.S. Court of Appeals. Parker Fielder was an authority on oil and gas taxation.

But Dean Page Keeton's recruits of the 1960s — young academics educated in the elite law schools of the East — were supplanting that generation, not only in the classroom but also in influence within the faculty. They were determined to make UT a national law school, and their scholarship was aimed at other academics, not Texas judges and lawyers.

Because the professor I replaced was a property teacher, that's the course I was assigned. I knew next to nothing about the traditional property subjects — things like fee tail, implied easements, the rule against perpetuities, and covenants running with the land — which originated in feudal times and hadn't changed a lot since. So I focused on modern issues like land use planning and landlord-tenant law. Fortunately my students were a very forgiving lot; if they realized I didn't know much more property law than they, they didn't rebel.

As the year progressed and they began hearing what first-years in other sections were studying in property, a few of them feared that they would be unprepared for upper level courses like wills and estates. I tried to assure them that all property courses were "selected topics in property" rather than a comprehensive survey of the field, and that they would be no more disadvantaged than those students who hadn't studied land use planning and landlord-tenant law. They weren't all persuaded, but I became increasingly convinced that what I was teaching would be more useful to them than the traditional estates in land, and I continued teaching property my way for seven years.

My interests and scholarship were aligned more closely with torts than property, but in the 1970s UT had a surfeit of torts teachers: Keeton, Green, Allen Smith, David Robertson, Jim Treece, Bill Powers, and Guy Wellborn. So I didn't get to switch from property to torts until some of those people retired or left. My scholarly output and my student evaluations improved when I was able to teach something I really liked.

———◆———

In my early years of teaching, most of the faculty gathered in the faculty lounge at 9 a.m. and 3 p.m. for coffee. Dean Keeton was usually there and often he brought up some issue that needed to be resolved. Views were expressed and agreements or disagreements would emerge. Keeton rarely revealed his opinion and when he later decided the issue, his decision usually was informed, though not dictated, by the discussion at the coffee hour.

It was an ingenious alternative to faculty meetings. It allowed the dean to measure faculty sentiment not just by numbers, but also taking into account each side's experience, standing in the faculty, stake in the matter, and intensity of feeling. Nobody had feelings hurt by being voted down, and Keeton got faculty input without being bound by it. And it minimized the need for formal meetings in which the length of time that a colleague speaks is often inversely proportional to the importance of what's being said.

———◆———

As long as the only women in the law school building were secretaries and a few librarians, one or two women's restrooms were sufficient. In the early 1970s that changed and we had a critical shortage of facilities for women. We solved the immediate problem by changing the sign on the door of one restroom from "Men" to "Women." To improve the décor, someone put potted plants in the urinals. I suspect that was not an official act, just the work of some pranksters.

The law school was busy year round. In addition to a first-year section for students who entered in the summer, a sizeable number of upper level courses were offered. This enabled people like me to graduate in 27 months. It also gave faculty members summer employment. By teaching in the summer, we could supplement our nine-month salaries: two-ninths of the regular salary for teaching a two-hour summer course, one-third for a three-hour course, and four-ninths for a four-hour course. Then a dean (I think it was Mark Yudof) got funding for summer research leaves, and once we could earn as much in the summer by doing research as by teaching, the summer courses pretty much disappeared.

We had long-established summer faculty exchanges with the University of Utah and the University of North Carolina; one of our faculty taught there for the summer and one of theirs came to us. Teaching a course in land use planning at UNC in 1976, I first encountered the view that government had no business limiting what people could do with their land. I hadn't expected to find any people more jealous of their property rights than Texans.

At Utah in 1977, living in an otherwise-unoccupied sorority house, I learned that Salt Lake City has burglars (or maybe sorority girls) with discerning taste. Someone entered the house through a window when I wasn't there and stole only one thing: my all-time favorite pair of boots — peanut-brittle tan Tony Lama's with burgundy-colored lizard wingtips.

———◆———

To get tenure I needed to publish a law review article by 1974. I was struggling with a piece about state constitutions when Mike Sharlot made a valuable suggestion. Mike saw a magazine article I had written about the effect that libel suits had on self-censorship in the press and said "why don't you expand that into a law review piece?" I did, and the resulting article in Texas Law Review got me tenure, put me on the radar of people in the media law world, and got me consulting gigs in a number of libel cases. Libel was a very active field in the 1970s and 1980s. I wrote numerous articles on the subject, culminating in one called "Is Libel Law Worth Reforming?" published in the Pennsylvania Law Review in 1991. History's implicit answer seemed to be no: major libel cases all but vanished for the next 25 years.

I invented an upper-level course I called "Communications Torts," and the "Law and Journalism" seminar I started in 1973 morphed into Communications Law and then into Mass Media Law. Marc Franklin began teaching Mass Media Law at Stanford at about the same time, published the first casebook in that subject, and invited me to join as a co-author in 1989. About the same time, David Robertson and Bill Powers invited me to join their torts casebook. Over the next 25 years we published a total of ten editions of those casebooks.

Of the 20 or 30 law review articles I published, the most significant was one called "The Origins of the Press Clause," published in the UCLA Law Review in 1983. When Mark Yudof was dean, he nominated it for a list of the 10 most important law review articles ever published (it didn't make the final list).

My article challenged what had become the conventional understanding of First Amendment history. For most of the first two centuries of American history, scholars had treated the Framers of the First Amendment as enthusiastic champions of free speech and press. Then in 1960, Leonard Levy published a book called *Legacy of Suppression*, in which he attempted to show that in fact they had a very cramped understanding of those freedoms and had intended the First Amendment to do very little. Levy was in the twilight of a long and distinguished career as a scholar. His view meshed with the urge of the time to debunk all accepted wisdom, and it quickly became the prevailing view among historians.

But I found a lot of evidence to the contrary. In the generation preceding the framing of the First Amendment in 1789, 11 of the 13 states had included ringing endorsements of press freedom in their state constitutions. Resentment against Britain's imposition of taxes on newspapers had played a large role in fomenting the revolution. Newspapers behaved as if the press was indeed free, criticizing governments and officials vigorously, and when prosecutions were attempted, juries often refused to convict. The Federalist Party's efforts to prevent Jefferson's election in 1800 by suppressing newspapers that supported him discredited that party in the eyes of the electorate for a generation.

After the article came out, I received a gracious letter from Levy, congratulating me and saying my article would force him to rethink his positions. But a few months later the UCLA Law Review published a piece by Levy, doubling down on his original argument and savaging my article, accusing me of plagiarism, distortion, and falsification of facts.

I was stunned by Levy's apparent about-face and furious at him for not allowing me to see his article before it was published. The law review at UCLA refused to give me a chance to respond. After I appealed to the UCLA dean, the law review did publish a rejoinder from me, but that was months later and by then Levy's attack had effectively neutered my article. Future scholarship on the subject either cited me with a "But see" to Levy, or vice versa.

It was my only experience with the kind of infighting that I gather is common in some academic fields, though not in law at that time. In subsequent correspondence, Levy indicated he considered the exchange just good hearty academic jousting, and said I was too thin-skinned. I guess I am; being accused of dishonesty gets under my skin.

The article about the origins of the press clause and another on freedom of the press that I wrote 30 years later were chosen in 2020 by other media law teachers for inclusion in a volume about the most influential articles of the last fifty years.

———◆———

When I joined the faculty, the law school was largely self-governing. The long-time dean, Page Keeton, set the policies and made the decisions after informal consultation with the faculty. Page hired me on the recommendation of some of my law school professors; I don't know whether there was an appointments committee; if there was, it just ratified his decision.

Page had his own power base among influential law school alumni, and through them, in the legislature. The law school had its own source of supplemental funds, administered by the Law School Foundation which Page had created. He had faced down the university regents several times when they tried to interfere with the law school; after that, neither they nor the university president were eager to take on Page.

We set our own requirements for admission and graduation, and our own calendar and schedule of classes (including some Saturday classes). We were proud of the many asterisks in the university's rules and regulations that said "Except in the School of Law."

Naturally the central administration resented our autonomy and the rest of the university envied it. They have been chipping away at it for forty years, and now it's mostly gone, although the law school probably still enjoys more independence than any other part of the university except the medical schools.

Since Page's era, internal committees have assumed an ever greater role in the law school's governance. I served on all the major committees except appointments: admissions, budget, tenure, and the building committee (twice) and chaired each of those at one time or another.

For many years members of the admissions committee read the applicants' files and voted to admit or deny. When we got sued over our affirmative action policies, the dean, then Bill Powers, put all the decisions in the hands of himself and the admissions dean. In litigation, it was too hard to explain decisions by six or eight different people employing different criteria.

The budget committee dealt with only one part of the budget, faculty salaries. Dean Mark Yudof created the budget committee to accomplish two purposes: to give him cover when he set professors' salaries, and to create an incentive structure to encourage scholarly productivity. To achieve the latter, every faculty member's publications for the previous year were read by at least one committee member, who evaluated the work and reported orally to the full committee in the presence of the dean. The committee then recommended in general terms the size of salary increase the professor should receive for the next year.

In terms of fair evaluation, the procedure left a lot to be desired, but it had an *in terrorem* effect: most of us wanted to impress our colleagues on the budget committee with our scholarly output, or at least avoid appearing substandard. So Yudof's strategy markedly increased the faculty's overall productivity.

Yudof didn't tell committee members what he had done with our recommendations, so we usually didn't know until we started the next year's evaluations and saw current salaries. When some of us noticed that he had ignored the previous year's advice, he changed the name of the committee to the "Budget Advisory Committee."

I always had reservations about the subjectivity of the evaluations, so the year I was chair of the committee I was secretly relieved when the central administration announced that there would be no money for raises the next year. That being the case, I told the committee there would be no point in our meeting, and we didn't.

There would still be a law school budget, however, and university rules required the chairman of the budget committee to sign off on the law school's request. The dean was always finalizing the document until the eleventh hour, so his practice had been to get the chairman to sign on a separate signature page which he would then attach to the request at the last minute. I warned him in advance that I wouldn't sign until I saw the budget, and he grudgingly complied.

But all it showed me was that modern governmental budgets reveal nothing to outsiders. In my journalism days we scrutinized city and school budgets so we could ask such questions as, "Why is the budget for fire department overtime going up by 50 per cent?" But that law school budget, and every other government budget I've seen since, employed codes and accounting methods that make it impossible for anyone but the cognoscenti to see meaningful figures.

———◆———

In my early years on the faculty it was the general (though not universal) expectation that anyone we hired would receive tenure after three or four years if he or she performed satisfactorily. I embraced that view wholeheartedly. Denying tenure to someone you have welcomed and worked beside and become friends with is a recipe for bitterness and tends to produce the kinds of divisions for which academe is notorious.

One of the years I was tenure chair there was no one up for tenure, so our work consisted only of monitoring and supporting young colleagues who would be up in a year or two. But another year we had three candidates were up for tenure, each of whom had a less-than-optimal case in some respect. I determined early on to help them get tenure.

I couldn't burnish their resumes but I could present them in the best light, which I did. Perhaps I should have taken a neutral stance instead of becoming their advocate, but if I had done so, we might have lost three people who, each in a different way, have each been valuable members of the faculty for 30 years.

———•———

In the late 1970s we had entering classes of 500 or 550 and the building was woefully overcrowded. Most of the classrooms had a few temporary seats; younger faculty (like me) were squatters for a year in the offices of senior colleagues who were on leave. Nearing exam time students had to compete for seats in the library.

When the university authorized a new building, Dean Ernest Smith appointed John Sutton chair of the building committee. I was the youngest member. We sat through many hours of meetings with the architects, who repeatedly told us that the design of the building was none of our business; we were just there to tell them what we would be using the space for. Some were university architects, some were from an outside firm.

Watching Sutton operate was eye-opening. The first showdown came when the university architects announced that new faculty offices could not exceed 150 square feet, per the university's rules. Sutton set about measuring the existing faculty offices, and determined that most were around 270 or 280 square feet. Telling our colleagues that they were going to move into rooms with half the space was a nonstarter, so Sutton found a solution. He had a survey done of the physical science departments, which found that in addition to their offices, the scientists had laboratories that brought the total space per faculty member to around 300 square feet.

"At the law school our offices are our laboratories," he told the architects. "When we're doing our research, we sometimes have dozens of open books laid out, so we have to have some tables." That, together with the veiled warning that the law school wouldn't be interested in the project if it would reduce offices to 150 square feet, carried the day, and we ended up with offices of close to 300 square feet.

———•———

There were many lesser conflicts, most resolved in our favor. Another major one came when the building was about done and it was time to discuss furniture.

The university architects announced that all offices would have gray metal desks with linoleum tops, metal filing cabinets and metal bookcases. Again, that was said to be university policy.

Our existing offices had wooden furniture of varying degrees of elegance or shabbiness, but only a few secretaries were stuck with metal desks. Sutton to the rescue: he got two new peopled appointed to the committee to advise us on decorating. One was Mary Alice Shivers, wife of the chairman of the board of regents. The other was her good friend, Martha Hyder.

Mary Alice didn't have strong views about decorating, but Martha did. Also, she and her oilman-husband, Elton Hyder Jr., were in the process of lending the law library some of the hundreds of antiques and art works they had spent years collecting throughout Europe. She didn't want their treasures embarrassed by cheap surroundings.

Mary Alice's presumed political clout and Martha's strong esthetic opinions quickly intimidated the university apparatchiks, and soon we were reviewing nice wood furniture, colorful fabrics, and vivid paints, all subject to final selection by Martha. A lot of people at the law school didn't like Martha's choices, but there is no doubt that the final product was far better than what the university's minions were going to give us.

———◆———

Sutton soon became dean, and his genius as a maneuverer was immediately required again. He had been appointed dean only after the president vetoed the faculty's choice. Resentment was rampant, and some faculty were threatening to leave. Sutton made two smart moves. First, before he took the job, he met one-on-one with unhappy professors. He explained that if he declined, the president might appoint someone even less acceptable to the faculty. He asked their advice, and almost all advised him to accept.

Second, when he did accept the job, his first move was to make Mark Yudof his associate dean with authority over all internal matters. Sutton knew that his own talents were far more suited to dealing with alumni and legislators. Yudof was in closer touch with the faculty, particularly the younger professors who were most doubtful about Sutton.

Sutton adhered to that division, gradually ceding more responsibility to Yudof, and five years later the transition to Yudof as dean was seamless.

———◆———

Thirty years later I was on another building committee, this time as chair. The digital revolution meant that the law library didn't need as much space for books, and the expanding faculty needed more office space, so two floors of the library were to be converted to offices. At first there was no building committee; the outside architects dealt directly with Dean Larry Sager, or his wife, Professor Jane Cohen.

Jane had a clear vision: she wanted steel and concrete, stark white walls, and gray industrial carpet — no wood paneling, no wood floors, no wall coverings. Larry was getting a lot of complaints from faculty, and eventually he acceded to calls from a number of faculty, including me, for a committee.

By that time Jane was deeply into implementation of her vision, and she wasn't inclined to yield. The architects and outside vendors had become accustomed to dealing with Jane. She continued to give orders without consulting the committee, and the committee's first chair had been too mild-mannered to fight her. When Larry appointed me chair, I understood that a big part of my job was to say no to Jane.

That was easier said than done. We often didn't know about orders she had given until it was too late to change them. Things came to a head one day when I walked into the new atrium and found small trees growing in horse tanks — galvanized steel ovals or circles that are used to provide water for livestock. I may have been the only one who recognized their original purpose.

I confronted Jane. "Yes, I ordered them," she said, explaining that it was now considered chic to repurpose these tanks to give interior spaces an industrial look.

"Jane, you can't order things without the committee's approval. You don't have authority to act unilaterally." But it turned out that the dean was not willing to create a stink (or perhaps a marital crisis) by countermanding her orders, so the horse tanks stayed. That was the last time she acted without the committee's approval, but by then the project was almost completed, and for better and worse, it bears the unmistakable stamp of Jane's vision.

———◆———

Early in my teaching career, the president of the university appointed me to the board that ran the Austin public television station, KLRN (its call letters are now KLRU). The station was owned by a non-profit entity but was deeply entwined with UT, which owned the studios, appointed several members of the board, and used the station's facilities in educating its radio-tv-film students.

The board had more than 50 members, and for a couple of years I did nothing but attend a meeting once or twice a year to ratify the actions of the executive committee, eight board members who made all the decisions.

That changed in 1979 when the general manager, Harvey Herbst, killed a program on natural childbirth because he thought the subject too delicate for public television. The program's producer was Bill Anderson (no kin), who had been a producer for NBC in New York and was eager to bring big-time ideas to the Austin PBS station.

An aggressive investigative reporter for the Austin *American-Statesman*, Gayle Reaves, got wind of the cancellation and called me to ask if it wasn't illegal censorship. I opined that it might be, and Anderson then asked me to try to get the board to reverse Herbst's decision.

Other station employees also complained of heavy-handed editorial decisions by Herbst, and Reaves aired their grievances in the newspaper. I enlisted the support of some other board members — Bob Jeffrey, the dean of the UT communications school, and Gus Garcia, a respected Hispanic civic leader.

We drove together to a meeting of the executive committee at a restaurant in New Braunfels. The board chairman treated us like interlopers and didn't want to listen to our concerns. But other station employees took their complaints to Reaves, and her newspaper stories eventually persuaded the chairman that he had to put a stop to it.

His solution was to appoint an investigating committee to hear the complaints and make recommendations to the board. His initial appointees were mostly members of the executive committee who had already made plain their disinterest in the complaints. In print Reaves called it an attempted whitewash.

We — the dissidents from the New Braunfels meeting — demanded that some of us be added to the investigating committee. When Reaves made clear that a whitewash wasn't going to silence her, the board chairman yielded and added Garcia and me to the committee.

The chairman of the investigating committee was Bob Roth, the bellicose owner of a commercial television station in San Antonio. At the beginning of the first meeting, he announced that the committee's hearings would be closed to the press. I had anticipated that, and had prepared a brief arguing that the Texas Open Meetings statute required the meetings to be open.

The board had hired Jimmy Meyers, a respected retired district judge, to be the investigating committee's counsel. He took my brief and asked to recess the hearing until after lunch. When we reconvened he said he believed I was right, and advised Roth that it might be illegal to exclude the press. That instantaneously transformed the proceedings from a whitewash into a forum for grievances (and made Roth hate me).

———— • ————

For a month we heard several dozen witnesses who had numerous complaints about the way the station was run. Roth bullied the witnesses and snarled at me, but each accusation gave Reeves new fodder for her relentless pursuit of the story, and the newspaper was treating it as a full-fledged scandal. By now other media outlets were also covering the hearings.

As such testimony is wont to do, it opened up new subjects for investigation. One concerned alleged misrepresentations the station had made to the Federal Communications Commission. Another involved fund-raising appeals that claimed there were funds available to match viewers' contributions when there weren't. Perhaps the most serious was that the station had allowed the university to control some of its operations in violation of the terms of its license.

As the evidence piled up, we won a crucial convert. Mary Ann Wooten was a housewife who was on the executive committee, probably because they thought a woman was needed to keep minutes. The board chairman put her on the investigating committee, perhaps thinking she would be a pliable vote. She was anything but. When she saw the problems that the investigation uncovered, she became a tiger. She had a tenacious memory, and often she pointed out inconsistencies in the testimony.

When the powers-that-be saw that they had lost Ms. Wooten, they realized that the game was over. The investigating committee voted unanimously to recommend that the general manager and the station manager be fired, that a review procedure be created so programs couldn't be killed based on one person's opinion, that the station ramp up its news and public affairs programming, and that the relationship with the university be restructured.

The board accepted most of the recommendations, but instead of firing Herbst outright, they created a management triumvirate of which he was a member. That infuriated many of the station staff who viewed Herbst as the Number One problem. I resigned from the board in protest, as did Ms. Wooten.

But the investigation eventually led to many changes, including Herbst's removal, the firing of the station manager, removal of the university from decision-making for the station, and severance of the Austin station from its sister station in San Antonio.

As scandals often do, this one produced some regrettable collateral damage. The station manager was an able young man whose offense was saying — on air during a pledge drive — that a donor had given money to match viewer contributions. When pressed, he was forced to admit that there was no match money at the time, although he had arranged after the fact to match the contributions with funds given for other purposes. That's probably the sort of fib that many a fundraiser has told when expected match money hasn't materialized, but it looks bad in a headline. The manager's next job in public television was in Juneau, Alaska.

Our scandal was pretty small potatoes — no crimes uncovered, no mysterious deaths, no political careers derailed. But it was front page news for a month, produced indignant editorials, and taught me a lot about the dynamics of scandals. Without the press, a wrong unearthed by an investigator is like a tree falling unheard in the forest. And a wrong uncovered by the press is just a story unless someone with power to do something about it takes action. This scandal had both of the necessary ingredients.

Until the 1990s there was a tradition of year-end skits performed by students in each of the year-long courses. The skits usually parodied the mannerisms or habits of the professor or riffed on some memorable event in the class. For me the most memorable skit was one that originated with a group of students who called themselves "The Wednesday Night Bar Association." They drank beer once a week at a bar called Mike and Charlie's, and I sometimes accepted their invitation to join them.

Fake Beauty Contestant, Torts Class

At first it was all guys, but a couple of women, Emily Little and Lisa Schafroth, heard about the outings and decided to integrate the group. They were welcomed, and eventually a few other women began to come.

On the last day of the year, my torts class was interrupted by Emily and another girl (I think it was Lauren, our favorite waitress at Mike and Charlie's) walking down different aisles to the front of the room, dressed as contestants in a beauty pageant. They were wearing short shorts and maroon t-shirts with diagonal white satin banners that said "Miss Wyoming." That was an allusion to a notorious case involving a parody about a fictitious Miss America contest in which the talent of the contestant from Wyoming was an ability to levitate men by fellatio, which she demonstrated by levitating one of the judges.

The contestants said I was to be the judge and pick the winner. I thought "this isn't going to end well," and I was trying to think of a way to abort the contest, when another contestant began sashaying down the aisle. She was trying to walk seductively, wearing heels, fishnet hose, a miniskirt, a blonde wig, and too much makeup. At that I panicked. I thought "Oh no, they've hired a stripper. How can I stop this?"

Only when she moved close as if to kiss me did I realize that it was one of the guys from the Wednesday Night Bar Association, Brad Friedman, in drag. By this time the class and the three "contestants" were convulsed in laughter, and I didn't have to judge.

Mount Bonnell Wedding

I've kept the satin "Miss Wyoming" banners as mementos of that skit.

Alas, the skits disappeared when year-long courses were reduced to one semester. I suspect that a semester wasn't long enough for them to learn that they could have fun together, but maybe it was because they chose not to spend time on anything that didn't advance their careers.

I once "officiated" at the wedding of two former students. Katrina Price had been my student in 1995 and had become a friend by the time she graduated. She was marrying another third-year student, and Katrina decided she wanted me to perform the ceremony. She somehow thought law professors had the same powers as ship captains. I told her I wasn't authorized to do that but she still wanted me to do it, so she investigated and learned that I could "marry" them and then they could go to the courthouse and sign some papers to make it official.

The wedding was at the top of Mount Bonnell on a beautiful day just after graduation in 1998. The families of both were present, along with many law school friends. We all climbed the steps to the top. Friends lugged coolers of food and drink up. I administered the vows they had written and declared them "husband and wife." The open-air reception was delightful. It was one of the happiest weddings I've ever attended. Unfortunately, events confirmed my observation that the length of the marriage is often inversely proportional to the excellence of the wedding. They were divorced within a few years.

———◆———

The members of the class of 1987 who had been in my torts class three years earlier were the most cohesive group I ever had. Karen and I had a house and a boat on Lake LBJ, and for one of the student fund-raising auctions I put up a water skiing outing for six. The students who bought it had so much fun they asked if we could repeat it the next year, and the year after that. After they graduated and moved away it became an annual reunion for the group, not only the original six but quite a few of their classmates. Those who married brought their spouses. It ended only when we sold the lake house.

A charter member of the Wednesday Night Bar Association took me aside one year and asked if he could have the lake house one night for a tryst with his girlfriend. By this time we had become good friends so I agreed and told him where to find the key. He later told me that only one thing had gone awry: I had neglected to tell him that the automatic sprinkler system ran every night; he had parked his car on the lawn with the windows down, so the next morning the interior was soaked.

———◆———

Two students from my property class in 1973-74 were charged with three felonies. Robert Campbell was a Vietnam veteran who first gained notoriety by coming to class with no shirt. Before the first semester was over he was charged with the rape of an undergraduate girl he had taken to the Texas-Texas Tech football game. He was freed on bond and came to me for advice. I told him not to discuss the case with anybody, including me, until he got a lawyer. But he came back several times and couldn't resist trying to justify himself. He didn't advance that cause with me when he said "It wasn't even a particularly athletic seduction." (Years later I learned he had similar conversations with other professors.)

I called some lawyers who I thought might help but before any of them were hired, the best lawyer Campbell could have hoped for came his way. Warren Burnett, legendary criminal defense lawyer from Odessa, was at the Law School to give a talk when someone told him about Campbell's case. I don't know what gained Burnett's sympathy but he agreed to represent Campbell for free.

While the rape case was pending, one day at the beginning of class I noticed two men in suits standing at the back of the room. When they saw Campbell enter the room, they arrested him. He was charged with intimidating a witness; he had asked (or ordered) one of his classmates not to tell the cops something he had told her.

As the trial date approached, the district attorney asked to talk to me and Byron Fullerton, the associate dean. Apparently Campbell had named us when Burnett asked him if he had talked to anyone about the case. With more chutzpah than legal foundation, I told the DA I wouldn't testify because I thought a student's conversations with a professor about hiring a lawyer should be privileged.

Asked by some students how he planned to keep Fullerton and me from testifying, Burnett said "I'm going to try to make lawyers of two law professors." To my great relief, I wasn't subpoenaed and didn't have to assert my shaky claim of privilege. Fullerton did testify; I don't know what he said.

At the trial Burnett used the classic "blame the victim" strategy. His cross-examination of the young woman was devastating. When asked, "Is it true that you drank six or seven vodka drinks Campbell had poured for you during the game?" she said, no, she had poured them out under her seat. His voice dripping with incredulity, Burnett said "None of people sitting next to you complained that they were sitting in a puddle? Were they wearing galoshes?"

The jury found Campbell not guilty on the rape charge. Apparently the witness intimidation charge was dropped too. Campbell didn't come back to law school, and a few months later he died of a heroin overdose. That he might have been a drug user wasn't a surprise to his friends, but some of them had a darker suspicion: They thought the young woman's father, a wealthy oilman, might have hired someone to forcibly administer the overdose.

The other student in that class who was charged with a felony, Robert Irby, was convicted of drug dealing. He drove a pickup with a little homemade wooden house on the back. We thought he lived in it, and maybe he did, but apparently he was also selling speed from it. When Irby was about to be sentenced, I and another of his professors, Jim Treece, wrote letters to the federal judge urging leniency. The judge wasn't as soft-hearted as we were; he sent Irby to prison.

＊

Students knew I liked honky-tonks, so some of them took me to a place called "Ed's Place" on the highway between Johnson City and Marble Falls. A very athletic student named David Randolph Smith made a bet that he could jump across our table from a flat-footed, standing start without touching the table. The table was about 30 inches high and equally wide. He cleared it, despite having drunk a few beers beforehand. The management didn't object to the table-jumping, probably because it was such a remarkable feat. But when some of us began arm-wrestling, they threw us out.

When John Sutton retired as dean in 1979, he announced that he didn't want the customary boring retirement dinner, but proposed instead that we go to the little town of Coupland for barbeque and dancing, and that the staff be invited too. I think the staff enjoyed the evening more than the faculty; two-stepping around the dance floor with beer-swilling locals seemed to make some of the professoriate a bit uneasy.

＊

In 1995 Karen and I were vacationing in Santa Fe with John and Laura Beckworth. John and I were standing on the sidewalk on the east side of the plaza while our wives were in one of the shops. Along came Bob Bullock, the lieutenant governor, who was also killing time while his wife shopped.

We chatted a while and he asked "What's going on at the Law School?"

I told him we were in the midst of a search for a new dean. "Who's it going to be?" he asked.

I said the faculty wanted Bill Powers. "That's pretty much unanimous."

Bullock's face clouded. "I heard he was pushing tort reform." A major tort reform bill had just passed over the strenuous opposition of the trial lawyers, who were major supporters of Bullock.

"I don't think Bill took a side," I said. "My understanding is that he was asked by the committee to help them with tort law questions. He didn't volunteer."

"That's not what I hear," Bullock said. "I heard he was on the side of the tort reform people and was responsible for a lot of the stuff that came out."

"I don't think that's right," I said. "He didn't insert himself, he was just a resource."

"Mike Gallagher says he was their adversary." Gallagher was the main voice for the Texas Trial Lawyers Association in the tort reform controversy. The TTLA was a powerful force in Texas politics at that time, and Gallagher was politically savvy.

"When Mike Gallagher speaks I listen," Bullock said.

When I got back to Austin I told Bill about the conversation. Shortly after that he withdrew as a candidate for dean. I'm not sure Bullock's opposition was his only reason, but it would have been reason enough. Bullock was the most powerful person in state government at the time. Few issues escaped his attention and he had a long memory. Sooner or later, he would have caused trouble for a law school dean he opposed.

———◆———

Gus Hodges was an old-school professor. He had a greying handlebar mustache, talked with a slow Texas drawl, and taught Texas procedure. I was never in his class but like everyone else, I heard about his method of dealing with unprepared students. The moment the student said "Not prepared," Hodges said "You're excused." That was his way of saying "you're to leave the classroom."

One year I decided to try a milder form of Hodges' method. I announced at the beginning of the semester that a student could say "Not prepared" once, but if it happened a second time he or she had to leave the room.

After a few weeks I called on a young woman (I'll call her Ms. Jones) who said she was unprepared. I made a mental note, called on several others, and a week or two later called on Ms. Jones again.

"I'm not prepared," she said.

"Well, you know the rule," I said, "you'll have to leave the room."

She said, "I won't go."

There was a collective gasp, as everyone (including me) wondered what would happen next. I collected my thoughts and said "Please see me after class."

She said "I won't see you after class."

Now everyone (including me) was shocked. I continued with the class, and later asked T.J. Gibson, the associate dean, what I should do.

"Did you announce the rule at the beginning?" he asked. I assured him that I did, a couple of times. "Then drop her from the course," he said.

At the beginning of the next class, I said "Ms. Jones, I need to talk to you after class."

She said "I told you yesterday, I'm not going to see you after class." Now we were all stunned.

After a moment's reflection, I said "well, then I'll have to tell you now. You're dropped from the course."

There was stunned silence. I went on with the class but it was clear the students were still in shock.

Ms. Jones stayed a few minutes, then noisily gathered up her belongings and stalked out. The door was at the front of the classroom, so her exit was seen by everyone.

She never returned. For the rest of the semester no one answered, "Not prepared." But I never announced that rule again; eviction was too distracting to the rest of the class.

Ten or fifteen years later I was at an alumni reception in Houston when a woman approached me. I didn't realize it was Ms. Jones until I saw her name tag.

"Remember me?" she said.

"Yes, I do."

She was cordial enough; we chatted for a few minutes and neither of us mentioned the episode in my classroom. She offered no excuses or apologies, and neither did I, but I've often wished I had asked her why she refused to talk to me.

———◆———

For a few years I hosted something called Story Hour. Once a week we sat on my veranda in the late afternoon, had a drink, and told stories for an hour or until the stories ran out. There was an open invitation to students, and I invited a few lawyers and judges, among them Lee Yeakel and Jan Patterson, then judges on the Austin court of appeals; Ronnie Earle, the district attorney; Max Sherman, former state senator, president of West Texas State, and dean of the LBJ School; Jack Hightower, retired Texas Supreme Court justice; former state senator Ike Harris, and assorted friends. Ann Richards came once just after she left the governor's office. The price of admission was one story — a joke or a funny story.

I quickly learned that most students aren't good story tellers. They seem to have an aversion to telling anything that requires more than ten seconds; their idea of a story is a one-liner, a pun, or a riddle. One notable exception was a student named Paul Turner. He was a yarn-spinner and a teller of tall tales. One, which I remember only in outline, started out as a memory of hunting trip with some buddies in his native Louisiana. They were hunting alligators in a bayou when one of Paul's companions accidentally shot off his big toe. The victim desperately wanted to find the severed toe in the hope that it could be reattached. There followed a gothic tale of guys searching through the weeds and water of the swamp, being bitten by strange insects and watching for snakes and alligators, until someone finally found the toe. They made their way back along the levee to their parked truck and put the toe in an ice chest. In his haste to get the victim and his toe to the hospital, the driver slipped off the levee and got the truck stuck in the mud. They were miles from any road or town, and this was pre-cell phones. They were finally rescued when one of them walked out of the swamp and fetched a truck — a toe truck.

I have a fuller memory of a joke Ann told: a missionary was walking across the African savanna from one village to another when he came upon a lion. He ran, and the lion chased him. The missionary looked back and saw that the lion was gaining, so he prayed: "Dear God, if it be Thy will, please put a Christian heart in the breast of this savage beast." Whereupon the lion dropped to the ground, put his head on his paws, and said "Dear God, bless this food to the nourishment of my body."

—————◆—————

Charles Alan Wright represented President Nixon when the House Judiciary Committee demanded the Watergate tapes and the White House invoked executive privilege to keep them secret. It was the most controversial legal dispute of the time and the students in Charlie's constitutional law class were thrilled to have a major participant as their professor. But Charlie dashed their hopes by announcing on the first day that he would not discuss the case or even the general subject of executive privilege.

He knew the case would require him to miss a few classes, but he calculated that by holding the class over for five extra minutes each day, he could make up for the missed classes. To further forestall questions he didn't want to answer, every day he continued lecturing as he walked up the steps to the exit and delivered his last words just as he went out the door.

I had the same group of students in my property class, so I heard a lot of grousing about Charlie's refusal to entertain questions about the biggest news event of the time. The exit to Charlie's classroom had double doors with large D handles on the outside. One day one of the students brought a short two-by-four and, after all the students and Charlie were in the room, slipped the bar in the D handles so the doors wouldn't open.

When the class ended Charlie walked up the steps, delivered his parting shot, and stiff-armed the door, but it didn't budge. The other students knew what had been done, and they held their breath, possibly expecting a lightning strike. But Charlie quietly walked to the other exit and left, never mentioning the episode to the class or the faculty. I have always believed the prankster was Scott Klippel, but he disclaims responsibility despite my assurances that Charlie deserved it for refusing to discuss the hottest constitutional issue of the day. Scott explains:

You don't tug on Superman's cape,

You don't spit in the wind,

You don't pull the mask of the old Lone Ranger
And you don't mess around with Charles Alan Wright.

———•———

Roy Mersky, one of the finest librarians any law school ever had, was also a First Amendment maven and ACLU activist.

Mersky's library amassed something he called "the First Amendment collection." The core of it was a "litigated literature" collection — books that had been subjects of famous court decisions, like Ulysses, Lady Chatterley's Lover, and Tropic of Cancer. But eventually it expanded to include a wider range of publications, such as Playboy and Penthouse. I'm not sure what the rationale for that was; if pressed, Roy probably would have said "I'm just trying to serve the interests of all the faculty."

When the keepers of the federal building in downtown Austin arranged lighted windows to make a tall cross at Christmas time, Roy complained to the feds. They shut down the display, but somehow made known who the grinch was. The city's leadership, its newspaper, and most of its citizens were outraged. Roy and his family received death threats.

———•———

For all of my 45 years on the faculty, secretaries — "faculty assistants" in later years — have each served five or six professors. Most have been very good, but occasionally they had peculiarities. My first year of teaching, I was assigned to a mousy woman whom I'll call Jewel. She was assigned to one or two visiting professors, a couple of retired professors, and me.

Her secretarial skills were excellent, and she was punctual and thorough. In those days before word processors, some professors dictated their letters and some produced rough drafts to be typed by the secretary, as I did. I learned to carefully review the typed letters that Jewel returned to me: she was so helpful that she sometimes rewrote them. When I asked about that, she would say "I thought it sounded better this way," or "I just made it clearer."

That may have been justifiable helpfulness, but what she progressed to next wasn't: she began to change the addressee. "I thought he would be a better person to deal with this," she might say, or "it's more important to inform this person." I learned that she did this to others too, and the associate dean in charge of secretaries knew, but didn't have the heart to fire Jewel. He just tried to assign her each year to someone who didn't know enough about her to object.

———◆———

Mark Yudof was a Philadelphian, conspicuously un-Texan. When he became dean in 1984, his predecessor, John Sutton, took him to Callahan's Western Wear and bought him a pair of cowboy boots. Mark wore them to his first few meetings with alumni; he said that helped persuade them that he was okay.

———◆———

After Sutton retired as dean and returned to the faculty, he and I went a time or two to the quarter-horse races at Manor Downs, a minor-league track near Austin. John's ability to pick winners by looking over the field was uncanny. He waited until the horses paraded in front of the stands, and then bet on the one (or two) that he thought looked most promising. He kept his betting money in one pocket and his winnings in another, so he could always determine exactly how much he had won.

Later we went to the Breeders Cup when it was run in Fort Worth, with Daryle and Cindy McGinnis, John's urologist Ned Stein from Houston, and some other friends. We turned out to be congenial travelers, so going to some major track became an annual event for the group. We went to River Downs in Cincinnati, Hollywood Park and Santa Anita in California, and Churchill Downs. John's son is a pilot and sometimes flew John and his wife Nancy to the city nearest the race. John loved to place exotic bets — exacta, trifecta, each-way, and boxed. We always tried to sit where John could get a good look at the horses before the race, but at these races he seemed to have more luck relying on the form sheets than on a view of the horses, maybe because at the big-time races the horses are more closely matched.

Daryle had been my classmate and John's student. He interrupted his law school career to go to Vietnam, where he flew cargo planes. After he came back from the war he finished law school and became a pilot for Delta. Eventually he was president of the Delta pilots union at the time of a bitter and protracted strike. By the time we were going to races, he had retired from Delta and was writing novels and traveling. Daryle and Cindy became close friends with John, and toward the end of John's life Daryle became his confidante.

———◆———

Bernie Ward was an immensely popular teacher of federal courts, remedies, and introduction to law (now replaced by civil procedure). He often taught two of those courses each semester. Introduction to law was a required first-year course, so one-fourth of each class — as many as 125 students — was assigned to him. His fed courts or remedies courses usually attracted 140 or 150 upper level students, as many as the classroom could hold. That meant that at the end of each semester, he had 250 to 300 exams to grade.

On Memorial Day in 1981 there was a major flood on Shoal Creek. Houses along the creek were flooded, several blocks of downtown businesses were inundated, one auto dealer's cars ended up in Town Lake, and fifteen people were killed. In the faculty lounge several days later, various faculty members were recounting their flood experiences. Bernie described how he had just turned onto Shoal Creek Boulevard, beside the creek, when his car encountered rising water and stalled.

"I got out and started up the hill toward the Temple [Beth Israel]. Then I remembered my bluebooks. They were on the floor in the back. So I waded back and put them up in the window above the back seat. When I want back the next day the car was full of water but the bluebooks were okay."

George Schatzki erupted. "Bernie, you fool. Don't you know that every law professor is entitled to lose his exams once in a career? It's a well-known rule. [There was no such rule, of course.] You blew your chance!"

Bernie was the most literate of my law professors. He often interrupted himself to quote a few lines from Shelley or Shakespeare. As students we marveled at his ability to call up pertinent passages at will and recite them from memory, with suitable theatrical inflection. As a professor, I soon learned the trick of having an apropos story, joke, or song lyric ready if the right occasion arose. I'm not saying

Bernie's poetic interjections were rehearsed, but neither am I certain that all of his felicitous asides were entirely spontaneous.

———◆———

Steve Susman taught at the law school for a couple of years in the mid-70s. He was an adventurer and an organizer. I've written elsewhere about some of the canoe trips he organized. He also organized a trip to the annual Sweetwater Rattlesnake Hunt. Steve and his wife Karen, Marc Grossberg and his wife, and I were in one car, and some of Steve's friends from the Houston art world were in another. As we trekked across West Texas, we began stopping at every Dairy Queen. First it was to get something to eat or drink; then it was because somebody needed to use the restroom, and then it became an attempt to see how many Dairy Queens we could visit. We were driving on non-interstate highways where every 20 miles or so there was a town big enough to have a Dairy Queen. We must have been insufferable — boisterous city people laughing extravagantly at things that didn't seem funny to anybody else.

It took us almost all day to go the 200 miles from Austin to Sweetwater but we arrived in time for the beauty pageant on the eve of the hunt. We called it the Miss Snake Charmer contest, but I'm not sure that was its official name. The 12 or 15 contestants came in all sizes and shapes. They appeared to be 16 to 18 years old, an age when walking across the stage in a swimsuit or evening gown would have been scary even for the most poised and self-confident girl, and many of these girls were anything but.

The high school auditorium was full of townspeople who probably all knew all the girls; some of them no doubt had daughters or sisters in the competition. Winning the contest that seemed so ridiculous to us may have been a high school girl's dream in Sweetwater. We made bets on which one would win, rolled our eyes when a fat girl walked across, and snickered at their earnest answers to banal questions from the emcee. We were loud and rude. It's a miracle we weren't hauled outside and given the thrashing we deserved.

I often think of that evening when I hear someone talking about the "intolerance" of small-town rednecks for outsiders. We got a few curious looks but nothing menacing at all.

The morning of the hunt we somehow got connected with a local oilfield worker who knew where there was a den of rattlers and had permission from the rancher to hunt them. Our guide had a pressurized spray can of gasoline, some small mirrors, and a few snake grabbers — sticks like groundskeepers sometimes use to pick up trash, with a handle like a pistol and a trigger that worked a pincer at the end.

The den was on the southern slope of a small mesa, well concealed by brush and mesquite. It took our guide a while to find it. It was under a small rock outcropping with an opening a foot wide but just high enough for a snake to slither through. The guide showed us how to angle a mirror just right to direct bright sunlight into the den and see some snakes. He then pumped the spray can and squirted some gasoline into the den.

In a few minutes the gasoline fumes started forcing the snakes to crawl out (a practice now condemned by conservationists). We took turns standing at the opening, catching a snake behind the head with the pincers, and lifting it into a cage. There were about 20 people in our party and we caught 21 snakes.

The guide then informed us that he had gained the rancher's permission by promising that we would clear the rattlesnakes out from under an old ranch house on the property. After a great deal of discussion about who was going to crawl under the house, we decided it would be sufficient to shine our mirrors under the house and if we didn't see any snakes, report that it was clear. We rationalized that cowardly but wise decision on the ground that it was unreasonable for the rancher to expect anybody to crawl around on their bellies in the dark looking for rattlesnakes. Or maybe it was just his joke on city folks.

Back in town at the hunt headquarters, we dumped our snakes out so they could be counted, weighed, and measured — there were prizes for the most snakes caught, the longest snake, and the heaviest. We didn't win any prizes, and we found out that hundreds or thousands of snakes in one place give off a nasty odor. We watched guys milk the snakes for their venom, cut off their heads, skin them, and deep-fry morsels of rattlesnake for those brave enough to taste it.

One of the duties of the new queen who had been chosen the night before was to get in an enclosure full of rattlesnakes and hold a mass of wriggling harmless snakes in her arms. The girl did it for a few seconds and then fled, crying.

Two of my students, Pete Geren and Paul Galvin, heard me taking about the rattlesnake hunt and asked to go the next year. There's a reason the rattlesnake hunt is always in early March: that's when it warms up and the snakes come of out of hibernation. But this time a norther blew in and it was snowing by the time we got to Sweetwater. The snakes don't come out unless it's warm; we didn't find a single snake the entire weekend.

Pete and Paul were good sports and didn't blame me for the aborted hunt. Forty-five years later, after a distinguished career as a congressman and secretary of the army, Pete endowed a scholarship in my honor at the law school.

———◆———

In each of my first forty years of teaching, I had 100 to 130 students in my first-year class. There was always one and sometimes two upper-level courses of 30 to 60 students each, sometimes more. In the last four or five years law school enrollments dropped and those numbers fell to 70 to 75 students in first-year classes and 20 or fewer in upper level courses. Allowing for students who took more than one of my courses, and for a few semesters when I had no students because I was on research leave, I calculate that I taught 4,500 to 5,000 students.

Looking back over those class rosters, the only thing more surprising than how many of the students I don't remember is how many I do. I was never able to memorize the names of every student, but at the time I could recognize them all by sight. There are still hundreds that I remember, most of them fondly.

For many years, visitors to my office have been perplexed by a bizarre pen and ink drawing hanging on the wall. It depicts a gigantic house in the shape of an inverted pyramid, towering over its neighboring traditional houses. It's about 24 by 30 inches, nicely framed, and it includes several images of me, the '57 Buick I was driving in the 1970s, and numerous grotesques.

The drawing was inspired by a case I taught in my property course in 1979. The case involved a zoning ordinance aimed at maintaining architectural harmony in a neighborhood. The ordinance was challenged by someone who wanted to build an unconventional house described by the court as being "in the shape of an inverted pyramid." Two students in the course, Mike McGinnis and Gil Reavis, got an artist named David Montgomery to do a whimsical interpretation based on the case.

Ready for Take off

That is one of many gifts my students have given me over the years, and I cherish them all. Michelle Crowson once asked me what kind of car I would like if I could have anything I wanted. I said a 1929 Duesenberg Model J roadster. At the end of the year, Michelle and her classmates from the class of 2005 gave me a 1:12 scale model of that car. It sits on a shelf beside my bed. There are other things — a wooden apple from April Lucas, a piece of pottery made by Bea Ann Smith, a huge silver belt buckle presented by Nelson Nease on behalf of the class of 1998, a voodoo doll from Katrina Price.

I have the "Miss Wyoming" sashes that Emily and Lauren wore across their chests when they dressed as beauty contestants in their end-of-year skit. They're white satin ribbons with the words "Miss Wyoming" spelled out in red and blue sequins — evidence, no doubt, of hours spent decorating them to avoid studying for exams. They now hang on a mannequin in my dressing area.

60th Birthday Party, Broken Spoke, 1999

One year my students gave me a hot air balloon ride for two. Karen and I showed up at daybreak at the designated take-off point east of Austin and were soon airborne, gliding westward on a slight breeze. But soon the wind picked up, carrying us a little off course. Our pilot was desperately looking for a place to land before we sailed out over the hill country where there were too many trees. He finally put us down in an open area of a manufacturing plant, where a security team wasted no time in telling us we were trespassing. I think the pilot persuaded them that landing there may have saved our lives.

For my sixtieth birthday, my torts students threw a party at the Broken Spoke. Fifty or sixty students came, and they invited my family and some family friends. The two-step was a mystery to some of the students, but not to Ross Fischer and Kelly Mayo. They whirled around the dance floor, revealing a Hill Country upbringing in which kids learn to two-step by the time they're six or eight. At that celebration, Vanessa Pogue gave me a quilt she had made, the squares embroidered with flattering things various students said about me. The quilt has hung on a wall in my office ever since.

The mementos will present some painful choices when I have to vacate my office.

———•———

(Writing about your life teaches you things about yourself. Writing this has shown me that students occupied a larger place in my life at the Law School than my colleagues or my courses or scholarship. Many of them became lifelong friends. John Watkins accompanied me on trips scouting for old cars before he went off to become a law professor himself. Milam Newby and his wife Tory house-sat for us one semester when we were abroad. Laura Prather represented us in some disputes with contractors and Kim Heilbrun represented us in a real estate transaction or two. John Beckworth, who wasn't my student but whom I met while he was in law school, became my co-counsel in a couple of libel cases and made me godfather of one of his children. Lyrissa Lidsky became a co-author on one of my casebooks before she became a law professor and dean. Jack Balagia labored with me in the media law field before he became general counsel of ExxonMobil. And Philip Bobbitt, one of my earliest students, became one of my closest friends, invited Karen and me to his wedding in Vienna, and several times loaned us his flat in London. After a couple of stints in the White House, he is now a law professor at Columbia.)

———•———

CHAPTER 5

Whitewater from Canada to the Big Bend

What might have been a fatal disaster began on a gorgeous fall day in 1969 and ended two weeks and a day later with improbable good fortune. In between were some harrowing moments.

Someone had told Ernie Stromberger about a fun canoe trip on the Guadalupe River upstream from Canyon Lake. Ernie was a reporter for the Associated Press in the Capitol Bureau when I joined the UPI Capitol Bureau in 1963. He and his wife Mary Gayle were the first friends we made when we moved to Austin and they became best friends for life.

Ernie arranged to borrow a canoe from a friend and tied it on the top of his car. We caravanned the 60 miles from Austin to the river in two cars, because we needed to shuttle one to the take-out point at a low-water crossing on FM 311 before taking the other car and the canoe to the put-in point ten miles upstream at Specht's Crossing.

Neither of us had done any whitewater canoeing, but we had read some instructions: put your valuables in watertight ammo boxes, take a roll of duct tape in case you have to patch a hole in your canoe, wear life jackets, tie everything to the canoe in case you tump, and steer to the wide side of bends in the river.

We took a gravel road from Highway 281 and parked beside the road just before it reached the river. Specht's low-water crossing was just that — no town, no houses, no parking lot, just a concrete structure wide enough for one car to cross if the water wasn't too high.

There was a big, slow eddy just above the crossing and we put in there, which meant our first maneuver was to get under the concrete crossing. There was barely two feet of clearance between the water and the roadway so we had to hunch down to get under.

Once clear of that obstacle, we floated leisurely from one set of mild rapids to the next. I sat in the front and Ernie tried to instruct me in the pull stroke, the J-stroke, and other techniques that the bow rower is supposed to use. As I recall, the most valuable service I provided was to use my paddle to push us away from rocks and trees just as we were about to hit them.

We had the river all to ourselves. It was a glorious ride. Giant bald cypress trees lined the banks, their knuckles edging into the water and their feathery branches arching over the river. (We realized later that we should have paid more attention to the debris lodged in branches 15 or 20 feet above the water.) We drank some beer and stopped a few times on sandbars to dump out water that splashed into the canoe in the rapids. The only sign of civilization was the Highway 281 bridge, high above the river a few miles downstream from Specht's.

After a few hours we reached our take-out point, loaded the canoe on top of my car, and drove back to Specht's to get Ernie's car. During that ride we agreed that it would be fun to bring our boys on a trip like this. His sons were six and eight, same ages as mine. We would take two canoes, he and I would sit in the stern and steer, our older boys would sit in the bow and paddle, and the younger boys would just be passengers.

Two weekends later, Ernie rounded up two canoes from acquaintances and we hauled the canoes and our sons to the same stretch of the Guadalupe. For the younger boys Ernie brought two little brightly painted wooden Mexican chairs with wicker seats. We tied them to the crosswise struts in the middle of each canoe to make seats for the youngest boys. I don't know the history of the chairs, but obviously they had already attained some status in the Stromberger household. "We've got to take good care of these," Ernie said, "Mary Gayle will skin me alive if anything happens to them."

This time we had to put in just below Specht's Crossing because the river had risen and there wasn't enough clearance to canoe under concrete roadway. There the water was swirling back toward the crossing so it was a little tricky getting everything and everybody into the canoes.

Ernie and his boys pushed out into the river first and promptly tumped. My boys and I were already into the current and I couldn't figure out how to get out of it, so we just floated on past them. By then I realized that this was a very different river than the one we had canoed two weeks before, and I should have figured out some way to abort, but I didn't and we continued to float rapidly downstream.

We made it through one set of mild rapids so I thought maybe we would be okay. But soon we approached a bend in the river and I could hear roaring water just beyond. By the time we could see it, we were swept into a frightening maelstrom. There were huge waves that we later learned to call haystacks. Water was crashing into trees and swirling around them.

We didn't just tump — the canoe was violently upended and Bill and I were thrown out. I had told the boys that in case we tumped they should try to stay with the canoe. Unfortunately John was trying to follow that advice while the canoe was cartwheeling among the trees. I could see flashes of his orange life vest as he clung to the canoe. I screamed at him to let go, fearing that he would be crushed against a tree or rock. Looking back upstream I saw Bill, clinging like a bear cub to a tree trunk in the middle of the stream, his paddle still in his hand.

I finally reached the canoe when it floated into calm water below the rapid, pried John loose, and got him ashore. The last I saw of the canoe it was floating away downstream, upside down. I parked John on the bank and frantically began trying to get back upstream to Bill. The current was too swift to wade against, so I took to the bank. It was steep, muddy, and choked with tall weeds. I was trying to watch the river too, in case Bill was floating down.

After what seemed like an hour, I got far enough upstream to catch sight of Bill — still clinging to the tree, paddle in hand. When I reached him all he said was "I was getting tired of holding on."

We fought our way through the mud and weeds to where I had left John, and the three of us climbed up to the top of the bank to look for a road. The road did not follow the river, so we struck out across some fields for a mile or so until we found it. We didn't know what had happened to Ernie and his boys, so l didn't know whether to walk back toward Specht's crossing or the other way.

While I was pondering, a station wagon approached. It stopped and the driver said "Lose your canoe?" He and his passenger had last seen their canoe wrapped around a tree, literally.

The driver turned out to be Dave Richards, the notable civil liberties lawyer. His passenger was Mike Sharlot, a UT law professor. I later shared many canoeing adventures with both of them, but at the time I had just started law school a few weeks earlier and I didn't recognize either. They helped us get reunited with the Strombergers, who hadn't lost their canoe but had wisely called it quits after they tumped close to the outset.

By now it was too late to go looking for our fugitive canoe, but Ernie agreed he would return with me the next day to search.

When we returned, we didn't even consider taking to the water to search; instead, we trespassed across farmers' fields parallel to the river, stopping the car now and then to walk to the river and scan the banks and sandbars.

Miraculously, we soon spotted the canoe. It was suspended vertically from a tree branch above the water on our side of the river. And there was the little Mexican chair, hanging by ropes from the strut we had tied it to.

I later canoed that stretch of river many times, sometimes with Ernie and sometimes with others. I learned to phone the Guadalupe-Blanco River Authority to check the water flow before setting out. Three hundred cubic feet per second was good; that's probably about what it was the first time Ernie and I went. Anything above 500 or 600 was dangerous. We later estimated that the day of the debacle with our sons, the flow was at least 1,000 feet per second.

———————◆———————

A few months later, Ernie and I teamed up again for a two-day trip on the Rio Grande through Mariscal Canyon, in the Big Bend. Charlie Schnabel or Dick Cory, or both, organized this trip for the Capitol Press Corps. Schnabel, sergeant-at-arms of the Texas Senate, was a consummate concierge for the senators: he could commandeer a lobbyist's plane for a senator's quick trip home, secure a private club membership, or get a senator a room in a sold-out hotel. Cory had been an important committee chair in the Texas House and was now a lobbyist for the beer industry.

By this time I had left the press corps for law school, but I was invited anyway, possibly on the assumption that I would soon flunk out of law school and be back in the press corps.

It was a VIP excursion. A private plane flew us to Alpine, where a bus from Sul Ross State College met us and took us to a ranch owned by an oilman named Bill Blakemore near Marathon, where we spent the night before heading to the river. We assumed the copious beer was furnished by Cory's clients. Who furnished the plane and the food was unstated; the rationale, or at least the rationalization, was that we couldn't be corrupted if we didn't know who our benefactors were.

Some of the college boys who worked for Schnabel as assistant sergeants trailered six or eight canoes out from Austin and had them waiting for us at the river. We put in at a place called Talley, which seemed to be little more than a candelilla "factory" on the Mexican side. The factory consisted of a giant iron tank over a fire, and piles of candelilla stalks waiting to be boiled to produce a valuable kind of wax.

The narrow canyon was lined with sheer 1,400-foot cliffs. At one point there was a cave high up on the Mexican side said to be occupied by "some hippies." There were a few mild rapids; the current wasn't swift and I don't recall that anyone tumped.

Rafting the Green River, Utah 1977

Once in the canyon, there was only one place to camp: a large sandbar on the Texas side. We beached our canoes there and retreated to the high point of the sandbar to build our fire and spread our sleeping bags. We could see only a slender slice of sky between the cliffs. There were a few flashes of light in the west which we assumed were from heat lightning.

We could occasionally hear the clink of donkeys' hooves on rock — smugglers, someone said, ferrying candelilla or possibly more lucrative cargo across the river and up the cliffs to accomplices farther north.

In the middle of the night someone shouted "Help, we're losing the canoes!" We got to them just as the current was beginning to float them off the sandbar, and pulled them to higher ground.

Those flashes we had seen were real lightning from a thunderstorm. In the bottom of the canyon we had been unable to see or hear the storm, but it rained enough upstream to silently send a rise down the river. I don't know what we'd have done if the river had continued to rise; there was no place to escape to. We stayed awake until we were sure the river had crested and then tried to get a few more hours of sleep.

The next day the Rio Grande was a different river. The water was swift and brown. There were supposed to be some rapids on that stretch but they apparently disappeared in high water. We had been told it was a half-day trip from our campsite to the take-out point, but the fast stream took us there in less than two hours and we were soon flying back to Austin.

———◆———

In the late 1970s, Bob Armstrong, then Texas Land Commissioner, organized a landmark week-long excursion through the Lower Canyons of the Rio Grande. Bob had a purpose: he wanted to persuade the Carter administration to designate the Lower Canyons a "Wild and Scenic River." Among the canoeists were a Carter aide and some of his fellow Georgians.

Like many of Bob's projects, this campaign took many years of effort, but it eventually succeeded. As a result the Rio Grande in the Lower Canyons is now protected from dams and development.

I can't resist digressing a moment for a brief shout-out to Bob Armstrong.

No one in my lifetime made more lasting contributions to Texas. As Land Commissioner, he turned an agency that had been used mainly for the previous commissioner's personal benefit into an engine of revenue for the state. Oil companies had been paying only a one-sixth royalty for their leases of millions of acres state-owned mineral rights. Armstrong made them pay one-fourth, netting hundreds of millions of dollars for the state's public schools and universities over the years.

Bob's love of the environment was personal and immediate, not abstract. He loved to fish, canoe, camp, and bird-watch. He was a dogged advocate for conservation and preservation of natural resources. He waged a 20-year campaign to persuade the legislature to acquire the 200,000-acre Big Bend Ranch and turn it into the state's largest state park. Later, as a member of the Parks and Wildlife Commission, he was an effective opponent of endless legislative efforts to starve the state park system.

Later, as head of the Bureau of Land Management and other federal land management agencies in the Clinton administration, he devoted the rest his active life to protecting public lands.

When I first knew him, he was a member of the Texas House, representing Austin. His desk was near the press table in the middle of the House chamber, and I suppose that's how we first got acquainted. Just before we both moved on to other venues, he invited me to accompany him on a fishing trip to Matagorda Island off the Texas coast. Also on the trip was another House member, James Nowlin, later a federal judge.

Bob flew us to the coast in a four-seater plane. Matagorda was uninhabited, with only an abandoned World War II airstrip to land on. As we descended, some feral goats appeared on the runway. Bob aborted the landing, gunned the plane, buzzed the goats to get them off the runway, and circled back to land. As I recall, we fished for a few hours and none of us caught a thing.

The excursion through the Lower Canyons was a decade later. Twenty or thirty of us canoed 80 miles through unpopulated territory in four long days during Thanksgiving Week, camping each night along the river.

The veterans on the trip were state Senator Don Kennard, chairman of the Senate Natural Resources committee, and Bill Kugle, a former state representative from East Texas. Kennard and Kugle and a couple of their friends were reputed to have been the first white men to explore the Lower Canyons, many years before our trip. Kugle's tombstone in the State Cemetery says "He never voted for Republicans and had little to do with them."

Joseph Lelyveld, a *New York Times* reporter who later won a Pulitzer prize and became executive editor of the *Times*, was Armstrong's canoe partner. The rest of us were just friends of Bob or the Lower Canyons.

Unlike the earlier catered trip through Mariscal Canyon, this one was a do-it-yourself production. We brought our own canoes, food, drink, and camping gear. Some of us formed subgroups — Mike Sharlot and I were teamed up with Dave and Ann Richards. The four of us rode out to the Big Bend in Dave's big International Harvester Travelall with a week's worth of camping gear stuffed inside and two canoes tied on top.

We were late arriving at the put-in point because along the way we hit a large javelina at 80 miles an hour and blew a tire. We had to back-track to a town and wait for a new tire to be installed.

The put-in was below Big Bend National Park, at the end of a rocky 15-mile desert road. We camped that night on a bluff over the river so we could get an early start the next day. When we awoke at dawn there was a light dusting of frost on our sleeping bags.

Our departure was delayed for a short time while we awaited the arrival of three young men from Houston who had said they were coming. Finally Armstrong said we couldn't wait any longer or it would be dark before we got to our planned camping spot at a hot spring 20 miles downstream.

At the first major rapid we encountered, Armstrong's canoe rammed head-on into a large boulder. Apparently Lelyveld didn't understand the importance of his role in the front of the canoe: even if you don't do anything else, use your paddle to push away from a tree or a rock before you hit it.

Armstrong was a sucker for the latest technology, and he had brought the latest in canoes: one made of a composite material that was supposed to be lighter than aluminum and stronger than fiberglass. Most of the other canoes were tried-and-true aluminum with lots of dents testifying to their endurance. If they sprung a leak, a roll of duct tape usually was sufficient to make a repair.

Armstrong's composite canoe had none of that resilience. The head-on impact caused numerous splits, the way the fibers in a stalk of bamboo separate if you ram the end of it into something solid. Bob used up the entire roll of duct tape he had brought, plus more borrowed from others, to patch the splits. He got the canoe back on the water, but it had no rigidity; it tended to flex longitudinally as well as sideways. That he was able to complete the trip in a floppy vessel was a tribute to his skill.

Each member of our team had a specific task — bring beer, bring whiskey, bring steaks. Ann's was to bring lunch. After a hard morning on the river, we pulled up on a sandbar ready to tuck into some hearty sandwiches. Instead, Ann pulled out a small tin of Vienna sausages and a package of saltines — her statement about being assigned a woman's task, I suppose.

We had to portage over some boulders that first day. We formed a sort of bucket brigade to help each other get the canoes over, but it was still a tough job. Each canoe was loaded with everything needed to camp for three nights and canoe for four days, all sealed up in big garbage bags tied down in the canoe. We usually had to hand the bags across separately to lighten the canoes, then tie everything down again.

It was almost dark when we reached our first-night destination. The hot spring was at the edge of the river on the Mexican side. We built a campfire and spread our bedrolls on a slight elevation 20 or 30 yards above the spring and the river. There was a lot of boisterous talk about getting naked and sitting in the hot water drinking whiskey, and some people did. But it was chilly and many of us were content to stay by the fire and treat our weary bodies to some welcome sleep, so I'm not sure who all the nudists were. I assume Ann was one, but I don't know for sure.

I was told that two who made themselves noticed at the spring were Kugle and his canoe partner, a voluble blonde 30 years his junior. While others sat quietly in the dark, passing the whiskey bottle, they cavorted noisily.

In the middle of the night someone was awakened by voices coming from the river. It turned out to be the three tardy young men from Houston. They had put in at mid-afternoon in the same place where we put in. All three of them and their gear were in one canoe. How they managed to run rapids and do the portage in the dark with an overloaded canoe was a mystery. They said their eyes adjusted to the dark and they could see a little.

The second night we camped on the Texas side, across the river from some primitive goat corrals made of vertical sticks stuck in the ground side by side. Two mysterious Mexican goatherds tended a few goats, paying us no attention. Someone said they were employed by a ranch 20 or 30 miles deep in Mexico. We couldn't see that they had any shelter or sources of food or water, but obviously they must have had. They were the only humans, in fact the only signs of human existence, we saw on the entire trip.

By the third night we had an emergency: almost all the beer was gone. One reason was that we drank more than anyone expected. Another was that when canoes turned over, sometimes the lid of a cooler flew open and cans of beer ended at the bottom of the Rio Grande. There was some bartering of food for scarce surviving beers, and people who had brought plenty of whiskey were very popular.

I have no distinct memories of the third and fourth days on the river, but I do remember the joy of reaching our take-out point at Langtry. Our vehicles were waiting for us there; I guess we must have paid some locals to ferry them the 150 miles by road from where we had put in to where we took out. We tarried long enough in Langtry to take a quick look at Judge Roy Bean's saloon, and then we made for hot showers at a motel in Del Rio, 50 or 60 miles downriver.

For dinner we crossed the river to Ciudad Acuna and a restaurant that must have rarely seen so many thirsty, hungry gringos. After dinner I don't recall that anyone wanted to do anything except hit the soft beds at the motel.

———◆———

Before she divorced Dave and got sober, Ann Richards was a fairly avid canoeist. Actually, I think she enjoyed the masculine camaraderie — the drinking, joshing, and storytelling — more than the canoeing; in the Richards canoe she was pretty much a passenger. Dave was an expert canoeist who needed little help from the person in the bow. I never saw her in a canoe with anybody other than Dave, and she was always in the bow. We called Ann "the Princess" because even in rapids, she sat serenely in the bow looking like the queen on a homecoming float, holding the paddle well clear of the water.

That's not to say she was unwelcome; she was a great raconteur and her sharp tongue often put down a long-winded braggart that we were all tired of listening to. And we saw the devastating wit that she later displayed in politics.

Dave had an insatiable appetite for new rivers to conquer. One day he called me, proposing to canoe the Medina, which was doable only after a rain. He said the river was on a rise and we could canoe it if we got there the next day. He rounded up two canoes and I met Dave and Ann at the town of Medina, northwest of San Antonio in the prettiest part of the Hill Country. My recollection is that Karen was my partner, but she doesn't remember making the trip so maybe some other Richards friend was in the canoe with me.

We put in just below the town and canoed to near Bandera. The river was so narrow that in places we could almost touch the banks on both sides. It was a lovely trip, just the burbling stream, lush vegetation on both sides, a few mild rapids, and no one else on the river. I don't think Ann's paddle was ever in the water.

If Ann ever went canoeing after the divorce, I am unaware of it. Single and sober, she got serious about politics and from then on she may have been too busy with her various official jobs. Or possibly she had no desire to canoe without Dave in the stern.

———◆———

The Lower Guadalupe, below Canyon Dam, is a better known white-water venue than the Upper Guadalupe that Ernie and our boys canoed. The Upper Guadalupe is scenic and pastoral, while the Lower is lined with houses and development. But the Lower has some class III rapids and offers more challenging canoeing.

When Steve Susman was a visiting professor at the Law School in the early '70s, he organized numerous canoe trips, usually including his wife Karen and members of the law faculty. He continued doing so after he returned to law practice in Houston. Steve was an adventurer, so he preferred the thrills of the Lower Guadalupe to the beauty of the Upper. Sometimes the thrills were too intense.

At one point there was a low dam across the river. All of the water usually rushed through a break in the middle of the dam, but on this occasion the river was a little higher than usual; in addition to the water going through the chute formed by the break, there was also a sheet of water tumbling over the top of the dam. Steve and most of the rest of us shot through the chute, but Mike Sharlot and Steve Van, sitting crosswise in the water waiting their turn for the chute, got carried too close to the dam and went over.

When they didn't emerge on the other side, Susman recognized that they were upside-down and caught in the hydraulic, the roll of water formed when some of the falling water rushes back toward the dam. Somebody quickly located a length of rope and Steve tied it around his waist. A couple of people on the bank held on while Steve waded into the water, fighting the current which was trying to wash him away from the dam. He carefully made his way close enough to the hydraulic to get a hand on Mike and Steve overturned canoe. The guys on shore pulled Susman and the canoe parallel to the dam, and Mike and Steve were clinging to the canoe.

They had been trapped in the tube of air inside the roll of water. When he got on the bank, Mike was badly shaken. He sat with his head in his hands for a while, and later he said "I thought I was going to die."

———————◆———————

Another Susman outing involved a dozen or more people, mostly connected with the Law School. We had cleared a major rapid and pulled up half a mile downstream on a sandbar. Counting noses, we quickly realized that Bob Hamilton, his wife Dagmar, and their daughter Meredith were missing. Bob was a professor at the Law School, Dag a faculty member at the LBJ School, and their daughter was a teenager.

Soon their canoe appeared, but Bob was not aboard. "He got mad and refused to continue with us," Dag explained.

We pieced together the story: Bob had no canoeing experience, but seeing men in the stern of other canoes, he had taken that position. Dag remembered a little about canoeing from her days at summer camp as a girl. In the rapids Dag had tried to tell Bob what to do but it hadn't worked and they tumped. Bob blamed Dag and she blamed him (unless your spouse is named Susman or Richards, canoeing together usually isn't good for the marriage).

We were trying to figure out where Bob had gone, when he appeared far up the river, wading and climbing over rocks. When he caught up to us, he said "I refuse to ride with that woman."

Someone else put him in the middle of their canoe. Dag took the stern of the Hamilton canoe and with Meredith in the front, they completed the trip.

———————

By the 1980s the Lower Guadalupe was ruined for canoeing by the armies of tubers that descended after a number of tube rental concessions opened along its banks. You couldn't line up your canoe to shoot through a rapid because if you did you would crash into a mass of people in tubes, clustered together like algae.

My friends and I never rafted any of the Texas rivers, I guess because canoeing was more of a challenge, and maybe also because rafting is no fun when there are long stretches of flatwater between rapids.

Rafting Flathead River in Montana with Bill

On northern rivers where the water is wilder, we did resort to rafts. Liz and I floated the Athabasca in Alberta, I did the Flathead in Montana with John and Bill, John and I did the Green River in Utah, and I did the Lochsa in Idaho and the Middle Fork of the Flathead in Montana. Except for the Green River trip which John and I did by ourselves, those were all trips with outfitters who did the paddling and rapid-running.

I saw no canoes on any of those rivers, but on the Lochsa trip our raft was accompanied by two guides in kayaks who performed amazing feats in huge rapids. That looked like great fun, but by then my river-rat days were about over.

CHAPTER 6

Carrying the UT Banner Afield

It was tough duty but someone had to do it. The assignment was to go to another law school in the U.S. or abroad for a semester or a year, teach or do research there, and live there and make friends. The purpose was to spread the UT brand, expose the UT professor to other scholars and new ideas, and encourage professors from other schools to visit UT for the same purposes. It still happens, but less frequently, possibly because now many professors have spouses who can't pull up stakes for a semester or a year.

My time at UT spanned the most transformative years the Law School had experienced up to that time. When I joined the faculty, only a handful of professors had national reputations. Texas was considered a good school, but not in the class with the best, or even the best state schools. A number of our graduates were nationally known, such as Supreme Court Justice Tom Clark, but we didn't have a large reputation outside Texas. Major East Coast law firms didn't recruit at Texas, and most of our graduates went to Texas firms. By the time I retired we were sending graduates all over the country, and other law schools recruited faculty who had graduated from UT or taught here. And as we are always eager to note, the school usually is ranked among the top 14 or 15 in the country.

Until the 1970s very few of our faculty ever taught abroad. But then two things happened: our growing reputation attracted more attention abroad, and interchange between U.S. law schools and foreign schools became more common throughout the law school world. I was a beneficiary of both those changes.

———◆———

High Table at Wolfson College Cambridge wasn't High Table at all by traditional standards. Wolfson, the newest of the Cambridge colleges, was not wedded to the centuries-old traditions of some of the other colleges. For example, instead of being seated at an elevated table at the front of the students' dining hall, the fellows and visitors at Wolfson's High Table dined in a separate room. But it was intimidating nonetheless.

I was invited to High Table when I was a visitor at Wolfson for about a month in 1988. Ten or twelve people, including Karen and one or two other women, were seated around a table. In the center on one side was David Williams, the principal of Wolfson and later vice-chancellor of Cambridge University. Sitting across from him, I quickly learned that High Table was not an occasion for friendly chit-chat, but for deft wit and intellectual competition.

I failed miserably. I had been in England for a couple of short vacations, but my ear was not attuned to the English accent, so I often had to ask for repetition. Allusions to important events in English history or major works of English scholarship were unknown to me. I'm sure the Brits thought I sounded like a back-country rube. The other Fellows tried a few times to engage me in conversation, but eventually they gave up. Williams finally alleviated my embarrassment by asking me some innocuous questions about the University of Texas and the state.

Fortunately a subsequent visit by Charles Alan Wright seemed to redeem the reputation of UT. As Geoffrey Hazard wrote upon Charley's death, Charley was an "unabashed Anglophile in look, demeanor, dress, diction, and erudition. And they loved him over there every bit as much as we have over here." Charley and his wife became close friends of Williams and his wife.

———◆———

For a student of libel law, England was a paradise. When I visited Queen Mary College in 1988, libel cases were in the news in England regularly. Elton John, before he became Sir Elton, received a £1 million settlement from the *Sun*, which had said nasty things about his private life. Jeffrey Archer, before he became Lord Archer, won a £500,000 judgment against the *Star* for saying he had contacts with a prostitute. Robert Maxwell, the media mogul, won a £225,000 judgment against *Private Eye*. (After winning these cases Archer and Maxwell were both disgraced.

Archer was convicted of fraud and repaid the money he had won from the *Star*, and Maxwell was found to have stolen millions of pounds from his employees' pension funds. As we're often reminded, reputation and character aren't the same thing.)

In the U.S., teaching defamation law has begun to seem like teaching ancient history because today few libel suits are brought and even fewer proceed to trial. But the seminar on defamation law that I taught in London had plenty of current material to draw on.

Useful examples seemed to leap out of the newspapers almost daily. One day the Evening Standard said Mike Tyson, the boxer, had been caught "canoodling with a lithe young woman." As is often the case with defamation, the issue turned on the readers' understanding of one word — canoodling.

The word was unfamiliar to me and I assumed it meant having sex. So did some of the foreign students in my seminar, but most of the British students thought it only meant necking or petting.

That raised a host of questions that occur in many defamation cases. If the statement is innocuous to most of the readers but defamatory in the eyes of some, can it be considered libelous? If it connotes sex only to people who misunderstand the word? (Professors have long illustrated this puzzle with the apocryphal story of Senator Smathers campaigning against Claude Pepper by telling backwoods audiences in Florida things like this: "Claude Pepper is a shameless extrovert. He practices nepotism with his sister-in-law. His sister has been a thespian in sinful New York. It is well known that before Pepper was married he regularly practiced celibacy.")

Does it matter what meaning the newspaper intended to convey? Does it matter whether the story appeared in a tabloid known for its interest in sex, so that the mere fact that the editors considered it newsworthy might lead readers to believe it referred to sex?

Does it matter whether the newspaper's readers are Brits who would understand that canoodling doesn't mean having sex, or foreigners who might think it does?

To readers who understand the word to mean something like "necking," or "petting," it wouldn't be defamatory. And even if the story did imply that the couple was having sex, is that defamatory under today's mores? Only if Tyson was married? Does the fact that the venue was a parked car imply that it was illicit sex? Does that depend on information about why people have sex in parked cars? About why celebrities have sex in parked cars?

After much debate, the consensus of the seminar seemed to be that the story wasn't defamatory.

———◆———

Painful experience seems to be the surest way to learn a country's peculiarities. Shortly after I arrived at Queen Mary College in 1988, I received an invitation to an elegant dinner honoring someone from Queen Mary. The entire staff (in England that means the professors, not the administrative staff) of the faculty of laws was invited. Karen and I were both excited to be attending a formal affair in London. We assumed the invitation included both of us, because in the U.S. no university would dream of excluding women from such a function.

When we arrived at the elegant hall we saw that places were assigned around a very large table — and there was not a place assigned for Karen, or for any other woman, even though there were several women on the Queen Mary faculty. Karen wanted to leave but someone said "Oh, I see we have a bit of a hiccup," and hurriedly rearranged seats so there was one for her.

Karen was not happy about being a pioneer for her sex, but my thought was "Good. It's about time for these people to join the 20th century." The dinner was delightful, and if the presence of a female interloper inhibited the celebration, I could not detect it. I don't recall that women were ever excluded from any other ceremonial occasion that we attended at London universities thereafter — or maybe I was never invited to a similar event again.

———◆———

During my first London gig we were invited to Philip Bobbitt's wedding in December in a mountain village outside Vienna. I had introduced Philip to the bride when she was my student at UT, assuring him that they were made for each other.

It was a destination wedding before that idea had a name. Forty or fifty guests, including Philip's aunt, Lady Bird Johnson, came to Austria from the U.S.

Before the wedding, we all spent a day or two in Vienna. We went to the Sacher Hotel one afternoon for the famous Sacher tort. One evening Karen and I went to the opera at the elegant Staatsoper. After the performance we discovered that it had begun to snow, and we walked back to our hotel in a magical winter scene.

A chartered bus took us all to Grunbach am Schneeberg, a snowy village in the Alps an hour or two outside Vienna. We all stayed in a quaint hotel and took our meals there as a group. An enterprising farmer brought his one-horse sleigh to the hotel one afternoon and offered rides for a small fee. Karen and I couldn't resist, so we got in the sleigh behind the driver and headed down a snow-covered lane away from the village. It was idyllic; no cars, no other sleighs, bells on the harness, the steady clop-clop of the horse's hooves.

We were warmly dressed and had a blanket, but before long we were cold. The farmer didn't speak a word of English. Karen's German was pretty much exhausted when the farmer asked "Where are you from?" and she responded "Texas." He recognized that, and said "Ah, Texas!" but couldn't understand when we asked him, after half an hour or so, to head back to the hotel. Several attempts to convey that we were cold and wanted the ride to end were unavailing; apparently he was determined to give us our money's worth. He didn't turn around until he was ready.

Thanksgiving dinner, Drapers Hall, London, 1988

The wedding was in a tiny unheated stone church. The bride bravely endured in a light dress long enough to say the vows, but the rest of us wore our overcoats.

Sadly, the marriage ended acrimoniously, and that ended my match-making career.

———◆———

When I visited at Queen Mary again in 1992, Mark Yudof was dean at UT Law. He was eager to establish a relationship with University College London like the one we had with Queen Mary, so he asked me to explore the possibility. I called UCL seeking an appointment with the dean of the faculty of laws, whose name I have erased from my memory. I was cold-calling, as it were, and that's even more unwelcome in England than here. They seemed to have trouble understanding why their dean might want to talk to someone from the University of Texas, so it took a while to talk my way in.

When I did get in to see him, the UCL dean was not happy to see me. While I tried to explain what we were proposing, he looked across the desk at me with an impatient and perplexed expression. It was plain he could not imagine why UCL, one of the premiere institutions in England, would want to have anything to do with the University of Texas, which I suppose he viewed as an outpost on the frontier.

I reported the meeting to Yudof, who fortunately wasn't discouraged. A few years later UCL welcomed us, possibly because we offered to pay the salaries of both the UCL professor who visited Texas and the Texas professor who visited at UCL.

———◆———

The idea of UT presence in London was so appealing to Yudof and a few wealthy alums that they flirted with the idea of buying a building there. I was invited to sit in on a meeting in London between a delegation of UT heavyweights and some UCL officials, and later was sent to check out the building, which as I recall was located on some prominent central London street such as Pall Mall or Oxford Street. Sadly the era of free-spending transatlantic ambitions at Texas ended before the dream of UT London could come true.

———◆———

By the second time I taught at Queen Mary in 1992, the school had absorbed another college and become Queen Mary and Westfield, and Graham Zellick had advanced from head of the law department to principal of the college. The principal is the chief executive officer because the nominal head, the chancellor, is a member of the royal family. In the case of Queen Mary College, the chancellor was the Queen herself, and she came to the college during my visit. The entire academic staff was invited to a reception in a very large hall.

Probably because he was eager to show off Queen Mary's internationalism, Graham took me by the arm and introduced me to the Queen. When she heard University of Texas, she said "I was there recently."

I said "Yes, I know, you were visiting Mrs. Johnson." I had seen stories in the paper before we left Austin about the Queen visiting Lady Bird and the LBJ Ranch. We exchanged small talk about Austin, the University, and Lady Bird. I wanted to introduce Karen but she was hanging back. When I tried to pull her into the conversation, she was anchored like a post, resisting. When she finally came a step or two closer, she responded to the Queen politely but made no effort to converse.

Meeting the Queen, Queen Mary College London, 1992

Later I recounted Karen's reluctance to a British friend, who instantly guessed the reason: "Karen was gobsmacked." Apparently about half of the Americans who unexpectedly meet one of the royals find their tongues tied and the other half find their tongues untied too readily.

━━━◆━━━

I'm chagrined to realize that what I remember best about that second visit to Queen Mary mostly happened somewhere else.

I spent a lot of time in the library of the Royal Institute of British Architects in Portland Place, far removed from Queen Mary. Earlier that year we had bought the lot our house now sits on in Austin, and I was beginning to think about the design.

The RIBA library was a treasury of books about Georgian architecture. I quickly realized that what is most commonly thought of as Georgian architecture — the Georgian townhouse — is totally unsuited to the Texas climate. It was designed to capture as much sunshine as possible, taking advantage of eighteenth-century advances in the manufacture of window glass. Its flat façade aimed to NOT shade the windows, exactly the opposite of what's needed in Texas.

But the Georgians also built country houses with porticos and verandas that in England weren't intended as defenses against the sun but could be adapted to that use in Texas. By the time we left London in December I had made conceptual drawings that evolved into the design of the house we built.

Ideas for the interior came mainly from two sources: Kenwood House and interior design books in the Queen Mary library. In the eighteenth century Kenwood House, a mansion on Hampstead Heath, had been the home of Lord Mansfield, one of the greatest English judges. Robert Adam created the interiors as part of a redesign of the house in the eighteen-seventies. I visited the house repeatedly and got permission from English Heritage to sketch interior details.

Queen Mary and Westfield had a trove of Georgian design books because Westfield College had specialized in interior design and when it was absorbed by Queen Mary its books came with it. There were books with extensive drawings of Georgian fireplaces, overmantels, entries, cornices, ceilings, door heads, screens, and bookcases. Some of those were so helpful that I later bought duplicates of those volumes from rare book stores.

If it sounds like I spent more time studying architecture than English law, I plead guilty. I did give a few lectures on tort law in Queen Mary's "private law" course and presented a colloquium on the effect of emerging European free speech jurisprudence on England's domestic law of defamation and privacy.

———◆———

Karen and I became friends with Graham Zellick, the principal of Queen Mary, and his wife Jenny. One summer they rented us their five-bedroom house in Hampstead, just a block or two from Hampstead Heath. With all those empty bedrooms, we invited friends to visit us. We told them we would furnish breakfast but they were on their own the rest of the time.

Those who came were Karen's 79-year-old mother and an 84-year-old friend, neither of whom had ever been abroad; Dwight Teeter, formerly head of the journalism department at Texas and at that time dean of the communications school at the University of Tennessee and his wife Tish; former Newsweek editor Jerry Footlick and his wife Ceil Cleveland, then a vice present of Columbia University; my former editor Keith Blackledge and his wife Joann; and Ordway Sherman, ex-wife of one of my college fraternity brothers.

Their visits sometimes overlapped, and although none of them had known each other previously, they got along beautifully. They went sightseeing, to museums and to the theater, and in the morning they would trade accounts of the previous day. Sometimes we went with them, but mostly we were just hosts.

The house had four floors, and the Teeters were on the top floor. One morning I heard a crash somewhere above, and then Dwight's plaintive voice calling down the stairwell: "David, I think we have a problem." While he was shaving, the bathroom ceiling had fallen in pieces around him. He wasn't hurt. A water storage tank in the attic had leaked and accumulating water had collapsed the ceiling. Dwight joked that I had booby-trapped him.

———◆———

Once when we were in London, we saw Bill and Diana Hobby taking communion at St. Paul's Cathedral. Bill was just finishing a long run as the highly respected lieutenant governor of Texas. Their daughter had been my student at the UT Law School. The daughter and her husband became our good friends, and the Hobbys, in their expansive way, treated Karen and me as part of their large extended family.

After the services, we visited with the Hobbys and their retinue of friends from Texas, and Diana invited us to join them for dinner that evening at Winfield House. Bill's brother-in-law, Henry Catto, was U.S. ambassador to the Court of St. James. Winfield House was the ambassador's official residence, a magnificent neo-Georgian mansion at the edge of Regent's Park. Actress Betty Hutton built it in the 1930s and gave to the U.S. government after World War II.

We arrived at the mansion agog at the prospect of meeting the ambassador, and our eyes only grew bigger when we were introduced to the other guests. One was Marmaduke Hussey, chairman of the BBC. Another was Lord Rees-Mogg, former editor of the London Times and at that time head of the Press Complaints Commission. Rees-Mogg's wife was there, or maybe it was Hussey's wife. There were half a dozen other guests.

After a dinner of many courses around an enormous mahogany table, we retired to the sumptuous drawing room, which looked like one of those gorgeous eighteenth century parlors in the movie *Amadeus*. American presidents were staring down at us from gilded frames on the walls. The carpet was soft as fine fur. We sat in plush chairs in those pale peach-gold-cream Georgian shades that can be recaptured today only at enormous expense.

I had been in the company of important people at political events and professional gatherings, but never in such an august social setting. Fortunately for me, the shared interest in the room was the media — the Hobbys and Cattos jointly owned a number of large television stations in the U.S., and Hussey and Rees-Mogg were pillars of the British media world. I had some knowledge of the media industries on both sides of the Atlantic, so as long as the conversation didn't stray too far from newspapers, television, and government media policy, I could nod knowingly and occasionally ask a pertinent question. But when it turned to fox hunting, of which Bill Hobby was enamored, or the Glyndebourne Opera, which Diana loved, I was completely out of my depth. And once the people they were referring to by first names got beyond "Rupert" and "Margaret" I was lost.

When I was at Queen Mary, Professor Basil Markesinis arranged for me to give a lecture at Leiden University on the right to privacy, and Professor Francesco Francioni got me a similar invitation to lecture at the University of Siena.

At all three universities — Queen Mary, Leiden, and Sienna — I learned that Europeans were more worried about data privacy (the accumulation of information about individuals by governments and companies) than media disclosures of intimate information, which was what most concerned American scholars at that time. This was one of several instances in which I saw legal issues in Europe that only later blossomed in the U.S. My audiences were probably disappointed that my talks didn't focus more on the threats to privacy that they feared most.

The audience in Leiden was sizeable, knowledgeable, and very much interested in ways to protect privacy from unwanted disclosures. They asked pointed questions and sometimes disagreed with me. In Siena, Francesco had to recruit an audience, and most of them were there more to please Francesco than to hear me. Francesco reminded me that there are few attendance expectations in European universities; I spoke in a course that had 700 students enrolled, but regularly met in a room that held only 50.

In Leiden the canals were not yet frozen so most transportation was by bicycle rather than skates. Sometimes Karen and I seemed to be the only pedestrians in rivers of speeding bicycles. A classic Dutch windmill was operating in the heart on the city, near an outdoor market with booths selling everything from fish to pies.

We took side trips to Delft and The Hague. In Delft there were houses with doors just a few inches above the water of the canal, to make it easy to skate out once the canal froze over. In The Hague we visited the Mauritshuis, a small gem of a museum packed with old masters, including Vermeer's *Girl With a Pearl Earring* and works by Rembrandt and Rubens, among others.

For my talk in Siena, Karen and I flew into Florence and spent a couple of days there before Francesco drove us to Siena. We stayed amid olive groves at the farmhouse of Francesco and his wife Susan outside Siena. Francesco drove us to San Gimignano, a walled medieval town famous for its fourteen stone towers built in the fifteenth and sixteenth centuries. In the Sant'Agustino, a thirteenth century church, we saw dozens of works by medieval and renaissance artists.

———◆———

Allen Neuharth, chairman of Gannett Newspapers, had global ambitions for freedom of the press, if not for his own newspaper empire. In 1992 the Freedom Foundation, supported by Gannett's charitable arm, decided that post-Soviet Russia needed a dose of American style press freedom. The Foundation sent a delegation of judges, lawyers, and media scholars to Moscow to meet with some Russian academics and editors of the emerging press in Russia.

The Glasnost that Mikhail Gorbachev had championed in the mid-1980s had given rise to a few newspapers, which, if not really independent, at least represented different factions. Yeltsin had sent Gorbachev into retirement in 1991, but there was still freedom in the air. Entrepreneurs were set up on the sidewalks charging tourists dollars for souvenirs they had bought for rubles at the state department store. It seemed like every Muscovite who owned a car was operating a bootleg taxi.

The heavyweights of the U.S. delegation were Gilbert Merritt, judge of the Sixth U.S. Court of Appeals, and John Seigenthaler, a confidant of Robert Kennedy who had become editor of the Nashville Tennessean. When Neuharth founded USA Today, he made Seigenthaler its editor, and by the time of the Moscow trip Seigenthaler was head of the First Amendment Center at Vanderbilt. Merritt and Seigenthaler were the only participants accompanied by their wives.

The scholars included Donald Gillmor of the University of Minnesota, Dwight Teeter, who had recently become dean of the School of Communication at the University of Tennessee, and me. There were two or three representatives of Gannett and the Freedom Foundation.

The Russians were mostly editors of the newly liberated newspapers, someone from a state-owned television station, some journalism teachers, and a judge or two.

We met on the campus of Moscow State University in a once-elegant building that had suffered many years of neglect. We thought our job was to impress upon the Russians what press freedom meant. We talked about resisting pressure from advertisers, maintaining distance from government officials, protecting confidential sources, and challenging prior restraints. We were all guilty of lecturing them, but the worst was Judge Merritt: he spoke to the Russian editors as if they were eighth-graders.

Finally, on the second day, a couple of the Russian editors grew bold enough to tell us what they saw as the main threat to press freedom in Russia: difficulty in obtaining newsprint. Sadly, there wasn't much we could do about that. But at least it gave us a more realistic view of the state of the free press in Russia. For the remaining days of the conference, we listened more and lectured less.

———————◆———————

The American delegation was put up at the Savoy Hotel, near Red Square. It was a bit run down, but apparently was considered a luxury hotel in Moscow at that time. Our hosts didn't want us to get sick, so they told us to eat only at the Savoy, which shipped its food in from Finland.

The doormen vigilantly excluded Russians from the hotel; we were told that was to keep out thieves and prostitutes, but we had some suspicion that the authorities thought it would be impolitic to let locals see what luxuries were available to foreigners but not to them. The no-Russians-allowed policy proved embarrassing when our group scheduled a dinner at the hotel with our Russian counterparts; a few of them were turned away before the doormen got the word that these particular Russians should be admitted.

We were warned ahead of the dinner not to try to keep up with the Russians' toasts; they tossed down many shots of vodka while we faked or sipped ours.

A Russian journalism professor from our conference and her husband, a man who worked for some government bureau, gave a party for some of us at their flat. It resembled a graduate student apartment in the U.S. — a kitchen in the living room and beads in the doorway separating that from the bedroom. A wicker chest served as a dining table and we ate dinner seated on cushions on the floor. The hosts were proud to have a flat that they didn't have to share with other people. They were friendly and tried to make conversation despite the language difficulty; I think they hoped their hospitality might win them an invitation to visit the U.S.

None of my colleagues were interested in visiting the Pushkin museum, so I ignored advice and took a taxi there by myself. The driver spoke a little English and seemed to wonder why someone who didn't speak a word of Russian wanted to visit the Pushkin.

In museums in France and Italy, I had found that names of artists, dates, and sometimes the titles of the works could be read without knowing the language, so I expected to be able appreciate the Pushkin's exhibits from the labels on the wall. But even the most familiar names were incomprehensible in the Cyrillic alphabet; the tour of the Pushkin was a good test of my ability to appreciate a work of art for its own sake, without knowing anything about it. I failed the test.

I made another solo excursion, to the Bolshoi Ballet. I know nothing about ballet so I have no idea whether it was good, but the music was enjoyable. The building, like many in Moscow, had deteriorated but signs of its former glory were still visible.

———————◆———————

One evening, at the hotel, we heard music coming from the direction of Red Square. Dwight Teeter and I went to investigate. What we found was a rock concert — gigantic speakers mounted on steel scaffolding opposite St. Basil's Cathedral, blaring rock music, thousands of young people, and hundreds of soldiers. The concert was sponsored by Coca-Cola. The Red Army provided the lighting, the generators, the scaffolding, perimeter fencing, and security.

Dwight and I bluffed our way in — acting as if we had a right to enter and silently daring 20-year-old soldiers to stop us. When we got through the fence and the cordon of soldiers, we found that a pretty Russian girl had come in on our coattails. Our quizzical looks brought only smiles from her. At first I thought she was just a teenager who had found a way to get in without paying, but when she stayed close to us I deduced that she must be a hooker.

Young men with girls sitting on their shoulders swayed to the music, but everyone looked somewhat uneasy, as if they weren't sure they should be comporting themselves so freely when surrounded by soldiers. As the evening progressed, that uncertainty seemed to dissipate and they looked like festive young people anywhere in Europe.

I was in favor of asking some girl to dance but none of them seemed unattached and Dwight wisely cautioned against risking a fight with a young man in Red Square surrounded by soldiers.

———————◆———————

The Freedom Forum had arranged for Bob Strauss, the U.S. Ambassador in Moscow, to host a reception for the American contingent at Spaso House, an elegant neoclassical mansion that serves as the ambassador's residence in Moscow. I remembered Strauss from 25 years earlier, when he was a member of the Texas Banking Commission and I was with UPI. He didn't remember me, but we had many mutual acquaintances. He obviously enjoyed talking to someone about back-home matters.

When he found out I was now a law professor, he had a mission for me. "The chairman of the Constitutional Court here is a bright young fellow. His name is Zorkin. I wish you would go see him and ask him if we can give him any help. Tell him I sent you. And give him my best regards."

To my amazement, Jim Collins, Strauss's top assistant, was able to arrange for me to see the chairman, Valery Zorkin, the very next day.

Talking through an interpreter was torturous, but Strauss's message got through, and Zorkin responded with a manageable request: "We would like to see your Supreme Court's opinions," he said. Since West Publishing Company was the publisher of one of my casebooks, I thought it would be no trouble to get them to make Westlaw, their online report of court decisions, available to the Constitutional Court.

I underestimated West's penuriousness. They wanted to know how the Russians were going to pay. It took several calls up the chain of command, before a West executive agreed that giving the court Westlaw for free would be a good contribution to democracy and the rule of law. "But only for one year," he said. "After that they'll have to subscribe."

The next year the constitutional court ruled that Boris Yeltsin's order dissolving the Russian parliament was unconstitutional. That precipitated the 1993 coup in which Yeltsin's tanks shelled the parliament building. Zorkin defended the court's ruling and was forced to resign. He continued to oppose Yeltsin's policies (for example, he condemned the Russian invasion of Chechnya), and in 1993 he was re-elected chairman of the constitutional court, a position he still holds.

———◆———

In 2003 the UCL-Texas exchange of law school students and professors that I had tried to arrange in 1988 became a reality, mainly through the good offices of Basil Markesinis, who had moved from Queen Mary to UCL. I was the first UT representative, probably because I was the only candidate who was free to go.

By that time the skeptical dean was gone and I was welcomed. Perhaps the most cordial gesture was arranged by Basil, who had not yet become Sir Basil. He persuaded UCL to allow Karen and me to stay rent-free in a flat at the top of the UCL law building in Endsleigh Gardens, just off Euston Road in Bloomsbury.

(Basil loved to tell about the letter he received from Buckingham Palace announcing that he was to be knighted. It asked several questions, one of which was "Can you kneel?" The next question, Basil said, was "Can you get up?")

The flat was of the graduate-student variety, two rooms with a kitchen down the hall, shared with another flat. The other flat was unoccupied much of the time and the minor inconvenience of sharing was more than offset by the location: a few blocks from the British Museum and the West End theater district, and just a couple of blocks from the Euston tube and Britrail stations.

I team-taught a course on mass media law with Eric Barendt, the leading British scholar in the field. We taught the course as a comparative study, with Eric teaching the English law and I the U.S. law, and with lots of discussion about the merits of each. Eric and I became friends and we have sometimes collaborated since.

———◆———

Karen and I took full advantage of the location. We went often to the theater and concerts at St. Martin's in the Field. Karen spent many days at the British Museum and I sometimes met her there for lunch. We went to the nearby British Library and Regent's Park.

Returning to UCL late at night after a concert or the theater, sometimes with a stop at a pub afterward, was a bit spooky. I had a key to the front door of the building, and had been warned to quickly pull the door closed behind us to be sure no one followed us into the building. The interior was dimly lighted and our footsteps echoed in the empty building. After we got off the elevator at the top floor, our flat was down a dark corridor. But nothing frightening ever happened.

———◆———

The Queen opened a new parliament in 2003. Ross Cranston, an MP who had earlier been Solicitor General, had offered me one of his two guest passes to the Queen's Speech, an elaborate ceremony that takes place whenever a new parliament is seated. A royal procession takes the queen from Buckingham Palace to the Palace of Westminster in a gilded horse-drawn carriage escorted by the Household Cavalry and dozens of other groups in colorful costumes that are silly by American standards but are steeped in British history.

Ross had been dean of the Faculty of Laws at Queen Mary College when I was there in 1988, and I had seen him again at a symposium in 2003. He apologized for being unable to offer a pass for Karen too, but passes were strictly rationed. She probably would have enjoyed the spectacle more than I, but the invitation was only for me.

I was to meet Ross at the entrance to the House of Commons to get my pass. Being a Yank, I woefully underestimated the extent to which the procession would snarl London traffic. I finally got out of the immobilized taxi near Trafalgar Square and walked, or ran, to the House of Commons, only to find my way blocked by guards. I was fruitlessly explaining that I had a pass waiting for me on the other side of the street, when Ross somehow found me in the throng and got me through the barricade.

Several hundred of us were seated in two or three long rows in the Royal Gallery between the House of Commons and the House of Lords. The Queen, Prince Philip, and numerous royal battalions paraded with great pomp through that Gallery, passing a few feet in front of us. This being England, there were no metal detectors, no bomb-sniffing dogs, and no armed guards.

The Queen's Speech is one of two occasions — the other is a coronation — when the Imperial State Crown — which is made of silver and gold with 2,688 diamonds and assorted rubies, sapphires, and emeralds — is actually on the Queen's head instead of posing to be admired by tourists in the royal jewel display in the Tower of London.

The Queen spoke from a throne in the House of Lords, reading a speech that was actually written by ministers of her government, outlining their plans for the Parliament. The speech sounded like a political party platform, because the Queen repeatedly said "My government will present a bill to do x x x," or "We will do x x x." Like the Oscars, the occasion is more notable for what you see than what you hear.

———◆———

I secured an invitation from the University of Stockholm to spend a month there in 2007, before going to London for the rest of the semester. I gave a lecture there on U.S. free speech law, and found that there was little the Swedes didn't already know.

A member of the law faculty at Stockholm arranged a luncheon with editors of leading Swedish papers. Swedish newspapers are subsidized by the government, a practice that has been anathema to U.S. newspapers. (I say "has been" because the current existential threat to newspapers has led some in the industry to rethink the matter.) The editors were as perplexed by American hostility to the idea of government subsidized press as I was by their acceptance of it.

"Ámerican editors fear that if they were financially dependent on the government, sooner or later the government would try to control what they say," I told them. "What keeps the government from interfering with your content?"

"They wouldn't dare," one of the editors said. "The public wouldn't stand for it."

I was skeptical, but they said the Swedish press has such a long tradition of independence that the issue rarely arises. I don't read Swedish so I couldn't look in the newspapers for hints of government meddling. But it wasn't only the editors who denied any interference; academics who might be more suspicious or more candid than the editors also insisted that government financial support hasn't led to censorship in Sweden.

———◆———

We had a flat near the city center, several miles away from the University. I rode the subway to and from, without being able to understand a word of Swedish. I just counted the number of stops between our station and the university stop, and got off when the train had passed the right number of stations.

That worked fine until one afternoon when the train didn't leave one of the intermediate stops. An announcement came over the loudspeakers. Some of the passengers got off but most stayed on the train, so I thought, "Well, these people apparently think the train is going to continue on, so I'll just stay aboard." But after a few more minutes there was another announcement and everyone got off. I followed but when I emerged from underground I had no idea where I was. I started walking in what I believed to be the right direction. After a few minutes some familiar buildings appeared and I was able to make my way home.

———◆———

When we arrived for our first visit in Sydney in 1998 and began looking for an apartment to rent, we found a listing for a place on Victoria Street in Potts Point, a desirable suburb just east of the central city. It was on the top floor of a high-rise with a panoramic view of the central business district, the botanical garden, and three iconic Sydney sights: the harbor, the opera house, and the harbor bridge. We were so thrilled with the place that until we moved in, we didn't notice that there was no door on the bathroom. No door, no curtain, no screen. We adjusted to the indignity ourselves, but when we wanted to entertain dinner guests we had to take them out.

I had gone to the University of Sydney Law School more or less uninvited. I had offered to go there at my own expense and teach a course or present a lecture if they would provide me an office. The response was enthusiastic but vague, and when I got there I found that I was to share an office and a computer with a visiting scholar from Germany who planned to be in the office using the computer every day.

That wouldn't work, so I telephoned the head of the law department at the University of New South Wales, Sue Armstrong, and asked if they would be interested in hosting me. She promptly welcomed me and provided an office and a computer. Our flat was convenient to the University of Sydney and a long bus ride from UNSW, but UNSW turned out to be a congenial home base and I eventually did a little teaching at both universities.

———◆———

The Law Department of UNSW was in a ten- or twelve-story high-rise built just before the influx of women into the profession, so it had a men's restroom on each floor beside the elevator, but only one women's restroom for the whole building. By the time I visited there in 1998, females outnumbered males among the students as well as the faculty. UNSW had accommodated the new demographic by switching a men's room to a women's on every other floor.

Faculty offices occupied four floors. My office was on one of the floors that had a men's room. After visiting with a colleague on another floor, as I approached the elevator, I decided to pop into the restroom. I absentmindedly assumed the restroom beside the elevator was a men's room, as it was on my floor.

I was in a stall taking care of business when I heard someone enter the restroom. When I heard the footsteps, I thought "Oh-oh, that click-click sounds like high heels." Their owner entered the next stall and I could see under the partition that the shoes were indeed high heels. About the same time, the wearer of the heels spotted my men's shoes, and exited the restroom like a rocket.

I pondered: Should I wait a while, hoping people would stop watching so I could slip out unnoticed? I decided against that, because if I stayed they might call the police. I decided the only course was to walk out and face the music. When I did, I saw that every women on that floor had positioned herself strategically to see the pervert when he emerged.

"Sorry ladies, I forgot which floor I was on."

———◆———

During my time at UNSW I was doing research for a book on invasion of privacy. They asked me to do a colloquium for their faculty on that subject. One of my major cases was Virgil v. Time, Inc., involving a daredevil body surfer. *Sports Illustrated* had said he demonstrated his fearlessness by eating insects, diving headfirst down stairs, and putting out cigarettes in his mouth. Virgil conceded that what SI said was true, but claimed that publishing it invaded his privacy.

Fearing that my audience might not understand what a body surfer was, I said "Apparently there are people who lie in the water and let the waves propel them to the shore head first."

After they stopped laughing, they informed me that Australian children learn to bodysurf about as early as American kids learn to ride bicycles.

———◆———

I blame Bill Clinton and Monica Lewinsky for the death of my privacy book. I had most of the book written before I went to UNSW, and planned to finish it there. My early chapters showed that the cause of action for public disclosure of private facts is practically nonexistent in the U.S. because very few people can ever meet the stringent limitations in the tort law itself.

In order to recover, a plaintiff must show (1) that the facts disclosed were truly private, and (2) that the disclosure was not of legitimate public concern. That sounds like a reasonable description of privacy, but to protect free speech, courts have made those very high hurdles. If the plaintiff has disclosed the information to even a few friends, she may no longer be able to complain about its disclosure to the public at large on the ground that it is no longer a private fact. In further solicitude for free speech, the courts are reluctant to hold that a disclosure is not a matter of public concern if the public is interested in it and the media consider it newsworthy.

If the plaintiff is a public official, almost everything is considered a matter of public concern on the theory that, no matter how irrelevant most people would consider it, some people might think it important. As to celebrities, almost everything is considered of legitimate public concern on one of two theories: (1) celebrities seek publicity and they therefore can't complain when they don't like what's said about them, or (2) what they do is a matter of public concern because they are likely to be role models for young people.

Sometimes courts rationalize this destruction of the privacy of public officials and celebrities on the ground that they have voluntarily surrendered their privacy, but of course that's circular: they surrender their privacy only because the law says so. Courts recognize that these rules give public figures little chance of recovering, but they often maintain that it is still viable for private persons.

My aim was to show that the right of privacy is illusory unless it protects public figures; they are the only people in whose private facts the media and the public have any interest. The rest of us are protected by the fact that nobody is interested in publicly disclosing our secrets.

The Clinton-Lewinsky scandal, which peaked while I was at UNSW writing my book, convinced me that I was whistling into the wind — we're not willing to protect privacy because we're too eager to know the dirt. And the "we" is not just the readers of tabloids. Ken Starr was supposed to be investigating some obscure dealings involving a failed savings and loan, but when Matt Drudge reported on some hanky–panky between the president and an intern, Starr and his staff of presumably mature adults — and most of the rest of us — quickly recognized that a sex scandal was a lot more interesting than financial dealings.

At a faculty colloquium at UNSW, I asserted that the law should recognize a difference between the public and private lives of public figures and celebrities. My Australian colleagues politely suggested that I was clinging to a quaint old-fashioned idea. I conceded, of course, that what the president and an intern did in the oval office wasn't private, but my colleagues weren't satisfied with that; they didn't want anybody telling them what they could and could not find out about public figures. It was clear to me that if there was ever a time when the private lives of public figures were off limits, that time had ended.

If I had paid more attention to the Europeans' emphasis on data privacy, I would have been better prepared 20 years later when data privacy replaced disclosure of private facts as the principal worry in the U.S. too.

———◆———

On the first really warm weekend of the southern spring — it was probably October — Karen and I went to Bondi Beach to soak up some sun. Bondi Beach is justly famous all over the world — a crescent of sand six-tenths of a mile long and 100 yards wide, so big that it doesn't seem crowded even when thousands of people are enjoying it, as was the case on this day.

We spread our blanket on the sand and were working on suntans when I noticed that two young women a few yards in front of us were conspicuously topless. They were not being discreet, in the way of women who unhook the straps on their tops only after they're lying on their stomachs: these women were flaunting their toplessness. Once, they stood up and vigorously shook the sand off their blanket, shaking their bodies just as vigorously.

Emboldened by their boldness, I asked Karen if she would take my picture with them. As I recall she said something like, "Are you crazy?" I pointed out that they were in plain sight of hundreds of people and didn't seem shy about their state of undress. Karen gave a sigh that I interpreted as acquiescence, so I approached the women.

"Would you mind if my wife took my picture with you? We don't see this sight very often in the U.S." They conferred a moment and then said "okay."

They posed on either side of me, facing the camera. When I said "thank you very much," one of them said "don't you want a shot from the back too?" So we posed again, with them facing away from the camera.

Spring on Bondi Beach, Sydney (Photo by Karen)

I sent one of the photos to Jim Wright, who had been my barber ever since student days. Jim posted it on the mirror in the Sportsman Barber Shop in Austin, and it stayed there for years. My colleague at the Law School, Jack Sampson, saw it and a few years later arranged his own visit to an Australian university. (There is not a shred of evidence that the latter was related to the former . . .)

———◆———

No visit to Australia is complete without a bush walk. We got ours courtesy of Sue Armstrong, who invited Karen and me along with several others for a weekend at her cottage at Jarvis Bay, on the coast south of Sydney. One afternoon she took us all to a nearby wilderness for a bush walk. We were following her single file when we met another party coming down the trail from the other direction. Sue stopped for a moment and chatted with the leader of that group. We couldn't hear what was said, and we soon trudged on.

Later someone asked Sue about that conversation. "He warned me about a death adder they had just passed on the trail."

Death adders are one of the deadliest of the many poisonous snakes in Australia; they are well camouflaged and lie still among the leaves, waiting for their prey to come to them. I'm not sure whether Sue was confident that the snake had moved away from the trail, or just didn't want to frighten us.

———◆———

Bond University had the only private law school in Australia. I was curious to see how much difference that made, so I arranged to spend a month there. It tended to confirm my impression that intellectual rigor of a school often seems to be inversely proportional to the quality of its climate and scenery. But I probably wasn't there long enough to have an informed opinion.

Bond was created to be the centerpiece of a housing development. Alan Bond, an Australian real estate developer, had observed that people like to live in communities near universities. So he acquired a large tract of mostly swamp land on the Gold Coast of Queensland, filled the swamps and funded the creation of a private university surrounded by pretty housing developments. The campus was built around a man-made lake, with attractive sandstone buildings and lots of green space.

Three years after the university opened, Bond's empire collapsed and he went to prison for fraud. Suddenly deprived of the patron it had counted on for operating funds, the university had to become entrepreneurial. Recognizing that Canada had too few law schools to meet that country's demand for legal education, the university recruited Canadian law professors to come to the Gold Coast and teach Canadian law to tuition-paying Canadian students. The prospect of spending the Canadian winter on the beaches of the sunny Gold Coast proved attractive to students and faculty alike, and Bond became an outpost of Canadian legal education.

Other innovative internationally-oriented programs followed, capitalizing on the spectacular location and the fact that Bond, as a private institution, wasn't subject to the tuition limits that restricted other Australian universities. Eventually Bond became quite international.

Once again, we were hospitably treated. A professor at Bond learned that I had some horses so he mentioned that his father, James Crowley, raised a breed called "Australian Ponies" on a farm a few miles inland from Bond. Karen and I were invited to visit.

The farm was down some country roads like those in rural Nebraska or Texas. The farm was hilly and green, lovely but not pretentious. The Australian Pony breed was developed from Welsh ponies. They were stocky like quarter horses but about three-quarter size. When we arrived a young woman named Nicole was riding a sorrel brood mare and James was exercising a black stallion named Doc in a round pen. Doc was smooth-gaited and collected, as if trained for show.

I was not invited to ride, which was just as well because the only saddles in sight were English.

———◆———

Of four visits to five different Australian universities, only one was slightly disappointing, and that was mostly my fault. I had contacted an acquaintance at Melbourne University about a possible visit there, and he put me in touch with an administrator in their law school who recommended that I teach a course in their LL.M program.

I agreed, not fully understanding that program. It was an innovation that a number of Australian law schools had adopted when the national government imposed draconian cuts in university budgets. Professors were able to boost their income by offering intensive short courses. Students could get a full semester's credit in one course by attending class from 9 a.m. to 5 p.m. for five straight days (or maybe it was two weeks) and then writing a paper.

The takers were mostly mid-career foreigners who could improve their pay grade with an LL.M. from Melbourne University. They paid hefty tuition, most of which went to the professor teaching the course. If the course attracted enough students, the law school would approve it without much further involvement.

I failed to appreciate how crucial this made the professor's salesmanship. There was plenty of demand for courses related to business or trade, but not for subjects further removed from careers in commerce. I spent a lot of time preparing material for a media law course that would be useful to media lawyers in a number of countries, but the time might have been better spent preparing a glowing catalog description that made the subject seem essential to every career. Only a handful of students signed up, so the course was cancelled.

UniMelb, as students called it, gave me an office and library access, so I did some research and writing. I gave a talk on threats to freedom of the press and attended numerous lectures by visitors and UniMelb faculty. But my interactions with other professors were fewer than at other schools and with students, nonexistent.

We cut the Melbourne visit short and I spent the last month at Murdoch University in Western Australia near Perth. On a home-exchange site, I made contact with a woman who had a flat in Cottesloe, a beach town on the coast near Perth. She said she probably would not come to Texas to use our house, but we were welcome to stay in her apartment because she would be away.

Her flat was on the top floor of a four-story building just across the road from the beach. The front was all glass, providing a panoramic view of the Indian Ocean, the beach, and the port of Freemantle a few miles down the coast.

We never met our hostess; she left the key with a neighbor and a note inviting us to also use her weekend cottage in the Margaret River wine district. Her note mentioned that she had a friend in Perth, a judge named David Anderson, who she said was eager to meet me.

Judge David Anderson and his wife were both life-long residents of Western

Australia and seemed to know most everybody of consequence there. We invited them to dinner and they invited us to a party at their house where we met a number of judges and other public officials. Wandering Americans were a bigger curiosity in Perth than on the east coast of Australia, and we soon felt like we were among old friends.

One of the benefits of academic visits is that they expose you not only to scholars at the host institution, but also to others who happen to be visiting there. For example, at Murdoch I got acquainted with Harold Luntz, one of Australia's leading torts scholars, who was at Murdoch for a short visit. He is a professor and former dean of the law faculty at Melbourne University and editor of the Torts Law Journal.

———◆———

Karen spent hours just looking at the Indian Ocean from the flat. The beach was busy with swimmers, sunbathers, surfers, and wind-surfers who tried to maneuver large kites to carry them out over the water. Offshore was a busy shipping lane for ships of all kinds going to and from the Port of Freemantle. A cruise ship the size of an apartment building passed by, as well as a U.S. battleship, submarine, destroyer, and aircraft carrier en route to R&R from the Gulf War.

When we went to the Margaret River wine country for a weekend, we traveled only during daylight. The car rental people had forbidden us to drive in that area at night because of the danger of hitting a red kangaroo, a species much larger than the familiar eastern kangaroo. We were told that after dark they were as likely as rabbits to bound across the road in the path of a car, and hitting one was about like hitting a horse.

The faculty at Murdoch were cordial and well-informed. It was soon after George Bush had infamously proclaimed the U.S. invasion of Iraq "mission accomplished." Like many other Australians, they were perplexed by Bush. I was often asked, in less blunt words, "What were you thinking when you elected him?" My answer was usually some variant of "I don't know. I was not one of those who elected him."

———◆———

The fabulous Cottesloe flat was not the only generous housing offer we received from the friendly Australians. While we were in Melbourne, a couple we had never met invited us to use their weekend cottage in Sorrento, on the Mornington Peninsula south of Melbourne. They contacted us through the home exchange site, but like the woman in Cottesloe were unlikely to seek a reciprocal stay in Texas.

We accepted the offer, and again we got a party as well as a weekend getaway. The owners, Cobien and Michael Watts, came to Sorrento while we were staying in their house and had several of their friends join us for dinner.

The '80s and '90s were the apogee of internationalism at the UT Law School. We had a number of regular visitors from abroad for a semester or a year: Alan Boyle from the University of Edinburgh, Jane Stapleton from Australian National University, Mexican legal historian Guillermo Margadant, Antonio Benjamin from the Catholic University of Brasilia School of Law, Ian Fletcher from Queen Mary, Barbara McDonald and Jenny Hill from the University of Sydney, Carl Baudenbacher from the University of St. Gallen in Switzerland, and Francesco Francioni from Siena University.

The most significant visitor was Basil Markesinis, who first came to us when he was at Queen Mary College in London. It was he who arranged for our first exchange of students with Queen Mary. Later he moved to UCL and established a student exchange there too. Basil came to UT every year for 20 years and taught popular courses. He and Jane Stapleton were elected to tenured positions at the Law School.

At one point, we had more than 50 students spending a semester at one or another of the London schools under established exchange programs, and many more at other universities abroad, mainly the schools from which we had faculty visitors.

The student exchanges with Queen Mary and UCL withered because of their success. The students paid their tuition to UT and UT paid it to the foreign schools. When the numbers in those programs reached 50, the loss of revenue was more than the Law School could stand, so the numbers of students was drastically reduced.

The diminution of faculty visitors from abroad is harder to explain. In some instances those faculty moved on to positions they couldn't leave for extended periods. Benjamin went to the National High Court of Brazil, Stapleton to Oxford, and Franchioni to the European Court. Margadant died, and others retired.

As I and others like me aged, retired, or died, so did our friends abroad. For whatever reason, not many of our younger colleagues visited abroad, so we weren't generating the contacts that promote a robust international presence. I think that's a huge loss, and I'm grateful that I came along during the brief window when UT Law was internationally ambitious.

I think I had more overseas visits than any other UT law professor, mainly because I enjoyed it and was available. Karen was working as the librarian at the Austin *American-Statesman*, which gave her a leave of absence the first two times we went to England. After that, however, she had to give up the job. She might have resented that if she hadn't enjoyed being abroad so much. She got to know London better than I did; she would leave the flat in the morning soon after I left and return home just before I arrived home in the late afternoon. She was very self-sufficient, arranging evening outings for us and entertaining herself at art museums and shopping while I was working. She made friends, played the world-famous organ at the Town Hall in Sydney, and charmed the couples we socialized with. She cheerfully endured the inconveniences of shared kitchens, bathrooms without doors, and unfamiliar groceries. So I wasn't merely available to go abroad; I had an enthusiastic traveling companion.

———◆———

In addition to the visits abroad, I visited at seven schools in the U.S. I had summer teaching gigs at Utah and North Carolina, and summer research leaves at Oregon, Washington, and Colorado. At Utah there was a sharp divide on the faculty between those who were Mormons and those the Mormons called Gentiles. The Mormons were generally older and more influential and the Gentiles were younger and more interested in the outside world. At North Carolina I taught land use planning to a class that was a mix of urban planning students, who were enthusiastic fans of land use regulation, and law students, who were generally opposed. Their discussions were previews of dozens of zoning debates I've seen since.

I visited for full semesters at William and Mary and Columbia. At William and Mary, where I taught a media law course in 1983, the students were noticeably better informed than UT students. They read newspapers and often came to class with questions or comments based on the day's news. Among the memorable personalities there was the dean, Bill Spong, who had been recruited by Lyndon Johnson in 1966 to defeat a U.S. Senator who had voted against the Civil Rights Act, and who was himself defeated for reelection in the Nixon landslide of 1972.

At Columbia I was a senior fellow in 1986 at the Gannett Center for Media Studies. The best aspect of that visit was the association with the other fellows, among them Jerry Footlick of Newsweek; Bud Benjamin of CBS; Susan Tifft and Alex Jones, then at work on their landmark biography of the Bingham family newspaper dynasty; and Sally Bedell Smith, who was then working on a biography of William Paley and later wrote biographies of Prince Charles, Queen Elizabeth, and Princess Diana. One of the memorable events of that visit was a retreat at the palatial Harriman estate on a mountaintop up the Hudson River from New York, the fellows and spouses gathered around a piano with Karen playing and Jerry Footlick leading the singing of show tunes.

CHAPTER 7

Junkyard Friends

Junkyard Jimmie was the meanest-looking man I ever knew. His face was deeply creased, grey-brown in color as if permanently stained by grease and dust. His sandy hair was slightly kinky and stood straight up. His eyes were bright blue, but one of them looked off to the side. The whites of his eyes were permanently bloodshot. His most unsettling feature was a jagged scar across both lips, which contorted his mouth when he spoke. I don't think I ever saw him smile.

I believe Jimmie did time in prison for killing a man, but I'm not sure why I think that. It may stem from a conversation one Christmas, when I took him a fifth of whiskey. He said he couldn't drink it but would give it to his friends. I recall him saying something to the effect that "I was drunk for 20 years, and it got me in trouble. After that, I never touched a drop."

I'm not sure whether the part about him killing a man came from one of his friends or was just my supposition. It didn't come from him. He was not a man to be proud of a disgraceful past, even if he had overcome it; when he spoke of having been a drunk and in trouble, it was clear he was ashamed of it. I never asked about it and he never mentioned it again. The scar remained unmentioned too.

———◆———

His name was Jimmie Robbin; I called him "Junkyard Jimmie," to distinguish him from Jimmy Davis, "Parts Jimmy" (more about him shortly). I met Junkyard Jimmie around 1977. He had a 1957 Buick in his junkyard in East Austin, and I needed a power steering unit to replace the leaking unit on my '57 Buick. At that time there weren't many reproduction parts being made for 1950s cars because they were not yet old enough to be collectable, but they were old enough to be finding their way into junkyards in considerable numbers. When you found a junkyard that had the right make and model, you went there and removed the part and paid the operator a few dollars for it.

'57 Buick at Lake Tahoe 1977

(By the way, you have to be careful about calling them junkyards; some of the proprietors insist that they are wrecking yards and what they contain is not junk.)

Junkyard Jimmie had a '57 Buick that still had its power steering unit. Jimmie's yard was behind a small-time used car lot on what was then called East First Street. Jimmie and the used car dealer shared a small concrete block building between the car lot and the junkyard. When I arrived and asked to see the car, Jimmie said "You wait here. I'll have to get the dogs in."

The junkyard was patrolled by two ill-tempered German Shepherds. If anybody but Jimmie came through the gate, they were trained to tear him limb from limb. Jimmie ordered them into a small, high-walled enclosure in one corner of the lot and assured me it was now safe for me to go through the gate.

The '57 Buick was parked next to the dog pen. I got a jack under it, jacked it up, propped it up precariously, and removed the left front wheel. Power steering units of that vintage were big heavy things, tightly sandwiched between the engine and the frame, bolted to the inside of the left frame member, connected by a pittman arm to the steering linkage, and attached by two hoses to the power steering pump.

I was lying on my back in the weeds with sweat, dirt, and grease falling in my eyes as I struggled to loosen connections that had been undisturbed for twenty years. The dogs did not like my proximity. They growled menacingly and frantically scratched the metal wall that kept them from me.

It must have taken me an inordinately long time, because Jimmie came out to see how I was doing.

"Let's make that easier," he said. "Get out from under there and I'll go get my wrecker."

He backed the wrecker up to the right-hand side of the car, extended the boom out over the car, and hooked its cable to the frame on the left side. He got back in the wrecker, drove it slowly forward while he winched in the cable, and rolled the car over onto its top. Now the underside of the car — and the power steering unit — was at waist height and easily accessible.

That was the beginning of a cherished friendship. At that time I had only one old car and Jimmie had only one wrecker, but we were both about to expand. Over the next few decades I owned 25 or 30 old cars, and Jimmie eventually moved to a larger lot in East Austin and operated 11 wreckers.

———◆———

Many academics' favorite leisure activity is reading — novels, history, biography. After spending most of my workday reading, I've always wanted to do something different when I get home. For many years, it was woodworking; I liked working with my hands and solving construction problems. But that's a solitary enterprise and I've always liked company, especially the company of working men.

Restoring old cars filled that need — getting acquainted with junkyard operators, mechanics, body and paint shop men, upholsterers, other old car enthusiasts, and going to car auctions. I didn't stop woodworking, but for 40 years I also bought and sold old cars, worked on them, showed them, and drove them. Eventually I owned a couple of national first-place winners, including one bestowed by the Classic Car Club of America, the pinnacle of the old car hobby.

But those early years of restoring junkyard cars put me in touch with the guys I most enjoyed hanging out with; maybe it put me in my natural social class.

Everybody in my family drove old cars. When son Bill began to drive I found another '57 Buick in a different junkyard, fixed it up, and Bill drove it to high school. Later Bill bought a 1972 Chevelle Super Sport. I bought a '66 Mustang convertible that son John drove. Later he drove a '65 Buick convertible and a '57 Buick station wagon converted to a pickup (more on that later, too.). Daughter Elizabeth drove a '67 Chevy, a '65 Mustang, and a '65 Corvair. Karen drove three different pink '57 Chevys. I had three '76 Cadillacs, a '64 Lincoln, a '57 Thunderbird, a '39 Chevy, a '53 Ford pickup, a '39 Ford pickup, a '57 Ford retractable hardtop, a '55 Cadillac, and half a dozen '57 Buicks.

I wouldn't have dared put my family in old cars if I hadn't known Jimmie. Old cars break down frequently, not only because they're old, but because cars of the 1940s, 1950s, and 1960s weren't as trouble-free as today's cars. Karen and the kids all carried Jimmie's card and knew to call him when they needed a rescue. If Jimmie couldn't fix the problem on the spot, he loaded the car onto his roll-back wrecker and delivered it to our house. If he was unable to answer the call himself, he sent his half-brother, Pig, or another trusted driver, with instructions to treat the car with extra care.

Jimmie's wrecker business made thousands of dollars, but he didn't trust banks; he kept the money hidden around his house. "I keep a loaded .38 under my pillow," he said.

I tried to help Jimmie one time, but it turned out that he didn't need me. The wrecker permit he had was only good in Austin and vicinity, and he wanted to be able to go statewide. That required a permit from the Texas Railroad Commission. I helped him file the application, and then we learned that a hearing would be required because a competing wrecker operator had filed an objection.

We rounded up a few people to testify for Jimmie, but they weren't needed. The administrative law judge, a young black woman, heard the competitor claim that Jimmie had violated his existing permit by picking up cars outside the prescribed territory.

The judge turned to Jimmie. "Jimmie, what do you say to that?"

Jimmie said "I can't swear that none of my drivers ever went too far, but they weren't supposed to. I make sure they all know what the limits are, and I'll fire them if they go too far."

After a little desultory conversation with Jimmie, she said "OK, you're going to get your permit." After she adjourned the hearing, she asked Jimmie and me to follow her to her office.

"Jimmie, I can tell you're an honest man," she said. "I could see that you weren't lying."

As we left, I told Jimmie, "I guess this proves that an honest man doesn't need a lawyer."

———◆———

Jimmie had a girlfriend named Kathy who helped around the office. Kathy's parents lived in a house in East Austin until her father died, then the mother lived there for a number of years until she died, and at some point Kathy moved in. When the house needed roof repairs, Kathy went to a bank for a loan but was turned down because the house wasn't in her name. She asked me to help straighten it out.

The house was still in the name of her father, who had died fifteen or twenty years earlier. Not only had her mother's estate never gone through probate, neither had her father's. And Kathy wasn't the only possible heir: she had a sister and a brother.

This was one time when I could actually help someone, though only after a lot of on-the-job training. I got affidavits from two neighbors who swore that Kathy's father and mother had lived in the house and that her mother had never remarried. Kathy's sister signed an affidavit renouncing any interest in the property. The brother had disappeared many years earlier and nothing was known about him; I have forgotten how that problem was solved, but it was, and Kathy got an affidavit of heirship that made possible a loan and a new roof.

When I was buying and selling a lot of cars, I got a car dealer's license, not to sell cars, but to avoid having to pay sales tax every time I bought one. To get the license, I had to have a car lot with proper zoning, a fixed address, a sign, and a phone.

Jimmie let me use a corner of his building on East Caesar Chavez Street. I put a sign on the front saying "David A. Anderson Classic Cars," and I got one of his phones listed in my name. I sometimes stored two or three cars there, but mainly it gave me an excuse to hang out on Saturday mornings with Jimmie, Pig, and Kathy.

———◆———

Jimmie had emphysema and heart trouble. He took Coumadin, which caused dark blood splotches under the skin on his arms. He was in and out of hospitals several times, had to wear an oxygen cannula, and eventually had to hire a woman to look after him at his home. He didn't smoke when I was visiting, but his stepbrother and girlfriend told me he hadn't quit.

The last time I saw him was in the hospital. He had persuaded someone to smuggle in a pack of cigarettes, and he was smoking even though he was hooked up to oxygen and various monitors. I said "Jimmie, if you don't stop smoking in here you're going to blow yourself up." He went right on smoking while we visited.

When I left, he said, "Goodbye, David." He had never said that before. The next day I learned that he had died during the night.

Until he died, I didn't realize that I loved Jimmie like a brother.

Jimmie's funeral procession went through Austin and up I-35 to Pflugerville, where he was buried. At every major intersection, a wrecker was stopped with the driver standing at attention beside it — not just Jimmie's wreckers, but those of his competitors too.

———◆———

I sometimes bought vehicles at collector car auctions: a '57 Thunderbird and a '76 Cadillac pickup at auctions in Austin, an '83 Jaguar and a '65 Buick convertible at auctions in New Braunfels, a '64 Lincoln sedan and a '68 Rolls Royce at auctions in Fort Worth, a '59 DeSoto convertible at an auction in Phoenix.

My favorite auctioneer was a one-eyed man named Von Reece. He was tall and rawboned, but aside from his missing eye (he didn't conceal the socket with a patch), his most striking feature was a protuberant lower abdomen. It pouched out so his belt buckle faced his head.

He was a shrewd but affable veteran of auto salesmanship. After years of running wholesale auto auctions in various Texas cities, he began auctioning collector cars. For a while in the 1970s and 1980s, he had the major old car auctions in the San Antonio-Austin-Fort Worth corridor, until the Kruse family with their national auction company moved in.

Von was a used car salesman at heart, wheedling, cajoling, and scolding bidders. It was a time when lots of guys who were making a little money and knew even less about cars than I were entering the old car market. One of the criteria they seized upon was "numbers-matching." Every car has a unique number stamped into the engine block and another stamped into the frame. The factory paperwork shows both, so it is possible to determine if the car has the engine that was installed at the factory. Often old performance cars, like early Corvettes, had their worn-out engines replaced by newer ones identical except for the number. Such cars are not, strictly speaking, "original," and are less valuable to some collectors.

At one Von Reece auction, someone interrupted the bidding on a car to ask "Do the numbers match?"

Von erupted. "What does it matter? It's a beautiful restoration. It has a correct engine. This matching numbers business has got out of hand. If the engine is correct, what does it matter what the numbers are? Matching numbers is for people who don't know cars. You have to know something about cars to judge the quality of a restoration. You don't have to know anything to read numbers. So guys who don't know anything can pretend they're knowledgeable and get all worked up about the numbers."

It wasn't a polite answer, but it captured the feelings of a lot of us.

———————◆———————

At a Von Reece auction in Fort Worth I bought a '68 Rolls Royce Silver Shadow. I hadn't even thought about buying a Rolls, and hadn't inspected this car before it came onto the auction block. But it was eye-catching and was selling cheap for a 10- or 12-year-old Rolls — $13,000 as I recall — so I bought it.

Now I had to get it to Austin. I had sometimes prevailed on one of my children to go with me to auctions and drive a car home if I bought one, but nobody had come with me to Fort Worth. So I had to recruit a driver. I got Von to announce, "If anybody would like to drive a Rolls Royce to Austin, see this man." That produced a volunteer, a young cowboy from Austin. I'll call him Clyde.

"I was going to hang around up here a few days, but I guess I could go on home," he said.

As the auction progressed, I began to think it might be better for me to drive the Rolls, in case it developed issues. All I knew about it was that it ran well enough to get to the auction block; if a problem developed on the way home, I might at least have some idea what it was. When I proposed to Clyde that he drive my van rather than the Rolls, he was a little miffed at my bait-and-switch, but he didn't back out.

So we set out caravanning from Fort Worth to Austin. We stopped somewhere for dinner — probably Hillsboro or Waco — and got acquainted. Clyde turned out to be a bull rider and sometime rodeo clown from Oak Hill, on the outskirts of Austin. I made the mistake of revealing that I was a lawyer.

"You are?! Maybe you can help me. I've got a little problem." He had got in a barroom fight and beat somebody up. I said "That just sounds like assault, you'll probably get a fine."

He said "They charged me with aggravated assault. I beat the guy up pretty bad." And he had a couple of previous arrests for beating people up. "They might send me away. I need you to represent me."

It's hard to tell people that yes, you're a lawyer, but you don't know enough to help with their legal problem. Abetted by our profession's insistence on issuing a single license whether the lawyer is to handle traffic tickets in municipal court or corporate mergers before the SEC, people think a lawyer is a lawyer. When you say you're not competent to handle their problem, they think you're just weaseling out.

I'm sure that's what Clyde thought, and it occurred to me that he might decide I deserved some of what had got him in trouble with the law. But we made it to Austin, and when I took him home I gave him the name of a lawyer who might actually be able to help him.

I didn't hear from him again; I hope that's because the lawyer did help him, and not because he was locked up.

———◆———

I often scouted for old cars in small towns near Austin, and sometimes I bought one that was not running to cannibalize it for parts. Once I stopped at a gas station in Kyle and asked about old cars that might be for sale.

"There's an old Buick out west of town," the guy said. "Belongs to Crazy Eddie. I don't know if it's for sale but it's been sitting there a long time."

I found the place, a small acreage with an unpainted shack and broken windows. The car was a black '57 Buick sedan that appeared to be intact. The place looked unoccupied. I went back to the gas station and told the guy that.

"Oh, he lives there all right. He's a nigger. He goes up north in the summer but he should be back here now."

So I went back to the place and this time I could hear sounds like someone chopping wood behind the shack. I called out but no one answered. The house was surrounded by tall weeds. I nervously made my way through the weeds, wondering just how crazy Eddie might be. I continued to call out but no one answered. When I got close enough to see through the weeds, I saw a large black man with an axe in his hands. He was as surprised to see me as I was to see him.

When I announced my purpose he was not exactly cordial, but civil enough.

"No, I don't want to sell that car. I'm gonna fix it up so I can drive it."

I told him that I had some '57 Buicks and they were fine cars, well worth fixing up. That warmed him up a little, and we chatted about Buicks. He said he had a sister who lived in New York and in the summer he went up there and lived with her. "They got good welfare up there, but it's too damn cold in the winter. So I come down here. I can't get nothing but food stamps here, but at least I don't freeze my ass."

I offered to help him find parts for his Buick, but he said he didn't think it needed anything. "I just need to get some gas in it and start it up. Right now I just keep my food in it so the rats don't get it."

There was no point in asking him to call me if he ever wanted to sell the car; a man who kept his food in a derelict car to keep the rats from getting it was not likely be able to keep my phone number handy.

———◆———

A year or two later I drove by Crazy Eddie's place and the car hadn't moved. So I stopped and reminded him that I was the '57 Buick guy.

"Oh yeah, I remember you. You wanted to buy my car."

I told him I'd still like to buy it. "How much you want to pay?" he asked. I told him I'd have to look at it first, so he took me to the car and opened the doors. I doubted that it would run, but it had a few good interior trim pieces and excellent rear bumper ends. I asked to see the trunk to see if the floor was rusted out. He had the key in his pocket and popped the trunk lid.

The trunk was full of boxes of Ritz crackers and jars of peanut butter. "I keep this stuff in here so the rats don't get it," he said. I was about to ask if that was all he ate, but decided it was best to act as if there was nothing unusual about his diet.

I offered him $100 for the car and he hesitated, so I upped the offer to $125. "I guess I might as well take it," he said. "I was gonna fix it up but I guess I'm not."

I counted out the money on the spot and told him that I'd send Junkyard Jimmie to get the car.

I told Jimmie to be sure Eddie had a chance to take the Ritz crackers and peanut butter before he hauled the car off. Jimmie said they were gone when he opened the trunk.

Several parts off that car found their way into the '57 Buick convertible I was restoring, and some years later I took the convertible by to show Eddie that parts of his car lived on. The shack was still there but Eddie wasn't, and the guy at the gas station said "I don't think he comes back here anymore."

———————◆———————

Parts Jimmy was a counterman at Austin Auto Parts on Red River Street when I first met him. When I inquired there for a part for an old car, I was always directed to Jimmy, because he had been in the business long enough to know a lot about parts for 20- or 30-year-old cars.

When Red River Street started to become gentrified, Austin Auto Parts closed down, and Jimmy bought their inventory of obsolete parts. More important, he bought all the old parts books, the six-inch thick loose-leaf volumes that contained thousands of part numbers, crossover indexes, and specifications.

Jimmy took it all to the one-car garage at his house on Bouldin Street in South Austin. I'm not sure how I found him there; maybe he left a notice in the window of the old Austin Auto Parts building. Somehow most of the old car aficionados in Austin found him and he did a thriving business. He had a large inventory of the most frequently sought parts — spark plugs, points, condensers, fuel filters, gas caps. Often he knew the correct part number without looking it up. If he didn't, he had the old parts books and could cross-reference part numbers. He was often able to find a current part number for an item whose number had been discontinued by one brand but was still available from another. He would then go to one of the parts distributors and bring the part back to his garage.

My entire family got acquainted with Jimmy. When a part was needed for one of the cars of my children or my wife, I could call Jimmy, and they all knew where to go to pick it up.

Jimmy wrote down purchases on a small pad, and he could add up a column of figures faster than an adding machine. He always went back over the figures to make sure he was right, but he always was.

Jimmy must have been about 70 when he left Austin Auto Parts and well over 80 by the time he died. I didn't know about his death; I hope some of his customers knew about it and went to his funeral to show appreciation for all he did to keep our old cars running. I don't know what happened to his inventory and his books. He had often said, when he thought about retiring, "I suppose I'll have to sell it for 10 cents on the dollar." I suspect he was right; it wasn't worth much without Jimmy's experience and knowledge.

———◆———

Pete Levchik lived on an acreage on the edge of Bynum, a tiny town between Waco and Dallas. His house and shop were surrounded by 50 or 60 rusting hulks of cars, mostly Buicks.

Pete had been a navigator on planes flying over Vietnam, and settled in Texas when he retired after 20 years in the Air Force. He had bad knees, which he blamed on his flying career. He also had heart trouble and other ailments, some of which he blamed on Agent Orange. He complained about the Veterans Administration health care, but he was unfailingly jolly despite his infirmities. He loved jokes about "Pollacks," of which he claimed to be one.

Around 1974 I started looking for a 1957 Chevy but before I succeeded, I found a 1957 Buick coupe. I liked the Buick, and after driving it a year or two I decided to try to find a 1957 Buick convertible. I placed an ad in the Buick Club magazine asking for help in finding one. Pete saw the ad and called me.

"I know where there's a real nice one," he said. "It's in Corsicana and I think the guy wants $200. It belongs to a guy named Po. If you want to look at it I'll take you over there. Po has a junkyard over there and he might not take kindly to a stranger poking around."

I thought there was a little disconnect between "it's a real nice one" and "it's in a junkyard," but that was a before I knew Pete. I eventually learned that he only dealt in junkyard cars, and to him "nice" meant restorable. "Real nice" meant fairly easily restorable.

We arranged to go to Corsicana on a Saturday. My sons, then about 15 and 13, went with me to Pete's place. Pete indicated that we should go to Corsicana in his pickup, so the boys squeezed in between us and we set off on farm-to-market roads. "I like to stay off the main highways because there's too many patrol on those."

I soon understood why — we were flying down narrow two-lane roads. My boys were having trouble keeping their seats when we went over humps in the road. John was sitting where he could see the speedometer and he later said we were going 80 or 90 miles an hour.

In Corsicana, the Buick was sitting close to the road in a small junkyard, looking forlorn. It was pale yellow, the top was in tatters, the passenger compartment was full of trash, and the chrome was dull. As Pete pointed out, there was only one small dent in the body and there was no visible rust. I told Pete it looked like too big a project for me, so we raced back to Bynum.

Compared to the hulks in Pete's yard, the car in Corsicana was indeed "real nice." Pete's Buicks were almost all covered with surface rust and many were missing wheels, doors, or bumpers. But Pete assured us that people were buying them regularly for restoration.

Pete was a scout. When he heard about an old Buick for sale, he hooked his pickup up to a flatbed trailer and went to check it out. As we saw when we went to Corsicana, he preferred to get there via secondary roads, where there were often old junkyards, old gas stations, and old farmsteads, and often those were home to old cars.

Pete's peripheral vision must have been superb; flying down a two-lane road at 80 miles an hour, he could spot an old Buick peeking out of a dilapidated garage or resting in the back row of a weed-choked junkyard. He made a mental note of those, and sooner or later he would return to inquire about them.

He sometimes got a car for nothing, if the owner had died and the widow just wanted the car hauled off. More often, he had to haggle a little. He carried a roll of $100 bills: "The sight of a Ben Franklin or two makes 'em think harder about selling," he said.

If the negotiation was successful, he winched the hulk onto his trailer and headed home. If he couldn't make a deal, he filed the car away in his mind to be revisited in a year or two.

His trips rarely took more than a day, although sometimes it was a 24-hour day. Even when he hauled a trailer-load of old bumpers, fenders, doors, hoods, trunk lids, and fender skirts to a national Buick meet hundreds of miles away, he rarely stayed more than a day. He would time his trip to arrive at the peak of the meet, sell or trade as many parts as he could, and then scurry home. He often had buyers lined up before the meet; Buick owners everywhere knew of Pete's stash and if Pete had a part they needed, they'd ask him deliver it to the meet.

I eventually bought the '57 Buick convertible from Po's junkyard and Pete fetched it home for me. He later hauled several other cars for me, including Crazy Eddie's Buick, a '57 Roadmaster convertible I bought from a farmer in Nebraska, a rare stick-shift '57 Buick I bought in Iowa, and some others that were just parts cars.

Pete's ability to identify Buicks was uncanny. The car I bought from Po's junkyard had been sitting outside for 10 years with the top down, and the floor was rotten so I needed a complete replacement. Pete to the rescue: Years earlier he had spotted a Buick sitting upside down about half a mile off the road, in a pasture near Godley, in North Texas. "It's a '57 Special," Pete said. "It's a coupe, so the floor should fit your convertible. There's no running gear so the floor is just looking up at the sky, waiting for you."

I asked Pete to go check it out, and he reported that it belonged to an elderly dairy farmer who would sell it. I went there and told the farmer I didn't want the whole car, just the floor. He agreed to let me bring a torch and cut it out, but insisted that I wait until it rained. "That pasture is pretty dry, and I don't want you setting it afire."

So in a few weeks, after a good rain, I rented an acetylene torch and drove to the pasture. I had no experience with cutting torches, so it took me all day to cut out the floor. I removed it in one piece all the way from the firewall back through the trunk. The pasture didn't catch fire and, as I recall, the farmer helped me load it onto the roof of my Ford van and tie it down. With a lot of trimming, it did fit my convertible.

———————

Pete's acreage was just a few miles off I-35, so I usually dropped in on him every time I came home from Dallas or Fort Worth. Whatever the time of day, Pete always offered me a beer and drank one himself. He loved dirty jokes, and political correctness did not limit his repertoire.

A (rare) clean sample: "A guy was walking on the beach and saw a bottle. He picked it up and out popped a genie. The genie says I'll grant you a wish, any wish, but only one. The guy says 'okay, build me a highway to Hawaii. I've always wanted to go there but I don't like to fly over water.'"

"The genie says 'Damn, that's tough. You realize it wouldn't be just the highway, I'd have to build gas stations and rest stops and motels and restaurants too. Isn't there something else I could do?'"

"The guy says 'Well, you could explain women to me.' The genie says 'Would you like that highway to be two-lane or four?'"

On one of these visits I was complaining that Buick didn't make a '57 pickup. "We could make one," Pete said.

"How are we going to do that?"

"Get a '57 station wagon and cut off the back half of the roof. You've got the floor and the tailgate. You move the back window up and make it the back of the cab. All it would take is a little cutting and welding."

"You know I can't weld or do body work," I said.

"I could rough it out and you could do the rest."

We discussed it a little further. I said "we'd have to start with a model 49, and that's going to be hard to find." For 1957 Buick had introduced the model 49D, a "hardtop station wagon," which eliminated the post between the front and rear doors. The pickup conversion would have to have that post to anchor the back of the cab. And the model 49 would be hard to find because hardtop model, 49D, was far more popular.

Pete said "well, let's see if we can find one."

A few months later he called me. "I found a model 49," he said, "and it's in real nice shape."

I agreed to buy it and Pete agreed to haul it from North Texas to his place. When I first saw it it was a station wagon, but by the second time it was beginning to be a pickup. Pete had cut off the rear half of the roof, welded the rear doors shut, and welded the rear window to the back of the cab. It was rough, but it was a start.

Pete hauled it to my place and over a few months I completed the transformation, had it painted dark green and white, and had the seat reupholstered. I took it to a few Buick meets and invariably somebody said "I didn't know Buick made a pickup."

When John turned 16, he drove it to school. It was the coolest vehicle in the parking lot.

———◆———

To keep weeds down around his old cars, Pete kept a few Barbados sheep (he called them "Barbie-does"). They looked like goats and the rams had horns. Sometimes he had a ram that didn't like people infringing on his space, and would lower his head and shake his horns as if he was about to charge.

"Just ignore him." Pete would say. "If you're not afraid of him he'll leave you alone."

Pete specialized in '41 and '42 Buicks, and only the largest of those, the Roadmasters, which had enormous straight-eight engines. His knowledge of them was encyclopedic; he could spot a 1941 radiator from 20 paces and tell you how it differed from a '42. Eventually he hunted his favorite models to extinction, and branched out into smaller models, Centuries and Specials, and even a few non-Buicks, which he disparaged heartily. He was especially contemptuous of Chevys; he called them tin cans.

One year I was driving my '57 convertible home from a national Buick meet in Dallas when I noticed the ampere gauge registering negative. I pulled off I-35 at Carl's Corner, near Waxahachie, and determined that the generator wasn't generating. It was Sunday morning so there was no chance of getting it repaired right away.

I was about 30 miles from Bynum, so I called Pete for advice about where to have the car towed to. "Don't do that," Pete said. "I think I've got one of those generators. Just sit tight and I'll bring it up there."

He did, and with his tools I switched my bad generator for his good one. I was back on the road in an hour or so.

———◆———

In later years Pete and his son P.J. built hot rods. Their last project was a '34 Terraplane, an orphan model built by Hudson only for six years. It had a late-model Lincoln engine and a Ford rear end.

Pete was at the mercy of the Veterans Administration for treatment of his various medical problems, and he complained that what they gave him was mostly delays and runarounds. The last few times I saw him the pain showed in his eyes. When he died, P.J. called me, crying, to tell me of the funeral plans.

It was a graveside service at the Bynum cemetery. P.J. was drunk and Mrs. Levchik seemed to be nearly comatose. A handful of Pete's neighbors were there. It was a sad end for a man who had helped dozens of people all over the country restore their old Buicks. I placed a memorial ad in the national Buick club magazine to let them know of Pete's demise.

———◆———

Easy Jack operated a huge junkyard in Universal City, near San Antonio. "Easy" was a terrible misnomer: Jack was a bundle of apoplexy, mostly aimed at his city council, which he believed was trying to drive him out of business with zoning ordinances, aesthetic regulations, and similar forms of "harassment."

I should never have let him know I was a lawyer; every time I saw him he harangued me with his latest beef. He didn't seem to believe me when I told him I wasn't the right kind of lawyer for his problems; like many people in the old car world, he thought a lawyer was a lawyer and should be able to help him. I did write a letter or two threatening dire consequences for the authorities if they didn't leave him alone.

Junkyard car in Mid-Restoration

Jack had eight '57 Buicks of various body styles and in various stages of deterioration. One was a Roadmaster convertible with a tree growing up through the floor. I bought the whole car to get the trim pieces specific to the convertible; those were stainless steel and in much better condition than the rest of the car. They wouldn't fit my Special convertible because the Roadmaster was larger, but I was able to sell them readily.

The other seven Buicks were various types of sedans of limited use to me except for parts like bumpers, wheels, jacks, engine parts, chrome trim items, and the large rear bumper ends that were prone to rust out because the exhaust came out through them. Jack was protective of his Buicks; at first he wouldn't let me scavenge from any car he thought was restorable. But eventually he came to trust me not to dismantle a good car.

Numerous parts from Easy Jack's found their way into cars I was restoring.

———◆———

I can think of only two bad experiences in junkyards. I was told about a large one near Mexia. When I got there, I found lots of cars and two young men in a trailer. They were both on telephones most of the time and I never got an answer to my question about cars I might cannibalize. I concluded they were selling something besides car parts.

One summer when I was teaching at the University of North Carolina I heard about a big junkyard somewhere near Raleigh. I had a '57 Thunderbird at the time and I wanted to find a "Town and Country" radio for it. "Town and Country" was Ford's name for a signal-seeking radio, just as Wonderbar was GM's name for the same thing.

When I called the junkyard, the proprietor said he thought he had a Town and Country in a '57 Ford station wagon.

When I got there, the entire junkyard was covered with kudzu. Occasionally a radio antenna or a roof peeked through, but many of the cars were completely covered. I asked if he knew where the '57 Ford was and he gave an approximate location. I asked if it was okay to poke around and see if I could find it.

He said "Sure, if you're brave enough. There's lots of snakes under there."

I asked how he got anything out of there. He said "We wait 'till winter. The kudzu dies back and the snakes aren't so active."

I wasn't brave enough to find out if he was putting me on. I told him I would come back in the winter, but of course by winter I was back in Texas.

———◆———

After 1990 or so, my junkyard adventures tapered off. For one thing, various restoration suppliers began making parts for 1950s cars so it was no longer necessary to prowl junkyards. For another, I moved to a different class of cars — like a 1937 V-16 Cadillac limousine and a 1930 V-16 Cadillac roadster — that aren't found in junkyards.

The V-16 Cadillacs were old enough and rare enough to qualify for the Classic Car Club of America. I showed the roadster at a few CCCA events and met some wealthy guys who owned classics like Auburns and Marmons, but they weren't as colorful, or as much fun, as my junkyard friends.

———◆———

CHAPTER 8

Moonlighting

Kenny Stabler, Hall of Fame quarterback who led the Oakland Raiders to a Super Bowl victory in 1977, was playing for the Houston Oilers later in his career when NBC broadcast a report accusing him of having thrown an Oilers game against the New York Jets. The principal evidence consisted of a photo of a sleazy looking character talking with Stabler after the game and footage of Stabler throwing four uncharacteristic interceptions during the game.

Stabler hired Nick Nichols, a celebrated Houston plaintiff's lawyer, to file a libel suit against NBC. Nichols had won Rudy Tomjanovich's suit against Kermit Washington for slugging Rudy in the face on the basketball court, but he had little experience in libel cases so he hired me to help him.

NBC moved to take Stabler's deposition. I went to Houston a few days early to help prepare Kenny. We warned him that in addition to innocuous questions about his background and football career, he would probably be asked questions that might be unwelcome, such as whether he had ever used drugs or been arrested. We thought he was ready, if reluctant, to be deposed.

The deposition was taken in a conference room at a law firm. On one side of the table were four lawyers for NBC and on the other, Nick, one of Nick's associates, and me. Kenny was visibly intimidated by the colliding armies of lawyers.

It quickly became apparent that Kenny was not going to be a good witness. He had trouble setting aside the renegade personality that had made him the face of the Raiders during the years when they were the bad boys of the NFL. He didn't like it that he was being interrogated when NBC was the defendant. His temper flared when he was asked about alleged misdeeds and he couldn't conceal his irritation at routine questions like "State your name." Worse, he often gave implausible answers to questions about minor transgressions, like "Do you drink?" or "Have you ever placed a bet on a football game?" We tried to assure him that it was more important to demonstrate honesty than purity, but he remained unnecessarily defensive.

The lead lawyer for NBC was John Koeltl (now a federal judge), whom I knew from the days when we were both on the editorial board of the magazine of the ABA litigation section. Koeltl was then with Debevoise and Plimpton, one of the country's leading libel defense firms. He wore thick, horn-rimmed glasses that magnified his eyes. When you spoke to him, he had an unsettling habit of staring at you for a few seconds before responding. I should have mentioned that to Nick and/or Kenny, but I didn't think to do so.

When the questions began, Kenny was defensive and hostile, but he was generally doing a good job. His answers sometimes defanged Koeltl's questions. For example, when Koeltl asked, "How did you get the nickname 'Snake,'" Kenny said "Because my junior high coach said I ran like one."

When he got to the heart of the matter, Koeltl said "You threw four interceptions. Can you explain why you had so many interceptions that day?"

"Those were all in the first half," Stabler said. "I was hung over." He explained that he and Fred Biletnikoff (and another former Raider whose name I don't remember) had gone to Manhattan the night before and explored the club scene, including the Lone Star Café and Elaine's. When they finally got ready to return to their hotel in New Jersey a few hours before sunrise, they couldn't find a cab, so they approached a limo driver and paid him $100 to take them. The game started at noon so they barely got to the hotel in time to go to the stadium.

"I wasn't really awake until the second half," he said.

After halftime, he threw five touchdown passes and no interceptions.

As for the gambler photographed with him, Kenny said "He's a jock sniffer. He's always hanging around. There are lots of guys like that."

But those were the few high spots of the deposition. Kenny sometimes gave answers that were inconsistent with what he had told us when we woodshedded him. When that happened, Nick would ask for a "brief recess," take Kenny out of the room and remind him of what he had told us, and repeat the advice about being honest. Then he would come back in and say "Mr. Stabler would like to amend his answer to the last question."

After that happened a few times, Kenny told Nick he didn't want to answer any more questions. Nick told him he was doing fine, but after one or two more of those episodes, Kenny said "I'm not going back in there. That man's (Koeltl's) stare is driving me crazy. It's like he can see right into my soul."

Nick explained that we would have to drop the suit if he refused to be deposed. "Okay, then drop it," Kenny said. "I'm not going to take any more of this."

What followed was a remarkable show of chutzpah. When we went back in the room without Kenny, and after all the times we had asked for recesses to set Kenny's testimony straight, I thought it was obvious that our client had pulled the rug out from under us. But Nick was nonplused. "What would you be willing to give us to drop this right now?" he asked. They paid $10,000, which was a pittance, but it was $10,000 more than I would have had the temerity to ask for.

———◆———

The case taught me a few things about network journalism. NBC had placed ads in New York newspapers offering to pay for photos of Stabler talking to anyone before or after the game. Their broadcast relied mainly on visual innuendo — a mug shot of the guy seen with Stabler, video of the guy slamming his door in the face of an NBC reporter trying to interview him, and video clips of Stabler throwing interception after interception. It omitted some inconvenient evidence: the mug shot had been taken 16 years earlier when the man was arrested for a small-time bookmaking offense; the attempt to interview him took place when he was awakened at his home at 2 a.m.; Stabler had thrown more touchdown passes in the game than interceptions; and although the Oilers lost the game, they beat the point spread, so anyone who bet against them would have lost.

I also learned a little about the life of sports heroes and other celebrities. When we went to dinner at a restaurant, the peace lasted only until other diners realized that, yes, that guy really is Kenny Stabler. Some fans came to the table just to ask for an autograph. Others wanted to chat. "I was at Super Bowl XI. You were terrific. Do you remember that touchdown pass you threw to Dave Casper? That was beautiful."

Kenny was unfailingly polite to the fans; it was the rest of us who had to ask them to let him eat in peace.

———◆———

A federal court jury in Las Vegas awarded Wayne Newton $20 million in a libel suit against NBC. NBC persuaded the trial judge to reduce the award to $5.2 million and appealed the rest to the Ninth Circuit. Newton's lawyer, Mort Galane, hired me to help defend the award. I was excited to work on the case, but I warned Mort that very few large libel awards survived on appeal.

When I met Newton, I was surprised at how boyish he looked, even though by then he had been a singing star for 35 years. He was tall and fit, tanned, with coal black hair perfectly coiffed. I could see why matrons swooned over him.

NBC had broadcast a report by Brian Ross called "Wayne Newton and the Law," about Newton's purchase of the Aladdin Hotel in Las Vegas. The segment purported to describe "the role of Guido Penosi and the mob in Newton's deal for the Aladdin," and implied that the mob was the real purchaser and Newton was only a front man. It included footage of two detectives staking out Penosi's house for undisclosed reasons, and an ambush interview in which Ross and a cameraman trailed Newton across a parking lot, peppering him with questions that he refused to answer.

Ross was the same reporter who had broadcast the false story about Stabler. I felt gratified years later when he was forced out of network news because of repeated errors. I only wished the Stabler and Newton stories had been his downfall.

Newton had testified that Penosi was just a fan and neither he nor the mob had any role in the purchase. NBC's implication was pretty clearly false; at trial Mort showed that Newton had borrowed the purchase money from a bank and the Nevada Gaming Commission had investigated and found no mob connection.

Newton, one of the most successful Las Vegas entertainers ever, was obviously a public figure, so he had to prove not only that NBC's accusation was false, but also that they either they knew it was false or recklessly disregarded the likelihood that it was false. The jury had found reckless disregard, but unlike most jury findings, that one could be rejected by the appellate court because it was a constitutional requirement.

My job was to help convince a three-judge panel of the Ninth Circuit to sustain the jury's verdict. That task was complicated by NBC's careful omission of any explicit statement of their implicit accusation; we had to show that they knew or were reckless in creating a false *impression*.

Mort was a New Yorker who had moved to Las Vegas and established a successful small-firm practice. I assumed that anyone who arrived in Las Vegas from New York in the 1950s and started a law practice, as Mort did, must have made his peace with the mob one way or another, but I never saw any evidence of mob connections.

He had won millions for his clients and was well-connected politically. He managed Nelson Rockefeller's 1968 presidential campaign in Nevada and was nominated for the federal bench by President Reagan but withdrew because he decided he would rather litigate. He was a close friend of Las Vegas Mayor Oscar Goodman and Senator Harry Reid, who testified for Newton at the trial. I learned of these connections only years later; Mort never mentioned them to me.

NBC's lead lawyer was the renowned Floyd Abrams, possibly the most successful libel defense lawyer ever. But his successes had all come on appeal; the Newton case was the first libel case he had ever tried to a jury. Mort considered Abrams an inept trial lawyer.

Later, at a conference of libel defense lawyers, I heard Abrams minimize his loss at the Newton trial by attributing it to the jury's prejudice in favor of a home-town hero. "The jurors rode on Wayne Newton Boulevard to get to the courthouse," he said. That was true, but it was also true that most of the jurors were newcomers to Las Vegas and some of them had never heard of Wayne Newton until the trial.

Mort was obsessed with the Newton appeal. He was an insomniac who worked on the case day and night. After being awakened by him at all hours, I finally persuaded him not to call me until 7 a.m. my time — 5 a.m. his time. Sometimes he was calling to tell me about a case or article he had found, but more often it was to try out an idea. "Talking about it helps me clarify it in my own mind," he would say. If I told him I was not at my sharpest at 7 a.m, he would say "okay, call me back in an hour."

Although I spent many hours writing memos and talking to Mort (for which I was well paid), I don't think my input was very valuable. I thought the key issue was whether a defendant could be found to have committed reckless disregard with respect to the impressions it created when there was no explicit defamatory statement.

There was no authoritative holding precisely on point, but there were a couple of instances in which the Supreme Court had affirmed judgments for plaintiffs in cases in which the defamatory sting was created by implications alone. I thought we should concentrate our fire on that issue and those cases, but Mort was unwilling to do that. He insisted on addressing at length every point made in NBC's brief.

The brief we filed violated every principle that law students are taught in their brief-writing courses. It was 121 pages long, almost twice as long as NBC's. It cited more than 160 cases and other authorities, many of them of little importance. Much of it merely quibbled with NBC's portrayal of the case or recited irrelevant facts (sample: "Born in Norfolk Virginia in 1942, Wayne Newton began singing professionally at age six.")

It was tendentious; showing that you passionately believe in the merits of your client's case might sway a jury, but it doesn't impress appellate judges. I tried to make these points to Mort, but he was so deeply and emotionally invested that it did no good.

The oral arguments were in the federal courthouse in Pasadena. Mort intended to argue the case himself, but wanted me to sit close behind him as he argued. I thought this meant he wanted me to whisper reminders to him, and maybe he did, but I should have resisted. My whispers just distracted him, as we both realized too late.

He barely spoke to me thereafter. Maybe that was because he realized that having me in Pasadena had been a waste of Newton's money. Or maybe it was because of something that happened after the argument was over. I noticed that one of the lawyers in NBC's camp was Rex Heineke, whom I knew from libel law conferences. When I shook hands and exchanged a few pleasantries with him, I saw that Mort disapproved; he believed fraternizing with the enemy was inexcusable.

He didn't call me even when the Ninth Circuit granted NBC's appeal and threw out the jury's verdict a few months later. I called him but he didn't return the call.

Before I committed treason in the eyes of the media defense bar by working for plaintiffs in the Stabler and Newton cases, I was hired by lawyers for a number of media outlets — Harte-Hanks, Storer Broadcasting, The Associated Press, Oklahoma Publishing Co., Freedom Newspapers, and Landmark Communications, among others.

Most of those were routine consultations or expert witness gigs, but occasionally something unexpected happened. Conrad Shumadine, an able media lawyer, hired me to be an expert witness in a case against his client, the *Virginian Pilot.* Just the previous year I had taught at the College of William and Mary, and when my friends there found out I was going to be in the vicinity, they gave a party the night before the trial was to begin. It was a good party, and in the festivities I somehow lost my reading glasses.

The party was in Williamsburg and the trial was in Richmond, 50 miles up the road. Conrad picked me up in Williamsburg and drove me to Richmond. On the way I told him of my lost glasses.

"If the courtroom is well lighted I should be okay," I said. I had just begun to use reading glasses, and in good light I didn't need them.

"Well, check it out after we get there," Conrad said.

The trial was in the Richmond federal courthouse, which looked like it had been built before the Civil War — old-fashioned lights hanging from high ceilings, dark paneling, and ancient mahogany furnishings. I knew that on the stand I would be handed documents and asked to read them, and I told Conrad I wouldn't be able to do so.

Conrad said "Run up the street to Talheimer's and get some glasses. It's only a few blocks."

When I got to Talheimer's department store, they only had two pairs of reading glasses in the power I needed. Both were shaped like cat's eyes, one with red plastic frames and the other with rhinestones embedded in gray plastic frames. I chose the latter, as the lesser of evils.

When I returned to the courthouse the proceedings had already begun, so I went directly to the small room reserved for witnesses waiting to testify. All the others there were fact witnesses, waiting to testify for the plaintiff.

Soon I tired of listening to their chatter and picked up a magazine, but it was too dark, so I had to put on my rhinestone glasses. At first no one noticed them, but eventually someone did, and pretty soon all of them were looking at me and tittering.

At midmorning there was a recess. I found Conrad, showed him my glasses, and told him, "You'd better settle this case, because putting me on the stand in these glasses is going to do you more harm than good."

Whether for that reason or not, the case was settled before I had to testify.

———————◆———————

Boris Berezofsky, a pal of Boris Yeltsin, emerged from the fall of the Soviet Union owning some of the assets previously held by the state, including Russia's largest auto dealership. Forbes magazine published an article that described him as "one of the most powerful men in Russia," and said he left behind "a trail of corpses, uncollectible debts and competitors terrified for their lives."

Berezofsky and an associate sued for libel in London, where the law at that time offered little protection for publishers. The English Court of Appeal had rejected the magazine's argument that the English courts were not an appropriate forum for a suit by a resident of Russia against a U.S. publication that had minimal circulation in England. I had written something decrying "libel tourism," the practice of American celebrities suing in England where American constitutional free speech protections didn't apply. A Forbes lawyer in New York asked me to help persuade the House of Lords throw out the suit.

Berezofsky's lawyers had cleverly stipulated that they were seeking damages only for harm to his reputation in England where he had extensive business dealings, and not for any harm done in Russia or the U.S. or elsewhere in the world. "What better place than England to sue for damage done in England?" was their theory.

That theory would not work in the U.S. because we have a "single publication rule," which says that for any libel there can be only one suit which encompasses the damages in all jurisdictions. I wanted to argue that the Lords should adopt such a rule for England, which would mean Berezofsky's London suit would have to include his damages everywhere. Since he presumably was best known in Russia and the vast majority of the readers were in the U.S., most of the damage to his reputation would have occurred outside England, and therefore either New York or Moscow would be a more appropriate forum.

But the Court of Appeal had rejected that argument and David Hooper, the London libel expert who was arguing the case for Forbes, believed the Lords would not be willing to take that step either. So we adopted a more modest strategy: we argued that the reputation of an international businessman cannot be subdivided into national components: in the modern world where business, travel, and communications are global, such a person's reputation is transnational.

We lost, 3-2. The majority said "all the constituent elements of the tort occurred in England. The distribution in England of the defamatory material was significant. And the plaintiffs have reputations in England to protect. In such cases it is not unfair that the foreign publisher should be sued here."

We much preferred the view stated in the dissent: "The plaintiffs are forum shoppers in the most literal sense. They have weighed up the advantages to them of the various jurisdictions that might be available and decided that England is the best place in which to vindicate their international reputations. They want English law, English judicial integrity and the international publicity which would attend success in an English libel action."

As a result of our failure, "libel tourism" continued until England revised its libel law to make it more in line with U.S. law. Berezofsky eventually settled for a groveling retraction in which Forbes said it hadn't meant what it clearly and emphatically had meant.

A few years later, Berezofsky was found hanged in his home outside London. The coroner was unable to decide whether it was homicide or suicide.

———◆———

They came every week or two to clean our house, two middle-aged white women named Mary and Irene. They both worked for the telephone company and came to us after work. They both drove late model Cadillacs and arrived separately; the neighbors must have thought we were rich to have cleaning ladies who drove Cadillacs. They each brought a tumbler full of clear liquid — vodka, I think. We called them the White Tornados because they whirled through the house and had it cleaned in no time.

One day Mary said "Could I talk to you? You're a lawyer, aren't you?"

When I said yes, she said she had been sued. She explained:

She collected antique glassware. One day she was in an antique store and spotted an antique Hummel plate in a display case. It was a rare one, and one she needed for her collection. There wasn't a price tag on it, but one was lying nearby. It said $30 — a real bargain because Mary knew that plate was worth several hundred dollars.

She asked the clerk if that tag went with the plate in question. The clerk, a young woman, said "Well, I don't really know, but I guess it must."

Mary said "I'll take it," and paid with a check.

The next day when the owner came in he noticed the plate missing and asked the clerk if it had been sold. When the clerk told him how much the customer had paid, the owner hit the ceiling. "That plate was $400!"

Mary's check was still in the register, so the owner called her and demanded that she return the plate or pay an additional $370.

Mary refused. "I asked the girl how much it was, and she said $30. I bought it fair and square."

The owner didn't think so, and sued Mary in small claims court. That's when Mary consulted me. "Will you help me? I've never been in court. I wouldn't know what to do."

I said "This isn't my branch of law, but I'll go with you and see what I can do. It sounds to me like you paid what the clerk asked and the owner's beef is with the clerk, not you."

So I researched offer-and-acceptance and apparent authority and went to the JP's courtroom with Mary. I argued that the owner had left the clerk in charge, the clerk had offered to sell it for $30, and Mary had accepted.

My legal research was wasted. The JP asked Mary, "Would you have paid $200 for it?"

Mary said "I suppose I would, but I bought it for $30." The JP asked the owner, "Would you settle for $200?"

The owner said "The price was $400."

The JP said "Yes, but your clerk sold it for $30. Would you rather have $200 than $30?"

The owner grudgingly agreed, and the judge told Mary to give the man a check for $170.

The Oklahoma Publishing Co. owned two newspapers, the *Daily Oklahoman* and the Oklahoma City *Times*. Both were aggressive forces in that state's politics. In an election for the U.S. Senate, their favored candidate was then-Gov. David Boren. Another of the eight candidates was George Miskovsky, and another was a marginal candidate named Points.

At a candidate forum that Miskovsky attended but Boren did not, Points claimed that Boren was a homosexual. The accusation was unsupported and Points had little credibility, but Miskovsky demanded that Boren address the charge. Both of the newspapers ran stories and editorials condemning Points and Miskovsky, and the *Times* ran a cartoon depicting Miskovsky holding a wind-up toy labeled "Points," whose arm was cocked to throw a mudball.

Miskovsky sued for libel contending that the stories, editorials, and cartoon implied that there was a conspiracy in which Miskovsky induced Points to make the charge so Miskovsky could benefit from it without having to take responsibility for it. The jury awarded him $1 million.

I was engaged to help convince the Oklahoma Supreme Court that the trial court should have dismissed Miskovsky's suit. The defense of the news articles and editorials was straightforward: Miskovsky was a public figure and there was no evidence that the newspapers were aware of any falsehoods regarding Miskovsky.

The cartoon could have been harder to defend, depending on how it was interpreted. As is often true in libel cases, the plaintiff was his own worst enemy. If he had simply alleged that the cartoon implied that Points was Miskovsky's mouthpiece, our job would have been tougher. It would have been hard to deny that implication, and Miskovsky might have been able to show that the newspaper knew that in fact Points and Miskovsky had acted independently.

By going further, and claiming that the cartoon implied a conspiracy between himself and Points, Miskovsky gave us two defenses: (1) the cartoon didn't imply that, only that Miskovsky had attempted to capitalize on Points' accusation after the fact; and (2) the newspaper certainly did not know *that* implication was false, because it wasn't. The Oklahoma Supreme Court agreed with us.

In most of my litigation it was hard to feel any sense of personal accomplishment because I worked through other lawyers; sometimes my name wasn't even on the pleadings or briefs. One exception was a libel suit against the Fort Bend (Texas) *Herald Coaster*, which I successfully handled in my own name.

The plaintiff was Norma Stewart, the official court reporter for the local district court. The newspaper had reported that she was ignoring transcription of records in criminal cases while she transcribed testimony in private civil depositions. The Houston *Chronicle* had published similar charges, and Ms. Stewart had sued both papers.

After the litigation against the *Herald Coaster* had dragged on for a couple of years, the publisher got tired of it and was referred to me by one of the state press associations. I replaced the local lawyer who had been handling the case for the newspaper.

From covering courts for newspapers, I knew that court reporters were generally underpaid by the county but made up for it with gigs for private lawyers who hired them to transcribe depositions in civil cases. So one of my first steps was to file a motion to require the plaintiff to produce her tax returns for the relevant years. Her suit claimed loss of income as a result of the newspaper coverage, so we were entitled to know what her income was. I thought there was a good chance she didn't report all of it, and if she didn't, she would not be eager to have her earnings on the public record.

After she ignored one request to produce the returns and responded to a second with an excuse based on a falsehood, I asked the judge to order her to comply, and he did so. She still stonewalled, so I filed a motion for sanctions, asking that the case be dismissed because of her defiance of the judge's order.

I knew the judge would be reluctant to impose so draconian a penalty, but would understand that until we knew how much income she had lost, we couldn't decide anything about our defense, or even whether we should offer to settle. The judge granted the dismissal.

By this time Ms. Stewart's initial lawyer had been replaced by a well-known Houston lawyer, who appealed to the Court of Appeals in Houston. The appeal raised procedural issues far afield from any expertise of mine, so I persuaded my friend John Beckworth, then a young Houston lawyer and later my colleague at the Law School, to help me. I argued the case (my only appellate argument) and the court upheld the dismissal.

I'm proud of that case because my strategy saved the client a lot of money. My fees totaled something less than $20,000. The case against the *Chronicle* went through the courts and up to the Texas Supreme Court twice before the *Chronicle* eventually won. They were represented by a major Houston law firm whose fees reportedly were over $1 million.

———————◆———————

My most notorious client was *Soldier of Fortune* magazine, which was sued by the son of a woman murdered by a reluctant hit man named John Wayne Hearn. Hearn had placed an ad in the magazine which led to the murder.

The ad said "Ex-MARINES-67-69 'Nam Vets, ex-DI, weapons specialist, jungle warfare, pilot, M.E, high risk assignments, U.S. or overseas. 404 991-2684."

The ad ran in the classified section of the magazine. One of the readers who saw the ad was a man named Charles Black in Bryan, Texas. He said he interpreted it as a help-wanted ad and phoned the number hoping to get employment, but learned when he called that Hearn was in fact seeking work himself as a security guard or bodyguard.

Black told Hearn that he needed to raise some money and offered to sell his gun collection for $5,000. Hearn went to Bryan to look at the guns, and while he was there Black offered to pay him $10,000 to kill Black's wife. Black had a girlfriend in California and wanted to get his wife out of the way.

Hearn said he initially declined. He had never killed anyone and wasn't eager to do so, but he was in love with a Florida woman named Debby. Sometime later, Debby persuaded him to kill her husband and her sister's husband. When he saw how easy that was, he was easily persuaded to kill Black for the money. So he went to Bryan and shot Black's wife, making it look like a botched robbery attempt. The authorities there bought the robbery explanation and closed the case.

But law enforcement officials in Florida eventually identified Hearn as the hit man in the two murders there. In their investigation they got Hearn's phone records and noticed a number of calls to Bryan. When they called the Bryan police they were told that the number Hearn had called belonged to a man whose wife had been murdered.

The Hearn-Black operation soon unraveled. Black was sentenced to death; Hearn was already in prison in Florida. When further investigation unearthed the *Soldier of Fortune* connection, the son of the dead woman in Bryan sued the magazine.

Soldier of Fortune had lawyers in New York, Houston, and its home base, Boulder, Colorado. The Houston lawyers recruited me. My job was to help write a motion that would get summary judgment in favor of the magazine.

Hearn and Black claimed that although the ad had brought them together, neither of them understood it as a solicitation for crime. My theory was that the magazine could not be liable for the same reason that a gun store would not be liable if two of its customers happened to strike up a conversation that led to a deal to commit a crime.

I tried to persuade Magazine Publishers of America, the industry trade organization, to file an amicus brief on our side. I told them that liability for publishing what appeared to be an innocuous ad was something that could threaten all their members, but apparently they preferred to keep their distance from *Soldier of Fortune*.

The federal district judge denied the motion and set the case for trial. I had no further involvement in the case. The plaintiff convinced the jury that the magazine must have known that its ads were being used to solicit criminal acts, and therefore should have rejected *Soldier of Fortune*'s ad. The jury awarded the son $10 million.

A lawyer less naïve than I later told me the summary judgment motion was doomed from the start. "Federal judges spend day after day hearing dull boring matters that people never hear about," he said. "When they get a case as juicy as this, they're not about to give it up."

As lawyers, we thought we were fighting for the survival of the magazine, but we underestimated the resilience of Bob Brown, its founder and owner. Brown struck me as a gruff paramilitary type in the mold of Clint Eastwood, but he must have also been a shrewd publisher. Somehow he was able to save the magazine despite the huge judgment, and soon *Soldier of Fortune* appeared to be more successful than ever.

Dave Richards is a distinguished lawyer who taught briefly at the Law School. He was a veteran of many controversial cases and knew a lot of litigation tricks, including some not found in the books. I learned one of those from him.

A state court judge in San Antonio had issued a patently unconstitutional prior restraint. A small newspaper in the Hispanic community had obtained a "trick list" compiled by Theresa Brown, a madam who ran a long-tolerated brothel. The list was a card file which included the customers' names and their sexual wishes.

The 3,000 customers were said to include some public officials, including judges, and other prominent citizens. The newspaper, *El Pueblo*, was planning to publish the list, or at least the names of those presence on the list was newsworthy. Pat Maloney Sr., a lawyer well connected in San Antonio political circles, filed suit to prohibit publication of the list and a local state court judge granted the injunction.

This was just a few years after the famous Supreme Court decision holding that the *New York Times* could not be enjoined from publishing the Pentagon Papers, a study of the Vietnam War that the government said contained classified information. If the *Times* couldn't even be enjoined from revealing national defense secrets, how could a newspaper be enjoined from publishing a trick list? The Washington-based Reporters Committee for Freedom of the Press got wind of the injunction and contacted me.

In the faculty lounge, I was lamenting the fact that the Pentagon Papers case gave *El Pueblo* little help. The paper would have to obey the unconstitutional injunction until it was reversed by a higher court. The newspaper couldn't afford an expensive appeal, and anyway, during the time the appeal would take, some other news outlet would most likely get the list and steal *El Pueblo*'s big story.

Most of my colleagues just commiserated with me, but Dave Richards spoke up. "Spurious removal," he said. None of us had any idea what he was talking about.

"It's an old labor lawyer's trick," he said. "When management gets a state court injunction against the union, and the union doesn't want to wait for an appellate court to overturn it, you just file a removal petition in federal court." We all knew that the filing of the removal petition instantly suspended the jurisdiction of the state court. But if there was no basis for removal, wouldn't management file a motion in the federal court to remand the case to the state court? And when the federal judge granted it, wouldn't the state court injunction be in force once again?

"Sure," Dave said. "That's why you have to be ready to do whatever it is you want to do as soon as you file the removal petition. You only have that window between the filing of the petition and the granting of the remand."

The gambit was as brilliant as it was devious. I had a little trouble convincing our local counsel in San Antonio that he wouldn't get thrown in jail, but eventually he acquiesced. Today "spurious removal" would be met with a few thousand dollars in sanctions, but at that time I didn't think the courts would hammer us for answering a patently unconstitutional restraint with a stratagem that was only slightly unethical.

In the day or two that it took to put the scheme in operation, the publisher began to get cold feet. It sounded to her like legal chicanery, which of course it was. Could I promise her that she wouldn't get in trouble? No, but we had Dave Richards' assurance that he had done it and got away with it.

She went along, sort of. We removed the case to federal court, but the publisher lost her nerve, and I couldn't blame her; if one of the published names turned out to be incorrect she might be sued for libel. *El Pueblo* was judgment-proof, but the publisher was not. So the paper published only 19 names and did not include any salacious details. Those named were mostly public officials, on the theory that they would be least likely to win a libel suit.

———◆———

One of my moonlighting gigs was a painful failure. I failed to win the release of the couple accused in the infamous Oak Hill child molestation case, Dan and Fran Keller, who spent 21 years in prison before they were finally cleared.

Gary Cartwright wrote a story for *Texas Monthly* showing that the prosecution of the Kellers arose from a group of therapists and parents who believed there was a vast network of satanic cults that controlled public officials and preyed on children. They believed in blood-drenched rituals in graveyards and "alters" who could control the minds of witnesses on the stand.

The story, published after the Kellers had been convicted, revealed facts that had not come out in their trial: the three-year-old girl who the Kellers were charged with molesting also said they stuck pins in the stomachs of cats, put a baby in a hole with skin and bones and blood running all over, cut up some babies, and drowned others in a swimming pool full of blood. She said the Kellers had the children in their day care center take off their clothes and had parrots "that pecked them in the peepee." She told of being buried alive in a cemetery, and of tigers who licked the children and then were killed.

A purported expert on satanic cults testified that children who have been abused often make up preposterous stories but their accusations about the abuse nevertheless should be believed.

A witness who was charged with participating in the abuse gave a statement under intense questioning, saying he joined the Kellers in molesting the girl. He recanted his story as soon as he walked out of the interrogation and did not testify at the trial, but the statement he gave during his questioning was presented at the trial.

The only physical evidence was described by an emergency room physician who testified that the girl had redness and tears around her vagina that were consistent with sexual abuse.

By the time Gary's story appeared, the Kellers had been convicted of aggravated sexual abuse and sentenced to 48 years in prison, but I thought Gary's expose would quickly bring the case to an end. I underestimated the reluctance of elected prosecutors and judges to side with "child molesters."

My friend Larry Wright, the writer who was later to win a Pulitzer prize for *The Looming Tower*, had just written a book, *Satan Remembered*, about a discredited case in Washington state in which a therapist working with adult women helped them "recover memories" of abuse by a parent many years earlier. His book was one of several that exposed a nationwide hysteria about satanism and child molestation.

After the *Texas Monthly* story came out, Larry called me and said, essentially, "Can't we do something to help the Kellers?"

The Kellers had already filed an appeal with the state court of appeals that didn't effectively connect the prosecution with the preposterous accusations of ritual satanic abuse, and it was not possible to file another brief in the Kellers' name.

After consulting colleagues at the Law School, I decided the only course left was to file an amicus brief alerting the court to the facts that made this look like another of the fantastic satanic cult claims that were cropping up around the country.

Larry and I recruited people to sign the amicus brief. We wanted amici who would be known to members of the court of appeals as sensible people and whose concern ought to get the court's attention. Larry recruited from his world of letters and arts, and I from my world of law and academia.

We got Marcia Ball, the singer; Steve Harrigan, the writer; Ricardo Ainsle, psychologist and writer; Rick Pappas, lawyer specializing in arts and entertainment; Betty Sue Flowers, a distinguished professor in the UT College of Liberal Arts; prominent attorney Karl Bayer; and three of my colleagues at the Law School: Bob Dawson, Mike Tigar, and Alex Albright. Larry and I also signed the brief. All of the signers were known personally by at least some members of the court.

We were able to get my Law School colleague Steve Goode, a recognized expert on the rules of evidence, to write the brief. Since most of the satanic stories hadn't been introduced at the trial, we knew that in addition to alerting the appellate judges to the taint of those preposterous claims, we would have to present a legal issue that the court could hang its decision on.

Steve spotted such an issue: the statement of the witness who "confessed" and implicated the Kellers and then immediately recanted, should not have been admitted because it was hearsay. Steve showed that the court's own precedents, as well as precedents from the Court of Criminal Appeals and the U.S. Supreme Court, said as much.

To our dismay, the court dismissed the points made in our brief in a footnote.

The next step was the Court of Criminal Appeals, where Steve represented the Kellers directly instead of on behalf of amici. That court simply affirmed the court of appeals. Both courts ordered that their opinions not be published in the official reporters; I'd like to think they were not proud of their decisions.

The other signers of the amicus brief were perplexed. They wondered if they had been sold a bill of goods by Larry and me. At least one of them feared that his participation would damage his career. Steve and Larry and I were disillusioned; we thought judges were supposed to be made of stronger stuff.

I saw very little more that could be done on the Kellers' behalf. The Actual Innocence Project at the Law School took a look at the case but they thought their resources were better saved for cases in which there was DNA evidence or some other concrete proof of innocence. When the Kellers were eligible for parole I wrote letters asking the Board of Pardons and Paroles to free them. But eventually I gave up, unable to think of other avenues.

One who didn't give up was Dan's sister, Mary Jane Avery, who stood by her brother through it all and stayed in touch with him. She continued to call me whenever she saw a news story or television report that she thought might be of some help. I often had to dash her hopes, one of the most painful tasks I ever had.

Many years later the emergency room physician who had examined the girl acknowledged that his report of signs consistent with sexual abuse was probably a mistake, caused by his inexperience at the time. A dedicated and persistent lawyer named Keith Hampton was able to use that information to get the Kellers' convictions reversed, and after 21 years in prison they were freed.

If I hadn't been so sure the judges would set them free once they saw the dubious circumstances from which the prosecutions arose, maybe it would have occurred to me to see if the physician had second thoughts about his testimony. But it didn't, and being unable to do anything about a clear miscarriage of justice was a lingering disappointment.

———◆———

Before she became my client, I knew Jewel only as the ex-wife of Ty Murray, world champion rodeo cowboy. But I quickly learned that she is not only a successful singer and songwriter, but a talented writer.

She wrote a best-selling memoir called "Never Broken," about her odyssey from a childhood in a remote cabin in rural Alaska, life as a homeless teenager sleeping in her car in Los Angeles while she perfected her musical talent with unpaid gigs in pizza joints, to such fame that she needs only one name.

A former student of mine, Randy Roach in Houston, enlisted my help in getting her soul-baring book published without losing a suit for libel or invasion of privacy.

I learned that a successful recording and touring musician needs a platoon of agents, managers, accountants, and lawyers as numerous as the staff of a small corporation. Jewel had an agent in New York and one in California, a business manager in Nashville, and lawyers in New York, California, and Texas. Organizing a conference call to discuss her manuscript was like planning a political campaign.

The manuscript was sensitive because she had written candidly about her relations with her mother, which had been strained for years and finally imploded. She wanted to be honest about the financial and logistical turmoil that had led to the breakup and describe truthfully the emotional cauldron left by the wreck. At the same time, she didn't want to exacerbate the schism.

As is generally true of publishers today, hers provided little legal or editorial help. As is also the norm today, the publisher insisted that she agree to indemnify them for any legal costs the book might cause them.

The easy course for an author in that situation is to scrub the manuscript of anything that might give offense to anyone. Authors who have asked me to vet their books have sometimes said "I don't want to get sued." I have a standard response: "Anyone with the $150 filing fee can sue you. I can't prevent that. All I can do is try to make sure you won't *lose* the suit, and possibly reduce cost of winning it."

It takes some fortitude to accept that. Jewel did, and she didn't get sued. Her determination to tell her story her way was gratifying. I regret that I only talked to her on the phone; a person with her spunk is someone I'd like to meet.

———◆———

My most important client was *Texas Monthly*. When Mike Levy, my law school classmate, founded the magazine in 1973 he asked me to be the magazine's lawyer. For 44 years I did prepublication review, and for most of those years I read everything the *Monthly* published, even when I was in England or Australia. I retired only when the second owner, Emmis Broadcasting, refused to pay the full amount of my fee.

After a few months of publication, Mike phoned me in a panic. "We've been sued. What should we do? Should I go someplace where they can't serve me?" (A conversation with Mike never has a preface — he assumes you know who's calling and sometimes, what he's calling about.)

I said, "The first thing we need to do is get a real lawyer." I recommended Jim George. Jim had finished a Supreme Court clerkship just a couple of years earlier, but he was already doing litigation and he was with a major firm, Graves Dougherty, which makes it easier to litigate. I wish I could claim sole credit for that marriage, but I think Jim was already on Mike's radar. Jim became a nationally prominent libel lawyer and formed his own firm, which still represents *Texas Monthly*.

Representing the magazine was an enjoyable, instructive, and rewarding gig. In the early years, an editor delivered the typewritten copy to me with editing marks, questions, and alterations in pencil. Those marked–up drafts, now in the archives of Texas State University, would make excellent material for an editing course; they show how a skillful editor turns rough copy into graceful prose.

Sooner or later, I worked with every *Texas Monthly* writer and editor and became friends with many of them. For 15 years, I sat in on the monthly editorial meetings, listening to writers and editors propose story ideas for future issues, and knock them down or flesh them out.

Karen and I were included in parties, picnics, and dinners. Through *Texas Monthly* I got acquainted with many of the finest writers in Texas — Gary Cartwright, Larry Wright, Steve Harrigan, Mimi Swartz, Bill Brammer, Al Reinert, John Graves, and Bill Broyles, to name a few. Brammer and Reinert babysat our house and our dog one summer.

———————————◆———————————

The first editor in chief, Bill Broyles, personally assigned and edited most of the stories in the earliest years. He was a genius at turning bright young lawyers, politicos, and newspaper reporters into writers. He later edited *California Magazine*, was editor in chief of *Newsweek*, wrote two books about the Vietnam War in which he had won a Bronze Star as leader of a platoon of Marines, and wrote screenplays for hit movies such as Cast Away and Apollo 13.

Every editor in chief proved that a magazine reflects the personality of its leader. Under Greg Curtis, who took over when Bill got burned out from the 15-hour days and always-looming deadlines, the magazine turned slightly toward more personal journalism, reflecting Greg's more private personality.

When Evan Smith arrived from New York in 1992, he was about as un-Texan as anyone could be. He talked too fast, was too abrupt, and didn't understand Texas. By the time he became editor in 2000, he and Texas had both become less parochial. Evan embraced and embodied the best characteristics of the new Texas.

Jake Silverstein was a Californian who quickly learned about things Texan, probably helped along by his previous experience as a reporter for a weekly newspaper in the Big Bend.

Texas Monthly alumni went on to illuminate many journalism outlets. Dominique Browning became one of five top editors at *Newsweek* (known as the "flying Wallendas"). Evan Smith co-founded the *Texas Tribune* and hosts "Overheard with Evan Smith," an interview program that airs nationally on public television. Nick Lemann wrote an acclaimed book about the migration of African-Americans from the South to the industrial North and later became dean of the Columbia School of Journalism. His recent acclaimed book is "Transaction Man," about the decline of the American dream. Jan Reid wrote "The Improbable Rise of Redneck Rock." Nate Blakeslee wrote "Tulia." Mimi Swartz co-wrote a book about the collapse of Enron. Robert Draper wrote "Dead Certain: The Presidency of George W. Bush." Silverstein became editor of the *New York Times Magazine.*

Bill Broyles and Al Reinert were nominated for an Oscar for the screenplay for Apollo 13, and Reinert wrote and produced "For All Mankind," a documentary about NASA's Apollo program. Andrea Meditch also produced award-winning documentaries. Emily Yoffe became a columnist for Slate and a contributor to *The Atlantic.* Larry Wright wrote "Thirteen Days in September," the definitive book about the 1979 Camp David accord between Israel and Egypt, and won a Pulitzer prize for "The Looming Tower," his book about the September 11 attackers.

The cachet of the *Texas Monthly* work brought me other prepublication review jobs for such periodicals as the *Texas Observer, California Magazine*, and *Third Coast*, and such books as "The Long Road" by Rico Ainslie and "The Empty Quarter" by D. M. Wilkinson.

Texas Monthly listed me as a contributing editor, I suppose because I sometimes gave editorial as well as legal advice. I wrote one cover story, a feature on the Highland Lakes. I can't say the cachet of that piece launched a career as a magazine writer, but it was fun.

———————

By 1980 *Texas Monthly* was making lots of money and Mike Levy was feeling expansive. A magazine called *New West* was struggling in California. It had been started by Clay Felker, who had launched *New York* magazine and was idolized by magazine journalists everywhere for his fearlessness and creativity. But *New*

West hadn't managed to equal *New York*'s success, and Mike saw an opportunity to replicate *Texas Monthly*'s success in bridging multiple markets.

Until Mike came along, no one had thought it possible for a single publication to serve such disparate markets as Houston, Dallas-Fort Worth, and San Antonio. The thinking was that readers in one city would have little interest in stories about the others, and advertisers would not pay to reach readers outside their own territory.

California markets were, if anything, even more sharply divided; southern California was very different culturally, politically, and demographically from northern California. *New West* published different editions for the two regions with separate offices and staffs. Mike thought what had worked in Texas would work in California.

I was the first representative of *Texas Monthly* to make a personal appearance at *New West*. I had two assignments, both aimed at reducing expenditures. One was to size up the editorial staffers to see which ones were expendable. The other was to get a handle on *New West*'s legal expenses, which were in the vicinity of $600,000 a year. *New West* was using the same New York law firm as *New York*, and apparently anyone on staff was free to consult the firm by phone on any story that they thought might cause legal problems.

A lawyer was exactly the wrong person to be the first face *New West* saw. The staff was proud of their magazine and wary of the intentions of the new owners. Beginning the relationship with a lawyer and cost-cutter sent an unwelcome message; it would have been better to send a respected writer or editor, someone like Bill Broyles, who might have been viewed as a kindred spirit.

Despite my desire to be understanding and sympathetic, I compounded the problem. I showed up wearing boots and a leather jacket, no doubt confirming to the staff that they were being taken over by Texas yahoos. I interviewed individual writers and editors, asking their views about the magazine and other staffers — evaluations that should have been solicited by an editor, not a lawyer. And that probably created suspicions that some staffers were currying favor with the new owners at the expense of their colleagues.

Remarkably, the staff was cooperative and courteous to me. The main offices for the magazine and for the southern California edition were on Rodeo Drive in Beverly Hills. For that first visit they arranged for me to stay at a boutique hotel in West Hollywood that apparently had once been a favorite of the movie world. I think they didn't realize that it had now become a sort of boarding house for gay men. To reach my room, I had to walk past the swimming pool. When I did, a dozen bronzed young men lying on their pool-side lounges raised their heads to see the new prospect.

Mike had asked me to take over pre-publication review temporarily, and that caused some consternation. The staff liked and respected the lawyers they had been dealing with in New York, and those lawyers, who had been billing all those phone conversations at hourly rates, encouraged their skepticism about having their stories vetted by some professor in Texas.

New West, like *New York*, had a reputation for aggressive, anti-establishment journalism which I generally appreciated. One of the establishments *New West* covered was Hollywood, and I discovered that they went after movie stars with the zeal that the Washington *Post* went after politicians, which I had a harder time appreciating.

One young woman was essentially a gossip columnist who believed her job was to show that the stars were all hypocrites or worse. She had an extensive network of chauffeurs, maids, hairdressers, nurses, and maître 'ds eager to dish dirt about the stars. She disagreed with my view that legal risks that might be tolerable in stories about misconduct in public office weren't necessarily tolerable in stories about the private lives of movie stars.

I continued to go to Beverly Hills once a month for several more months. I paid one visit to the offices of the northern edition in San Francisco. The staff there was wary not only of a Texas takeover, but also being subsumed into the southern California operation. That was a well-founded fear, for after only a few more months the northern edition was discontinued and the merged outlet was renamed *California* magazine.

After a few months I recruited Steve Shiffrin, a young constitutional law scholar at UCLA, to do *New West*'s pre-publication review, and I had no more to do with the magazine. The experience did, however, cure me of an anti-California bias. The lawyers and journalists I met there were topnotch, and I saw little of the phoniness that I had associated with Californians.

———◆———

Compressing 45 years of moonlighting into one account makes it sound more extensive than it was. Most of the time my only regular outside work was for *Texas Monthly*. The university required us to report outside employment annually; I always estimated 10 hours per week maximum, and on average I didn't exceed that. In the early 1990s I began rejecting most outside assignments because I got tired of answering the phone and flying to meetings. Returning to the quiet of academic life reminded me why I had chosen teaching instead of practice in the first place.

———◆———

CHAPTER 9

Rodeo from Outside the Arena

If I had pursued my youthful dream, the life described in the preceding chapters wouldn't have happened. As a young man in Nebraska, what I really wanted was to rodeo. My elders warned that a life in rodeo will only make you dissolute, disappointed, and possibly disabled. What saved me was not that advice, but lack of talent. If I had been any good at all, I probably would have banged around for a few years until I got crippled up and had to beg for a job driving a truck for a stock contractor.

My few forays as a contestant showed little promise. I bucked off a steer at the Curtis rodeo when I was nine and bucked off a bull at Ogallala when I was 21. I was shown up by my sister when I was ten or eleven: we both rode calves at the Gothenburg rodeo; when my calf stumbled after a few jumps, I bailed; a minute or two later, Nancy (two years younger) rode her calf far down the arena to wild cheers from the crowd.

What I really wanted was the trappings of the rodeo life: criss-crossing the vast spaces of the West from one rodeo to the next; towns throwing off their staid workaday habits for a few days during their annual rodeo; honky-tonks crowded with revelers for those few days; fast-living, hard-drinking, fist-fighting cowboys; the pageantry of rodeo parades on downtown streets and grand entries under wide western skies; hours of boredom punctuated with a few seconds of heart-pounding excitement; and no one telling me what to do.

I've experienced most of those as a lifelong fan, but I've always felt a little guilty about doing so without paying the price that my elders warned about. I've watched rodeos from the San Francisco Cow Palace to the Boston Garden, from the Calgary Stampede to San Antonio, and from the National Finals to the lowliest amateur contests. Always, I feel a little awkward. I'm not like my neighbors in the seats who have to be told that a bronc rider can't touch the horse with his free hand, but neither am I a rodeo cowboy.

———————◆———————

When I was working for the North Platte *Telegraph-Bulletin* in 1959, I covered the Buffalo Bill Rodeo. I wrote a front-page feature about a crowd-pleasing stunt put on by the clowns — brothers Gene and Bobby Clark — and their young sons. During the calf roping, after a roped calf had been untied, they put an eight-year-old boy aboard and let him try to ride the bucking calf. He rode a few jumps and then "got piled," as he put it.

My interviews with the fathers and sons produced good quotes and the story ran with some cute photos. A few years later when I applied for a job with *Time* magazine I submitted that feature as a writing sample. The interviewer said something like, "Charming, but not exactly *Time* material."

That fall I went back to Harvard. When the rodeo came to Boston Garden in October, I went there to look up a steer wrestler named Don Fedderson, who was from Nebraska.

[Right away, I see that I need to explain the evolution of rodeo terminology. In my youthful memories, the events included calf roping, bulldogging, and steer busting (or steer tripping). To put a kinder, gentler face on the sport, the powers-that-be changed some names. Calf roping became tie down roping, I suppose to soften the image of baby calves being caught by the neck and jerked down. Bulldogging became steer wrestling, which actually is more descriptive because the event no longer involves bulldogs but does involve some wrestling. Steer busting is now called steer roping (not to be confused with team roping, which also involves roping steers, but by two ropers instead of one). Steer roping still uses a horse to throw a steer down hard enough to make him lie still while the roper ties his legs. And all too often there is literally some busting; a sled is kept at the ready to haul steers whose legs have been broken out of the arena so spectators don't have to watch them hobble on three legs. What rodeo does to animals began to trouble me more in recent years, and what it does to men, even more.]

In a hotel connected with the Garden, I came upon some cowboys loung-ing against a stack of hay bales in the lobby. They told me where I could find Fedderson, and he gave me some tickets. My friends found it hard to understand why I was cutting class to go to a rodeo.

Boston Garden and Madison Square Garden were two of the country's big-gest rodeos at that time, so I suppose most of the big names were at Boston, but I only remember one: Benny Reynolds, the 1958 Rookie of the Year whose aw-shucks manner charmed millions when he was a contestant on a television quiz show.

———— ◆ ————

After I graduated and moved to Texas, I didn't feel completely at home until Karen and I went to the Fort Worth Stock Show in 1963. I remember the hair ris-ing on the back of my neck during the grand entry in Will Rogers Coliseum. We went to the Fort Worth rodeo almost every year for the next 50 years.

At the rodeo in Coleman that summer, Karen and I were in the press box over the chutes, allegedly covering the rodeo for the San Angelo *Standard-Times*. Access to the stairway leading to the press box was through the pens behind the chutes. As we were leaving after the performance, Karen stepped off the bottom stair just as a rodeo bull charged around a corner into the pen. She froze and the bull was so startled he stopped short, then trotted around her.

Karen has gamely gone with me to the Fort Worth Stock Show rodeo, and when the kids were young I often dragged them along: Liz to Calgary in 1984; John to a little rodeo in Vernal, Utah, put on by the local ward of the Mormon church; and all of them to small-time Texas rodeos in places like Mason, Llano, Lockhart, and Stonewall. But I've always been happy to go alone if necessary.

Cheyenne Frontier Days used to be a must for ranch people from all over Wyoming, Colorado, Nebraska, and South Dakota, as well as cowboys from ev-erywhere. In the 1960s Mother and Dad went with Karen and me a couple of times.

Dad's ability to find people he knew was uncanny. During Frontier Days we were staying at a motel on old Highway 30 when Dad noticed a license plate in the parking lot with a number indicating it was from Lincoln County, Nebraska.

Dad kept an eye on that car until its occupants came out, and surprise, surprise! The woman was one of my grade school mates from Union School.

I went to Frontier Days several times in the 1970s when it was a rowdy bacchanal befitting its name, with drunks and fights in the streets. I went once or twice in later years after locals, tired of hooligans breaking windows and urinating on sidewalks, had rebelled and insisted that it be domesticated. I preferred the earlier version, but I didn't have to live there.

———◆———

Musical acts during rodeos have never been a favorite of mine. Once in the early 1970s I took a group of my faculty colleagues to a small rodeo in Georgetown, near Austin. In the middle of the rodeo an attractive young redhead came into the arena and sang.

"I don't know why the producers think they have to put on some second-rate musical act to get people to come to the rodeo," I groused. Bill Powers never let me forget that the redhead turned out to be a very young Reba McIntyre.

Instead of having a musical act during the afternoon rodeo, at Cheyenne they had a separate concert in the evening, often with top-flight acts. One I saw was Dolly Parton, who gamely went on singing even though her voice was repeatedly drowned out by jets of the Wyoming Air National Guard taking off from an adjacent airfield. Another was Waylon Jennings, who had to pause for an hour because of a rain shower that soaked the stage.

A rodeo just as iconic as Cheyenne is the Pendleton Round Up. My cousin Harold Booth and I went there a few years ago. The arena is huge, three or four times the usual size, and instead of soft dirt, it's grass! I suppose the thinking is that the bronco-busters of old didn't have soft places to land, so neither should today's cowboys.

What I remember best about Pendleton is the horsemanship of the queen contestants. They came into the arena at full gallop from a runway under the stands, carrying a flag, and jumped a low railing before lining up in the middle of the arena. They must be descendants of the female bronc riders who competed in rodeos up until the 1930s.

My all-time favorite arena is at Galisteo, New Mexico. It sits in a wide grassy valley, far off the highway, with no concrete, trees, light poles, or buildings in sight. The air is thin and dry, and the sky is pale and limitless. In the distance are some low mountains. The stands and the chutes are unpainted wood. It reminds me of small town arenas 70 years ago. Not surprisingly, the arena has been used in movies about old-time rodeo. It's also seen its share of rodeo reality — a young saddle bronc rider, father of two small children, was killed there a few years ago when the horse kicked him in the head.

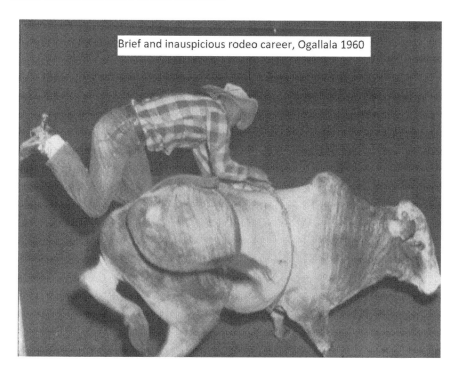

Brief and inauspicious rodeo career, Ogallala 1960

The best competition is at the National Finals, where the year's top 15 contestants in each event compete for ten days on the best stock from all the contractors' strings. My friend Bill Reid went with me to the NFR in Oklahoma City around 1970. On the first night, we stood outside the sold-out coliseum at the state fairgrounds trying to buy tickets. A wicked norther had just blown through. We took turns, one standing out of the biting wind on the lee side of the building and the other standing at the curb to accost anyone who might have extra tickets.

After I had stood at the curb calling "Tickets, anybody got extra tickets?" until

I was half-frozen, Bill motioned me back. It turned out that the cowboy who had been standing silently beside Bill had tickets he wanted to sell but was too shy to advertise the fact until Bill finally struck up a conversation with the him.

I went to the National Finals several more times in the 1970s, and once in the 1980s after it moved to Las Vegas, but curiously, I don't have many clear memories of it. I do remember the many disabled cowboys among the spectators: men with casts holding their arms extended, casts holding a leg rigid from the hip down, in one instance an upper body cast with a halo holding the man's head rigid. They were no doubt men who had dreamed of making it to the National Finals, but not as crippled spectators.

———◆———

On one of those trips I drove my '57 Buick and stayed through the final performance on Sunday afternoon. It had again turned bitterly cold in Oklahoma City. As I drove through southern Oklahoma that night, I marveled at what good gas mileage my Buick was getting — the gas gauge had barely moved.

A few miles south of the Red River, I ran out of gas. With a flashlight, I stood beside the car, hood up, trying to flag someone down. By now the cold front had reached north Texas. Car after car sped past. At first I was outraged, but then I realized that people weren't likely to stop in the dark for some guy in an ancient car parked beside the interstate highway in the middle of nowhere.

Finally a car stopped — an old Ford Falcon sedan. Crowded into it were six fat adults, men and women. They said it was 10 or 12 miles to the next town, and they would take me there. "There's a gas station there, maybe it'll be open."

I sat in the back seat with one of the large women in my lap. They were country people, roughly dressed, plain talking. When I told about my misleading gas gauge, one of them explained: "In those old cars, sometimes you have enough water in the gas tank to freeze up the sending unit."

By the time we got to the town, it was close to nine o'clock and the only thing open was one gas station. The guy sold me a two-gallon gas can and said he would buy it back if I was able to get it back before he closed at ten. He couldn't drive me to my car because he was alone in the station.

I was preparing to hitch-hike back up the interstate highway to my car, worried that if I didn't get back before the station closed, the two gallons of gas might not be enough to get me to the next open station. My rescuers in the Falcon said never mind, we'll take you back.

They did, and I got back to the station in time to fill up. I offered my rescuers some cash, but they refused. "No, we're just glad to help. Next time, you help somebody."

I think of those people when I pass someone with car trouble, but usually I'm like the people who whizzed on past me, afraid to stop in the dark, or in too big a hurry, or with no room in their car.

———◆———

The most successful stock contractor during my years of going to the National Finals was Tommy Steiner, second generation of a four-generation rodeo family. The patriarch, Buck Steiner, once showed me a clipping of himself riding a bucking bull backwards. I wouldn't have believed it, but the newspaper had a photo of him doing it. "They paid me ten dollars a head. Crowds loved it," he said.

Buck lived to be 101. He spent the last 60 years or so of his life at his leather goods store in Austin, Capitol Saddlery. By the time I knew him he was in his seventies and spent his days sitting in a wooden office chair, keeping an eye on his customers and the wealth he had accumulated. It was said he owned over 100 parcels of land in Austin and environs.

When he was even older, he took up with a woman 50 years his junior, which precipitated a horrible family fight. Some of his descendants sued to have him declared incompetent, fearing he might give her his hundreds of millions. After an ugly court fight, she got a home site on the family's gorgeous XS Ranch near Bastrop (and probably a few millions to boot).

Buck's son Tommy started performing as a trick roper at age 10. In the 1940s he began producing rodeos and by the '70s had the best bucking stock in the business. The hundreds of bulls and broncs ran on about 10,000 acres of prime real estate near Austin. More than 400 of them were selected for the National Finals.

Then, in the 1980s, he abruptly quit. I surmise that his financial advisers told him that no matter how much he loved rodeo, it was insane to devote hundreds of millions of dollars worth of land, equipment, and stock to the paltry profits that came from producing rodeos.

Tommy's son Bobby was world champion bull rider in 1973, then did what rodeo champions almost never do — he promptly retired. Bobby's son Sid won the world championship in steer wrestling in 2002 and then followed his father's example by immediately retiring.

A few years later I went to the XS Ranch and bought two quarter horses from Sid. Central Texas ranches are often mostly mesquite and cedar, but the XS was thousands of acres of lush rolling grass, just across the Colorado River from the suburbs spreading south from Austin. It looked like it belonged in Montana.

In a pasture near the horse barn was a big contented-looking Mexican steer. "That's the steer I had in the last go-round of the NFR," Sid said. "I won the World because he took the fall real easy, so I bought him."

Now that ranch and another just as fabulous on Lake Austin have been sold for housing developments. The development on Lake Austin is called Steiner Ranch. The family's rodeo history is memorialized at the Steiner Steakhouse, which sits on a small piece of the Lake Austin ranch. It's an insufficient monument to a remarkable rodeo family.

In 1975 I spent nearly a month going from one rodeo to the next — Cheyenne Frontier Days, then the Wyoming State Fair at Casper, then the Last Chance Roundup at Helena, Montana, then the War Bonnet Roundup in Idaho Falls, then Pikes Peak or Bust at Colorado Springs.

I suppose my inspiration was Larry McMurtry's novel, *Moving On*, about a would-be photographer roaming from rodeo to rodeo. In fact, my cover story was that I was taking pictures. I did take a few undistinguished photos with my little box camera, but my real mission was just the roaming. I had a Dodge window van with a bed in the back and cute little blue and white checkered privacy curtains made by Karen. When possible, I camped on the rodeo grounds. (Camped is a bit of an exaggeration; I did no cooking, just parked the van to sleep).

Of all the hundreds of miles driven, the dozens of performances watched, and the raucous nights in honky-tonks, I have only sketchy memories:

- In Cheyenne, the strange scenario I described in the chapter on honky-tonks: a beautiful tall shapely blonde in a silver lamé pantsuit came in a bar crowded with cowboys, danced with a few of them, left with one, then came back wearing a gold lamé pantsuit.
- At Casper, communal showers graciously provided on the grounds for the many of us sleeping in our vehicles.
- Trying to sleep parked in a national forest near Helena, with the temperature falling toward freezing before sunrise.
- Subsisting on crackers and cheese and Olympia beer, and in western Montana and Idaho, fat Bing cherries from roadside stands.
- After the final performance in Idaho Falls, heading south through the night on a two-lane highway in a caravan — the stock contractor's 18-wheelers full of broncs and bulls, pickup campers and horse trailers of contestants, and the RVs of contract acts.

That's as close as I ever got to "going down the road," as rodeoing is called in that world.

Blood is Thicker than
Time and Distance

It was the most surprising letter I ever received. It said "Hi. My name is Mona. I'm your cousin, in Norway." That was the first contact between our American and Scandinavian families in 50 years, and the beginning of the first continuing family relations in a century.

My father had a bundle of letters, handwritten in Swedish, to his mother from her father and siblings in Sweden, mostly in the 1890s. In the 1990s I got them from him and hired a Swedish woman in Austin to translate them. That was easier said than done, because they were in "old Swedish" which she didn't fully understand; she eventually took them to Sweden and got help from some of her elderly relatives.

It was a year or more before I got the translations, but it was well worth the wait. The letters were heart-rending. My grandmother's parents, Sven and Brita Stina, had been relatively prosperous farmers until the hard times of the 1880s, when they went broke. Sven signed some kind of guarantee for a friend and lost the farm when the friend defaulted. The bankruptcy broke up the family. Two of the sons went to Oslo, one of the daughters became a maid in Swedish households, and a son went to Seattle and after a few years was never heard from again.

———◆———

One of the Oslo brothers helped pay for my grandmother Elisabeth, 18, and her sister Minna, 16, to come to the U.S. The girls came in 1893, promising to stay only a year or two, but it soon became clear that they wouldn't be back. There was some plaintive talk of the parents coming for my grandmother's wedding in 1896, but that was a pipe dream. They never saw each other, or even talked by telephone, for the rest of their lives.

They exchanged letters which took six weeks or more to be delivered. The parents' love and longing cries out in their letters. Here's a sample, from one of Sven's letters: "We have your photograph hanging on our wall so that I never leave or enter the house without seeing your peaceful face and thinking that if only we could talk to you for one hour only it would be such a great joy."

We have none of Grandma's letters to them, but their references to what she had said in her letters indicate that she was just as anguished.

———◆———

Among the letters was a cryptic notation of an address in Oslo of one Erling Nordstrom. I had never heard that name and had no idea who he was, but I suspected that the note might have been written by my grandmother for my cousin Roger Booth, who had been the only family member ever to visit the Scandinavian relatives. He went to Oslo for a weekend in the 1950s when he was in the Army stationed in Germany.

I wrote a letter addressed to "Erling Nordstrom or anyone with knowledge of his whereabouts." I included my address, fax number, and an explanation of who I was. Several months passed with no response.

When my letter arrived, Erling Nordstrom had been dead for many years. His widow had moved away from the address 12 years previously, but the efficient Norwegian post office tracked her down. She didn't read much English so she set the letter aside.

What happened next was a serendipitous intervention by Mona Nordstrom, Erling's daughter. While visiting her widowed mother, Mona noticed the letter and asked to read it. She could have dismissed it as a weird missive from a nutty American, but she didn't. She replied to me by fax, and the rest is most welcome history.

———◆———

Mona speaks English fluently; she had been a career flight attendant for Pan American Airways and had lived in the U.S. (She, like the other Scandinavians I call cousins, was actually a second cousin; our fathers were first cousins.)

We corresponded for a few months and Mona invited Karen and me to visit her, which we did in 2000. Mona and some other relatives rented a hall in the Sonja Henie Art Museum in Oslo and arranged a dinner in our honor. They invited other members of the Norwegian and Swedish branches of the family, and several dozen came. Some of them had never met each other.

Two memories of that occasion stand out. I wanted to make a good impression so I bought a Norwegian dictionary and learned a few phrases. When I rose at the dinner and began to speak in my halting Norwegian; they began to laugh, and someone shouted "Speak English! We all understand."

The second memory is of my surprise at learning how well educated and successful they were. The understanding in our branch of the family always had been that we were fortunate that our grandparents had escaped from the poverty and backwardness of the old country. But the new-found relatives in Scandinavia included an architect, a doctor, a dentist, sisters who owned an apartment house, a couple of retired CEOs, and several people in the creative end of the television business. Most of those on my side — we who were thought to have been so fortunate to escape from the old country — were farmers or workers.

———◆———

Some of the Norwegians had been to the U.S. or had stories about Americans. Ellen Weidemann, wife of my cousin Aksel Nordstrom, told me a story about her father who had been a prominent Oslo businessman. He owned some timber properties in the American South, and on one of his business trips to New Orleans, he met a beautiful mulatto woman named Delia and brought her back to Oslo. He was a widower who enjoyed showing off his new mistress. Delia was a flamboyant woman who wore bright yellow dresses that highlighted her dark skin, a novelty in all-white Oslo.

They were the talk of Oslo for a month or two, but when she tired of the Norwegian winter, she went home. As Ellen told the story, her father escorted

Delia to the pier, kissed her goodbye, and then turned and brushed his palms up and down as if to say "That's that."

Someone told a story about Dagmar, Lillemor, and Borghild, beautiful daughters of my grandmother's brother Johan. In their youth, the three girls were living together in a flat in Göteborg when a salesman came to the door selling men's toiletries. The one who answered the door (I don't remember which of the sisters it was, but I'll say Borghild) said "Oh, there are no men living here." One of her sisters said, "You shouldn't have told him that, he might come back at night and do us harm." So Borghild called down the hall after the salesman, "But we have men here at night!"

(We made two more trips to Norway and Sweden, staying either with Mona or her cousin Eva Nordstrom. On one trip we visited not only Mona and Eva, but also Göteborg, which was my grandparents' jumping-off point when they emigrated and is the namesake of the Nebraska town where Karen and I went to high school. All the trips were memorable, but I'm not sure I can say what we did on which trip, so I'm collapsing them.)

———◆———

Interest in the family's roots seemed to be contagious. One of Mona's and my cousins, Wenche Nordstrom, hosted a dinner at her place in the country outside Oslo and invited many of the relatives. The dinner was ostensibly in honor of the 800th anniversary of some notable event in Scandinavian history. We were introduced to the custom of drinking toasts of aquavit, which reminded me of the endless toasts of vodka in Russia.

Our cousin Dag Ringestad enlivened Wenche's dinner by insisting that tradition required the person offering the toast to down his drink and throw the glass backward over a shoulder without looking. When he demonstrated, his glass hit a mirror on the wall behind him and shattered it. With characteristic aplomb, Dag offered no apologies.

Mona showed us many attractions of Oslo, among them the sculptures at Frogner Park, the Royal Palace, Oslo Fiord, a 13th century stave church. Some of the cousins organized a family outing to Sweden, and twenty or more of us caravanned across the border. Eva Nordstrom, the cousin who was an architect in Oslo, had done some research on the family.

Eva knew some of the places mentioned in the letters to my grandmother. One was the small church in Järbo, little changed from the time both of my grandparents were baptized there. My paternal grandfather, Carl Anderson, and my grandmother were cousins. His family also lived near Järbo until they emigrated to the U.S. in 1882. Grandpa's parents settled in the Loup River Valley of Nebraska; that's why Grandma and Minnie (as she was called in the U.S.) chose that as their destination. But we have no letters from my grandfather's family and little information about their descendants in Sweden.

We attended services in the Järbo church, which reminded me of the thriving little country church my family attended when I was a child. Standing at the simple altar where my grandparents had received the sacraments more than a hundred years earlier made me feel a physical continuity with them..

———◆———

 We found the farm where my grandmother's family had lived. The old buildings were gone, but we found a bronze marker inscribed "Lonkken" — "strongman," my paternal great-grandfather's nickname. (Why this marker for my *paternal* grandfather was on the farm of my grandmother's family was and remains a mystery. But my grandparents both hailed from the Järbo area and their families were related. Maybe that's explanation enough.)

Eva hosted all of us at her farm while also tending her sheep. She had just begun renovating the neglected house and she clearly had labored heroically to make it presentable. We supped on a table spread with Eva's prize possession: a linen tablecloth that my grandmother had woven for her parents. They apparently had given it to Eva's grandfather, Johan, perhaps in gratitude for his having paid for their daughters' passage to the U.S.

Eva was quickly becoming the family historian. She and Mona took us to Mellerud, a town where an elderly man had accumulated hundreds of family histories and compiled them into a beautiful leather-bound book called "Järbo-Adeln." There is an entry for each family, showing dates of births, deaths, marriages, and emigrations, with cross references to other families with whom they were related. The records came mostly from local churches, which until the 20th century were the official repository for births, marriages, and deaths, and apparently also for emigrations.

The book's title means "Järbo nobility," a reference to the 18ᵗʰ century, when Järbo was famous for its horsemen. In 1714, when the Swedish empire extended across most of Europe, the Järbo horsemen fetched King Karl XII back from Turkey to deal with some emergency at home. They were reputed to have made the trip across Europe in 30 days, and were rewarded with titles of nobility. Alas, as far as I can tell, none of my ancestors were among the Järbo horsemen.

Eva's farm in Sweden

I bought the book and used the entries to produce several family pedigrees going back to the 16ᵗʰ century. Eva put her artistic talents to work and drew a lovely multi-colored tree — literally, a tree — of the descendants of Sven and Brita Stina, Eva's and my great-grandparents.

———◆———

The most colorful of the Norwegian cousins was Dag Ringestad, son of Johan's daughter Dagmar. He was retired from a successful textile business and was married to a much younger French woman, Michelle. Dag invited us to lunch at their house in north Oslo. After four hours and many bottles of champagne, we feasted on traditional Norwegian foods. ("Feasted" is a bit of an exaggeration. We sampled the reindeer, whale, and other novelties rather gingerly and tentatively.)

In addition to the cousins of my generation, several of the younger generation joined us for the various events — Wenche's daughters Britt and Hannah (university students); Aksel's sons Steinar and Gudmund, Aksel's daughters Carina (a writer for a comedy show on Norwegian television) and Cecilie (producer of television programs for young people) and Cecile's three young daughters; and Dag's niece, a lovely 20-year-old aspiring actress whose father was a renowned opera director.

The young people seemed as different from American young people as other Europeans of their generation are. But when the older Scandinavians talked, I could close my eyes and imagine I was hearing my older American relatives. The similarities in mannerisms, speech patterns, and physical traits was uncanny. Even their outlook on life and their sense of humor seemed familiar.

But curiously, they were more like my grandfather than my grandmother. Like him, they tended to be tall, rangy, blond, blue-eyed. Grandma was petite, with dark hair and big brown eyes; she may have been descended from some of the foreigners captured by the Vikings many generations back. Grandpa's personality fit the Swedish stereotype: taciturn, austere, gruff. But my grandmother's personality was the opposite, and these were Grandma's people. They were warm, voluble, and lively. A few were a little skeptical of Americans, but most were open and embraced Karen and me as long-lost kin.

———◆———

Why are the family of my Swedish grandmother almost all Norwegian? Grandma and her sister Minnie, and my grandfather and two of his sisters who had also emigrated to the U.S., were all proud of their Swedish ancestry and spoke Swedish to each other. I don't recall any of them even mentioning Norway.

It turns out that this too was a result of the splintering of the family after the bankruptcy. When Johan and Anders left the farm for the city, they went to Oslo, possibly because Anders had a Norwegian girlfriend. Oslo wouldn't have been an entirely alien destination because Norway at that time was a Swedish possession (it didn't gain independence until 1905), but they would have been Swedish-speakers in a place where Norwegian was the language.

Another mystery was why the relatives included numerous children but few husbands. Swedish women apparently concluded (somewhat ahead of American women) that husbands are overrated. In updating pedigrees to the present, I needed to know who was married to whom, but I found that even close relatives often didn't know. And the women, married or not, usually kept the name Nordstrom or reclaimed it upon divorce. Two of Aksel Nordstrom's children, one male and one female, took his wife's surname, Weidemann.

Conversations with my Scandinavian relatives over those days cleared up some mysteries involving names. Until they married, the surname of my grandmother and her sister was Svenson or Svensson (sometimes Anglicized to Swanson). I knew about the traditional patronymic naming practice in Sweden: the son of a man whose given name was Lars automatically took the surname Larsson and a daughter became Larsdotter. So my grandmother should have been Svensdotter, not Svenson. I surmised that when she arrived in the U.S., someone, possibly an immigration official, chose to ignore that. But I learned that around the end of the 19th century the Swedes themselves began using "–son" for girls as well as boys.

The larger mystery concerned the name Nordstrom. In their letters to my grandmother, her brothers signed their names Nordstrom, not Svenson, and most all of the relatives we met, men and women alike, were named Nordstrom. Her father's early letters were signed Sven Eriksson, but later he signed as "S.E. Nordstrom."

The name change apparently happened with the breakup of the family after the bankruptcy. As long as people lived on farms or in villages, they could be identified by their father's name, sometimes supplemented by the name of their farm or village, e.g., "Svensson of Stora Torp." But when Sven's sons Johan and Anders went to Oslo, the names of their father and their farm didn't suffice to identify them, so they apparently just picked the name Nordstrom. Their father may have followed suit once he was no longer identified by his farm.

Recently I've learned of a more compelling reason for the name change: In 1901 Sweden passed something called the "Names Adoption Act," requiring all citizens to adopt inheritable surnames—names that would pass down intact instead of changing every generation. Many families adopted their current patronymic surname as their hereditary family surname (that's why many generations of descendants of my paternal great-grandfather Anders are Andersons) and many others chose a name from nature (Nordstrom means "north-flowing stream").

———————◆———————

We invited our Scandinavian kin to visit us in the U.S. In 2001 my sister Elaine organized a reunion of 50 or 60 descendants of my Swedish grandmother, and a few of the Norwegians came — Mona, Cecilie and her husband Erling Kjaernes, and their three young daughters. It was reminiscent of the dinner at the Sonja Henie Museum in Oslo a year earlier. We had dinner in a large hall in a state park in eastern Nebraska. I saw some cousins I hadn't seen since childhood, and met some of the younger generation for the first time. It was the first time the other Americans had met any of their Scandinavian relatives, except for Roger Booth, who had met Mona on his weekend visit in the 1950s.

At that reunion, Mona met my father for the first time. It was a sight to behold; they weren't strangers getting acquainted, they were like long-lost friends reunited. The rapport was instinctive and instantaneous. They talked for hours. Afterwards, Mona often said "Arnold is a real cowboy."

After the reunion dinner Mona, Cecilie and her husband Erling (not to be confused with Mona's father Erling) and their daughters visited the farm of my cousin Norman Anderson in Nebraska and the farm where my grandparents had lived. Cecilie, Erling, and their daughters then spent a couple of days in Colorado with Karen and me. I took them horseback riding in Rocky Mountain National Park; that, and the farm visit, may have satisfied their curiosity about the agrarian life of their U.S. relatives, because they haven't been back.

I'd like to say that since then there have been many visits between the two branches of the family, but that has not been the case. Elaine and her husband, Rich Peters, visited once and met a few of the relatives, and so did two of my young second cousins, but that's all.

My great-grandparents'
church in Jarbo, Sweden

Mona has returned to the U.S. many times, but none of the other Norwegians have come. Maybe it's because I haven't pressed them insistently enough. Or, quite possibly they think the rest of the American kin are likely to be no more interesting than Karen and me. But I think it's also something I've noticed among my friends in England and Australia: America is not as attractive to foreigners as it once was. Our politics, our guns, our inequality and our commercialism aren't very beckoning to them.

All of the Scandinavians I've mentioned so far are descendants of my grand-mother's brother Johan, who was the most successful of her siblings. He went to sea in the early days of steamships and later parlayed his knowledge of steam engines into a position at a steam-powered factory. He soon opened a store selling work clothes and tools to factory workers, and from there he became a successful businessman in Oslo. Johan and his wife Helga owned a large apartment building, which was inherited by his granddaughters Eva and Wenche Nordstrom. It was slightly run-down when Karen and I saw it, but still had traces of elegance.

Grandma's brother Magnus emigrated to the U.S. and made his way to Seattle about the same time she came. At one time there was talk that he would pay for his parents to come to the U.S. for a visit, but about 1900 he dropped from sight. I surmise that he was one of the thousands of immigrant fishermen, miners, or railroad workers whose death was too insignificant to warrant notifying next-of-kin in the old country. Relatives of such people erected a monument in their memory in Seattle. On a visit to the University of Washington in 2006, I arranged to have Magnus's name added to the memorial.

A third brother, Anders, had a long career with the street department of Oslo. According to family lore, he was something of a hero of the resistance during the Nazi occupation of Norway in World War II. He apparently published, or at least distributed, an underground newspaper, which could have got him in big trouble.

We met Anders' grandson Per on one of our visits. Per and his wife Unni hosted a lunch for us at their beautiful home, but what I remember best was their daughter Tine. All the Scandinavian relatives are handsome, but Tine was breathtakingly beautiful. She looked a little like Julie Christie but was down-to-earth and charming.

(One of the many similarities between the U.S. and Scandinavian families is the use of the same given names over and over. There was Per's wife Unni and Mona's sister Unni (recently deceased), and Mona's father Erling and Cecilie's husband Erling. On our side there was my grandmother Elizabeth (or Elisabet), her daughter Elizabeth, our daughter Elizabeth, my cousin Harold Booth's wife Elizabeth, and Harold's sister Elizabeth. And my great-great uncle Carl Anderson, my grandfather Carl Anderson, and my uncle Carl Anderson.)

———◆———

The one enduring bridge between the Scandinavian and American families has been Mona. She hosted Karen and me on all of our visits, usually at her lovely flat in Oslo but once at her farmhouse in Sweden. Sometimes together with Eva, Mona took us to numerous historical and family landmarks in Sweden and Norway. She keeps us informed of events among the Scandinavian kin, and comes to Austin once or twice a year. She visited my sister Elaine in Nebraska and keeps in touch with her by email.

I have more contact with Mona than with any of my American relatives outside of my immediate family, and I feel as close to her as to those I've known all my life. I suppose one reason for that is Mona's generous personality, but another is the mysterious tie of kinship.

Mona's daughter Katrine was a student at the University of New Orleans in 2005 when Hurricane Katrina struck. When Katrine was ordered to evacuate, she gathered up some clothes and essentials for herself and her three-year-old child for what she expected to be a few days' absence and drove to Houston. When the days turned to weeks, Mona told us of Katrine's plight and we invited her to come stay with us in Austin.

Katrine was a lovely, vivacious twenty-something with an adorable little girl, Sol-Marie, who is equally fluent in Norwegian and English. They stayed with us a few weeks, and when it became clear that their home in New Orleans was not going to reopen anytime soon, they settled in Austin. They're still here, and they've become good friends not only of Karen and me, but also of our son Bill and his wife Stella. Mona comes to visit them occasionally, so now there's a permanent link between the two branches of the family.

Having grown up in Norway, Katrine is an accomplished skater. There's not much ice skating in Austin, so she took up roller derby. She quickly became the star of the league. Her nickname was "Hurricane Katrina" and her jersey said "Kategory 5."

———◆———

Karen's paternal ancestors also emigrated from Sweden and settled in Nebraska. Family lore says they came from a town called Kisa. Fifty years ago a second-cousin visited that town but so far as we know made no contact with any relatives there.

So Karen's Swedish family is lost, just as mine would have been but for a series of happy fortuities. Connecting with my Scandinavian family has been the most precious and gratifying chapter in a life filled with wonderful experiences, and it wouldn't have happened had my grandmother not kept those letters from her family, had my father not given them to me, had my translator not been able to find some people who knew old Swedish, had the Norwegian post office not tracked down Erling Nordstrom's widow, had Mona not answered my long-shot letter, and had Mona and other Scandinavian cousins not been as enthusiastic as we about reestablishing family ties.

A NOTE ON MEMORY

The first recollection of an experience is a memory; each time you revisit it thereafter what you get is a memory of a memory. And a memory is like a soft piece of clay: each time you retrieve it, you change its shape ever so slightly. Worse yet, the mind abhors a blank, so when memory fails, imagination sometimes supplies the missing piece. I've been lovingly excavating memories for most of my 81 years, so I'm sure there are some of these distortions in this book. I can only say I've done my best to hew to reality.

Made in the USA
Coppell, TX
24 August 2020